Exclusion from school

D1043343

Exclusion from school

Inter-professional issues
for policy and practice

Edited by
Eric Blyth and Judith Milner

London and New York

Dedication to
Dinah Gill

First published 1996
by Routledge
11 New Fetter Lane, London EC4P 4EE

Simultaneously published in the USA and Canada
by Routledge
29 West 35th Street, New York, NY 10001

Routledge is an International Thompson Publishing company

© 1996 Eric Blyth and Judith Milner, selection and
editorial matter; individual chapters to their contributors

Typeset in Times Ten by
Florencetype Ltd, Stoodleigh, Devon

Printed and bound in Great Britain by
Clays Ltd, St. Ives PLC

All rights reserved. No part of this book may be reprinted
or reproduced or utilized in any form or by any electronic,
mechanical, or other means, now known or hereafter
invented, including photocopying and recording, or in any
information storage or retrieval system, without permission
in writing from the publishers.

British Library Cataloguing in Publication Data
A catalogue record for this book is available from the
British Library

Library of Congress Cataloging in Publication Data
A catalogue record for this book has been requested

ISBN 0–415–13277–0

Contents

Figures and tables

Contributors

Catherine Benson	Research Assistant, Middlesex University
Eric Blyth	Principal Lecturer in Social Work, The University of Huddersfield
Tony Booth	Senior Lecturer in Education, The Open University
Cedric Cullingford	Professor of Education, The University of Huddersfield
Howard Firth	Head of Educational Support Service, Social Services Department, Hampshire County Council
Philip Garner	Senior Lecturer in Special Education, Brunel University
Dinah Gill	Registered Psychologist, School Connections Ltd., Auckland, New Zealand, until her death late in 1995
Carol Hayden	Research Officer, Social Services Research and Information Unit, The University of Portsmouth
Christine Horrocks	Research Assistant, The University of Huddersfield
Pippa John	Teacher, Barnardos/Avon County Council Child and Family Support Centre, Bristol
Wendy Marshall	Senior Lecturer in Social Work, The University of Huddersfield
Judith Milner	Senior Lecturer in Social Work, The University of Huddersfield

Lynda Mitchell	Advisor for Special Educational Needs, Education Department, Wakefield Metropolitan District Council
Jeremy Monsen	Professional Tutor, Department of Psychology, University College, London, and Senior Educational Psychologist, Kent County Council
Jenny Morrison	Research Assistant, The University of Huddersfield
Joan Normington	Headteacher, Westfields Pupil Referral Unit, Kirklees Metropolitan Council
Carl Parsons	Reader in Education, Christ Church College, Canterbury
Susan de Pear	Special Educational Needs Coordinator, The Matthew Arnold School, Surrey
Chris Searle	Formerly Headteacher, Earl Marshal School, Sheffield
Martin Stephenson	General Manager, Cities in Schools
Margaret Stirling	Headteacher, Underley Hall School, Kirkby Lonsdale

Preface

BEYOND THE MORAL PANIC

The idea for this book developed from a conference, 'Behaviour Problems in Schools and Exclusions: Education and Social Work Responses', held at the University of Huddersfield on 14 and 15 July 1994. The conference itself was prompted by evidence of increasing concern amongst both professionals and a wider audience about the behaviour of young people in and outside school, subsequently highlighted by newspaper headlines such as 'Expulsions spiral as schools fight "yob culture"' (Preston, 1994a). It brought together teachers, governors, elected members, support staff from education and other services and researchers from across the United Kingdom to share information about innovative and successful interventions.

This book contains – in expanded and updated form – a selection of keynote speeches and workshop material originally presented at the conference, providing accounts both of professional practice and of academically oriented research. Drawing on their evidence and experience the contributors to this book produce suggestions for improved practice.

The book is divided into three parts, the first of which contains seven chapters identifying trends and providing a theoretical overview. In the first of these Eric Blyth and Judith Milner highlight trends in exclusion practice and discuss the possible effects of recent legislation and policy initiatives on schools and allied professionals. In 'Stories of exclusion: natural and unnatural selection', Tony Booth argues that formal definitions of exclusion serve to divert attention from the wider range of exclusionary practices used in schools – including those relating to discipline, difficulties in learning, race, gender and disability – which need to be taken into account if we are fully to appreciate the social, psychological and educational character of exclusion. Chris Searle, headteacher of a multi-racial inner-city high school, considers the relationship between the decline of comprehensive education in the United Kingdom, the rise in market forces, and the consequent increased use of exclusion following the Education Reform Act 1988. He argues passionately for a refocus on child-centred practices in education.

Margaret Stirling, providing another 'headteacher perspective', presents findings from on-going longitudinal research in a Midlands local authority into the effects of government educational policies on disadvantaged pupils. Echoing Chris Searle's observations, she draws on research evidence which shows how these pupils are adversely affected by a competitive education system. Increasingly susceptible to exclusion from school, many children receive part-time teaching or no education at all for lengthy periods. The evidence cited in this chapter provides further support to Tony Booth's assertion that formal exclusions are merely the tip of the iceberg and that potentially many more children than those formally excluded from school may be denied education under circumstances of dubious legality or morality. Stirling's research also reveals the particularly high risk of exclusion to which black (African–Caribbean) boys, and children and young people 'looked after' by local authorities are exposed. These issues are developed in more detail in the next two chapters, by Blyth and Milner and by Firth and Horrocks. In the former, the authors report on an in-depth analysis of one school's discipline management system which raises issues about the inter-relationship between sexism and racism which, they suggest, contributes to the disproportionate number of exclusions experienced by African–Caribbean boys.

Firth and Horrocks review the evidence concerning the educational disadvantage experienced by young people looked after by local authorities and, in particular, their increased exposure to the risk of exclusion compared to their peer group. They outline action which has been taken in one local authority area to improve the educational experiences of such young people and identify the tasks which need to be undertaken by the corporate local authority 'parent' to ensure that 'looked after' children and young people receive good quality educational experiences.

In the final chapter in this part Wendy Marshall provides a theoretical examination of the power relationship between children and adults. The implications for understanding interactions between professionals and children is explored as are the ways in which children can be understood as agents and the forms of power available to them.

The second part of the book, 'Consequences of exclusions', contains five chapters which highlight the financial, economic, social, psychological and educational implications of exclusion.

Carl Parsons reports on a research study funded by the Joseph Rowntree Foundation into the costs of exclusion from primary school, thus highlighting and combining two previously neglected aspects of exclusion research. Through illustrative case material this chapter reveals the extent of inter-agency involvement with children excluded from primary schools and begins to estimate the real cost of exclusion when the demands made on the families of excluded children and on the services of agencies other than schools and education are taken into account.

Lynda Mitchell draws on her research in one local authority area – providing illustrative case examples – to examine the disruption to educational careers when considering the delay ('waiting time') that exists between different stages of the exclusion process between the pupil's exclusion, the local authority conference and LEA decision, and the pupil's return to full-time education.

Cedric Cullingford and Jenny Morrison report on research investigating the educational experiences of young offenders in custodial institutions. This research explores the relationship between truancy and exclusion and, like Tony Booth's and Margaret Stirling's chapters, identifies a hitherto hidden aspect of exclusion, that of 'psychological' exclusion, which may occur even though the young person remains physically present in school and which, in the experiences of the young people interviewed, almost invariably precedes formal exclusion.

Susan de Pear and Philip Garner, in a chapter which draws on interviews with a small group of excluded pupils and their teachers, consider the relationship between exclusion from school, listening to pupils and school effectiveness. The authors conclude that, despite recent official rhetoric concerning the need to involve pupils in decision making and taking responsibility for their behaviour, those at greatest risk of exclusion are also those less likely to be involved in decision-making processes; while teachers and pupils may hold different interpretations of the events leading up to exclusion, they hold similar views on what constitutes potential solutions to the problem.

Pippa John presents an analysis of research using unstructured interviews with six young people educated at an off-site support centre for excluded pupils. The main theme to emerge from this is the young people's dissatisfaction with the way that their teachers relate to them, contrasting this with their experience of the centre. The chapter argues that young people experiencing emotional and behavioural difficulties have low self-esteem and that this is a crucial factor in understanding their behaviour. It outlines the pupils' proposals of what may have helped them to remain in mainstream schooling/education and concludes with recommendations which challenge teachers, schools and the government to re-evaluate traditional practice and policy.

The final part of the book, 'Preventive strategies and policies', contains five chapters. The first, 'The Staff Sharing Scheme' by Dinah Gill and Jeremy Monsen, outlines the development and rationale of an action-based project designed to increase teacher-effectiveness in the management of children with behavioural difficulties and to enhance the effectiveness of educational psychologists by changing the focus of their role. The Staff Sharing Scheme was originally developed in schools in New Zealand, by one of the authors, at a time when additional resources to support children with difficulties was limited and schools were expected to re-examine the management and use of their existing resources. It has subsequently been implemented in several English schools. The Scheme provides a model for developing a school's capacity for dealing with children presenting behavioural difficulties. It teaches school staff both process and content skills and leads to the whole school community being involved in managing problems.

Catherine Benson's chapter, 'Resisting the trend to exclude', draws on research conducted in one local authority which sought to examine the processes involved with, and influences on, exclusion and reintegration into mainstream schooling. This research reveals three major typologies of beliefs which are held by head-teachers about the role of education and of schools in the lives of young people and which appear to help to explain the diverse rates of exclusion between different schools. Benson concludes that additional support should be provided for the minority of headteachers who represent a 'collective resistance to the ... growing tide of exclusions'.

Carol Hayden's chapter, 'Primary school exclusions: the need for integrated solutions', provides a further contribution focusing on exclusion of primary-age children. She develops a key hypothesis that pupils in greatest need of social and educational support are those most vulnerable to exclusion, providing case studies to illustrate how a multi-disciplinary approach can be mobilised to prevent exclusion.

Joan Normington's chapter specifically focuses on inter-agency relationships and describes, from the perspective of a pupil referral unit (PRU), how such inter-agency collaboration can make flexible use of available resources. The author resists the concept of the PRU as a 'dumping ground' for pupils unwanted within mainstream schooling and explores how the availability of support can reduce formal exclusion and assist in the reintegration of excluded pupils into mainstream education either at school or in further education.

Martin Stephenson's concluding chapter outlines the origins and current work of Cities in Schools, a national charity operating in several locations in England and Wales, which facilitates the mobilisation of community resources, including local commerce, voluntary and statutory services, to provide innovative, cost-effective and flexible projects to prevent exclusion or to reintegrate into mainstream education children and young people who have been excluded or are long-term non-attenders.

Eric Blyth and Judith Milner

Acknowledgements

Eric Blyth and Judith Milner would like to thank their colleagues in the Centre for Education Welfare Studies at the University of Huddersfield for their encouragement and enthusiastic support in ensuring the success of the conference, 'Behaviour Problems in Schools and Exclusions: Education and Social Work Responses', which inspired the publication of this book. In particular they wish to thank Sheila Baxter, Ernest Dews, Alan Dunkley, Arthur Giles, Alison Hodgson, David Hoyle, Cherry Platt, Steve Stubbs, John Taylor and Joe Wilson.

They also wish to thank Kathleen Smith for her efficient word processing of the text of this book and for her patience with the vagaries of their – and other contributors' – handwriting.

Carl Parsons is indebted to the Joseph Rowntree Foundation for a grant which supported the research upon which Chapter 8 is based. Ideas expressed in this chapter are not necessarily those of the Foundation. Thanks are due also to Carl Parsons' colleagues on the research: Louise Benns, Jean Hailes and Keith Howlett. Particularly valuable advice on costing methodology was provided by Jenny Beecham and Charlotte Salter.

Dinah Gill and Jeremy Monsen wish to acknowledge the helpful suggestions of Marie Bell, Stewart Clark, Nora Frederickson, John Moore and Rosemary Rees in the preparation of Chapter 13.

Carol Hayden extends thanks to the Education and Social Research Council for funding (grant no. R000 23 4837) the research project on which Chapter 15 is based.

Part I

Trends and theoretical overview

Chapter 1

Exclusions
Trends and issues

Eric Blyth and Judith Milner

INTRODUCTION

Exclusion is the means by which the headteacher of a school can prevent a child or young person from attending the school, either for a fixed period (not exceeding fifteen days in any single school term) or permanently. It is, therefore, school driven. It does not refer to a child or young person absenting him or herself from school, for example by truancy, although the school can achieve this outcome by excluding a truant.

Despite agreed concern about exclusion from school – from the government, the teaching profession, parents and the media – accurate comprehensive national data concerning exclusion have not been readily available. The Department for Education (DfE) itself undertook a study of *permanent* exclusions from state schools for the academic years 1990–1 and 1991–2 (DfE, 1992a, 1993), reporting a rise of approximately 32 per cent (from 2,910 to 3,833) over this period, although on the basis of the first year's data alone the Department had claimed that 'too many' children are excluded for 'too long' (DfE, 1992a, p. 1). In addition the study revealed that certain groups of children and young people were at greater risk of exclusion than others; that variation in exclusion rates between schools could not simply be explained by differences in intake or the socio-economic characteristics of catchment areas; that existing procedures for the management of exclusions (including legal obligations) were not always adhered to, and that alternative educational provision made for many excluded pupils was subject to 'unacceptable variations in both quality and quantity' (DfE, 1992a, p. 1).

These findings are broadly supported by contemporaneous surveys conducted by two professional teaching associations, the Secondary Heads Association (SHA, 1992) and the National Union of Teachers (NUT, 1992). The latter's conclusion that official figures underestimate the actual number of excluded pupils have received further strong support. For example, a poll of Local Education Authorities undertaken on behalf of the BBC suggested that approximately 66,000 exclusions (of all types) take place annually (BBC, 1993). Extrapolating from the results of the first Office for Standards in Education (OFSTED) inspections, involving 428 English secondary schools, Preston (1994a) suggests that, in 1992–3, the number of permanent exclusions could have doubled from the previous year. However, it needs to be recognised that these particular inspections included those of schools about which the government had particular concerns and are not, therefore, necessarily a representative sample.

Researchers involved in smaller-scale studies have identified various strategies which help to mask the true prevalence of exclusion. Stirling (1992a, and in this volume) provides evidence of the phenomenon of 'informal', 'unofficial' exclusions although, since these may never be recorded and may never be notified to the Local Education Authority (LEA), the prevalence of such practices remains difficult to quantify, and may sometimes be portrayed as child and parent-friendly strategies. An illustrative example concerns a child who was 'excluded' from school for several days following misbehaviour in school. However, in a letter to the parents the point was made that the school was not making the exclusion 'official' in light of the child's previous good behaviour and the parents' previous cooperation. Further evidence of the existence of 'informal' exclusion is confirmed by the observation of the Secondary Heads Association that problems may be 'resolved' – and the stigma of exclusion avoided – by parents agreeing to withdraw the pupil and trying to place him or her in another school (SHA, 1992). Cohen and Hughes (1994) also note the practice of unofficial 'internal' exclusions where the pupil remains on the school premises but is prevented from participating in routine school activities with his or her peers.

Given the sensitive nature of exclusion from school, it is important, therefore, neither to underestimate nor overestimate its prevalence and impact. It remains true that the vast majority of school-age children and young people will not be subject to exclusion from school. Nevertheless, certain groups are at considerably greater risk of exclusion than others, and the educational, social and emotional implications for those who are excluded can be considerable.

PUPILS 'AT RISK' OF EXCLUSION

The research evidence indicates that those who are at disproportionate risk of exclusion are: secondary school-age pupils, boys (especially African–Caribbean boys); pupils with special educational needs; and children and young people in local authority care.

There is limited detailed national data concerning the age distribution of excluded pupils, although most attention has been given to pupils at secondary school. In the DfE study (DfE, 1992a, 1993) 87 per cent of permanently excluded pupils were of secondary school age in 1990–1 and 86 per cent in 1991–2. Nevertheless the rising numbers of exclusions from *primary* schools – described in some areas as 'dramatic' and 'notable' – is giving cause for concern (OFSTED, 1993b; see also Parsons and Hayden in this volume).

There is a notable discrepancy between the numbers of boys and girls excluded from school. In national studies boys are between four and five times more likely than girls to be excluded (DfE, 1992a, 1993; SHA, 1992), although Parsons *et al.* (1995) note that the gender difference is even greater at primary school age – 12:1 in 1993–4 and 21:1 during the autumn term 1994. When gender and *ethnicity* factors are considered together, however, it is evident that African–Caribbean boys are most at risk of exclusion, although the overall picture is incomplete because not all LEAs record the ethnic background of excluded pupils (Cohen and Hughes, 1994; CRE, 1985; DfE, 1993; Mayet, 1992; Nottinghamshire County Council, 1991; NUT, 1992). In the DfE study, African–Caribbeans made up approximately 2 per cent of the general school population but between 8.1 per cent (1990–1) and 8.5 per cent (1991–2) of all permanently excluded pupils. Similar, if not more extreme, trends are evident from data from individual local authorities (Mayet, 1992; OFSTED, 1993b).

Sivanandan (1994) views this as racism but there is also resistance from within the education system to the notion that high rates of exclusion are the result of racism (see, for example, Varnava, 1995).

The operation of racial discrimination is complex and its relationship to exclusion from school needs to be considered in relation to both masculinity and power issues (Cooper *et al.*, 1991; Blyth and Milner, and Marshall in this volume).

As Booth (in this volume) indicates, the relationship between pupils with special educational needs and exclusion has been little explored to date. Pupils with formal statements of special educational need under the provisions of the Education Act 1981 accounted for between 12.5 per cent and 15 per cent of permanently excluded pupils in the DfE study (DfE, 1993) although only about 2 per cent of the school population had such a statement during this period (DfE, personal communication). Apart from the survey conducted by Parsons *et al.* (1995) information about exclusion from *special schools* is not readily available. The latter shows that in the 1993–4 academic year, 4.1 per cent of all permanent exclusions were from special schools, rising to 6.1 per cent of all permanent exclusions during the autumn term 1994. What is perhaps more revealing about the exposure of pupils in special schools to the risk of exclusion is Parsons *et al.*'s calculation of the rate of exclusions from primary, secondary and special schools for 1993–4: 0.031 per cent, 0.35 per cent and 0.46 per cent respectively (Parsons *et al.*, 1995).

However, even though these figures recognise the increased exposure to exclusion of pupils with *formal* statements of special educational need, they do not acknowledge the risks posed to those children and young people who may have special educational needs but who have *not* been assessed and whose needs have not been formally identified. Given that the full assessment process can take over a year (ILEA, 1985; Searle, 1994) it is hardly surprising that researchers have found schools increasingly resorting to the speedier exclusion procedures, sometimes using the latter in an attempt to secure additional resources for the child or young person (Cohen and Hughes, 1994; Searle, 1994; Stirling 1992a, b; Todman *et al.*, 1991).

The final group of children and young people considered to be at particular risk of exclusion are those in public care, entry to which has itself been described as an 'educational hazard' (Social Services Select Committee, 1984). The educational experiences of these children and young people are likely to be demonstrably worse than those of their peers, whether they remain within mainstream education or are educated within social services establishments, and whether they are accommodated in foster homes or residential establishments (Audit Commission, 1994; Colton and Heath, 1994; DES, 1992; DoH, 1991, 1992; Heath *et al.*, 1989, 1994; Jackson, 1987, 1989, 1994; Sinclair, 1994; SSI and OFSTED, 1995; Stirling, 1992a, b). Changes of placement and returning home, frequently requiring a change of school, erect further educational hurdles in the path of the young person in public care (Bullock *et al.*, 1994; Firth and Horrocks in this volume).

In her study in the Midlands, Stirling found that many children in local authority care (in both residential and foster care) were excluded from school (Stirling, 1992a, b). Maginnis (1993) attempted to quantify the risk of exclusion to which children and young people in residential care in a Scottish local authority were exposed. These children and young people accounted for approximately 0.3 per cent of the total secondary school population in the region but 23 per cent of all permanently excluded pupils. The results of work we have recently undertaken with a number of local authorities show that there are variations between authorities concerning the degree of risk of exclusion to which 'looked after' children and young people in residential accommodation may be exposed. In one authority where it was possible to compare the rates of exclusion for children and young people in residential care with those in foster care, the former had almost a 1 in 3 chance of being permanently excluded from school while those in foster care had a 1 in 47 chance of being permanently excluded. In a joint review of the education of 'looked after' children, the Department of Health Social Services Inspectorate and OFSTED record their 'grave concern' about: 'the high percentage [25.6 per cent] of the children at [Key Stage] 4 who were excluded from school or who did not attend on a regular basis' (SSI and OFSTED, 1995, p. 13).

That these are not particularly new phenomena is indicated by the findings of Galloway *et al.* (1982) that nearly a quarter of the excluded pupils in their Sheffield study had been in local authority care at some stage in their lives. However, the relationship between exclusion and the public-care system has a further dimension since educational disadvantage, especially non-attendance and exclusion from school, increases the risks of a child or young person entering the public-care system (Bennathan, 1992; Parsons in this volume; Parsons *et al.*, 1994; Sinclair *et al.*, 1994).

THE IMPACT OF EXCLUSION

There has been long-standing concern about the adverse effects of children missing school in both the short and longer term (see, for example, Carlen, 1985; DfE, 1992b; Hibbett and Fogelman, 1990; Hibbett *et al.*, 1990) and contemporary research on juvenile delinquency has made explicit links between delinquency and certain aspects of school behaviour such as truancy, 'troublesomeness', dishonesty, aggressiveness and bullying (see, for example, Farrington and West, 1990). Exploration of the relationship between delinquency and exclusion from school is of recent origin (see, for example, Searle, Stirling, and Cullingford and Morrison in this volume), although anecdotal evidence abounds; most dramatically the DfE prediction that excluded children 'may be drifting into a life of juvenile crime' (DfE, 1993, p. 1). The National Association for the Care and Resettlement of Offenders (1993) has highlighted the potential crime-prevention role of schools that limit exclusions 'by holding on to and engaging disaffected pupils' whilst the Association of Metropolitan Authorities has observed:

> LEAs in the cities, in partnership with other departments and agencies, are beginning to be more aware of the social consequences [of exclusion]. Exclusion can represent the last departure point, particularly for boys, before they become entrenched in an alternative culture of crime.
>
> (AMA, 1995a, pp. 25–6)

The stakes concerning this relationship were raised considerably following a widely published letter from Sir Paul Condon, Commissioner of the Metropolitan Police, to leaders of the black community expressing concerns about the rise in crimes of violence against people in the context of reductions in crimes reported to the police in London: 'It is a fact that very many of the perpetrators of muggings are very young black people, *who have been excluded from school* and/or are unemployed' (Condon, 1995 – our emphasis).

Carlen's (1985) research tracing the origins of female offenders' criminal careers to admission to local authority care for non-attendance at school are echoed by Graham's review of the research evidence that a young person's delinquent career is 'at least partly contingent upon rejecting or being rejected by the school' (Graham, 1988).

The educational futures of many children and young people excluded from school is open to question. Headteachers appear to be increasingly reluctant to accept students excluded from other schools and relatively few permanently excluded pupils are readmitted to another mainstream school (NUT, 1992; Parsons *et al.*, 1995; SHA, 1992; Stirling, 1992a, b) – a practice which may correlate with increasing independence from LEAs (SHA, 1992). So, for some parents at least, the highly vaunted concept of *parental* choice is little more than a rhetorical device disguising the reality of *school* choice. At the same time it is clear that, following the introduction of the Education Reform Act 1988, a differentially stratified state education system has created 'schools which can afford to turn away certain clients and other schools that must take any they can get' (Ball, 1993, p. 8).

There is evidence of considerable delay in providing educational alternatives for some pupils who may find themselves in 'educational limbo' (DfE, 1992a, p. 8.; see also Mitchell in this volume). Some young people may reach school leaving age whilst still excluded (Hackett, 1992) while others completely disappear from the world of formal education (SHA, 1992).

Alternative forms of educational provision away from mainstream school may be of dubious quality as, in the light of adverse economic pressures, many LEAs are being compelled to reduce *existing* provision and support services (BBC, 1993; Garner *et al.*, 1990; Lloyd-Smith, 1993; NUT, 1993). The two major forms of alternative education provision for excluded pupils are placement in a special unit, which since the implementation of the Education Act 1993 is now referred to as a Pupil Referral Unit (PRU), or home tuition.

Historically the place of special units has been questionable (see, for example, ACE, 1991; Cooper *et al.*, 1991; DfE, 1992b; Mongon, 1988), as demonstrated by OFSTED: 'Units and their pupils occupy an ambiguous legal twilight zone and, although this offers some freedom to manoeuvre and the ability to be flexible, children are poorly served' (OFSTED, 1993a, p. 9). Tomlinson is even more scathing of the impact of 'special' provision: 'To be categorised out of "normal" education represents the ultimate in non-achievement in terms of ordinary educational goals' (Tomlinson, 1982, p. 6).

It is clearly too early to determine whether PRUs will be able to overcome the evident shortcomings of special provision and early evidence of their performance is mixed, as demonstrated by Stephenson's critique of PRUs in this volume, Normington in this volume and Parsons et al., 1995.

After provision of education within a special unit/PRU, home tuition appears to be the next most common type of provision – and more so for pupils excluded from primary than secondary schools. However, home tuition is rarely provided at a level which equates with 'full-time' education (Parsons et al., 1995).

Finally, there is evidence that excluded children may be placed at increased physical and emotional risk (Cohen and Hughes, 1994); a graphic illustration being a 10-year-old boy, Joseph Kenny, excluded from school for fighting and sent home, who was killed by his psychotic father in March 1994 (Alderson, 1994). That the impact of exclusion may also be felt by other family members – aggravating financial problems and increasing emotional tension – has also been highlighted by Cohen and Hughes (1994).

REASONS FOR EXCLUSIONS

Current evidence indicates a wide variety of circumstances resulting in exclusion from school. Despite well-publicised concerns about levels of violence in British schools and risks to other students and staff (and often vividly portrayed in contemporary media representations of school life such as *Grange Hill* and *Hearts and Minds*), exclusion for violent behaviour remains at a relatively low level (DfE, 1992b; Gale and Topping, 1986; Imich, 1994; NUT, 1992). However, the issue of violence in school and the way in which it is identified and 'processed' requires more sophisticated and detailed analysis. For example, bullying is experienced by many school children (see Smith and Thompson, 1991) but is not always reported and those instances that are reported are subject to various filtering processes. Concern about levels of physical and sexual violence directed towards staff (Norman, 1993) has also to be seen in the context of current constraints on schools to promote a positive image which militate against the reporting of violence in schools. According to a representative of one professional teaching association: 'Staff are not reporting violent incidents because they are under pressure from their school to hush attacks up' (Brook, quoted in Hirst, 1993).

Generally exclusion is associated with issues relating to the management and control of pupils. What emerges is the role of 'disobedience in various forms' (DfE, 1993) – a constellation of negative, disruptive, insolent and uncooperative behaviours (DfE, 1992a, 1993; NUT, 1992). In many instances the event precipitating exclusion may be relatively trivial but provides the 'final straw' for a deteriorating relationship between pupil and staff. For example, in our own work we became aware of a teenage girl excluded for a fifteen day 'block' for refusing to remove an earring (see also BBC, 1993; Channel 4, 1993; Cohen and Hughes, 1994; Garner, 1994).

Although the formal evidence indicates a fairly consistent pattern of the antecedents of exclusion, these should be treated with at least a degree of caution. Recorded categorisations are, by definition, the *official* rationale for exclusion and specific behaviours will be interpreted and coded to fit acceptable descriptions and categories of behaviour. Such coding will also be influenced by the existing nature of pupil/teacher interactions and allow considerable scope for individual interpretation, not to say idiosyncrasy, which is no doubt responsible in part for some of the school differences in exclusion rates (McManus, 1995).

VARIATION IN EXCLUSION RATES BETWEEN SCHOOLS

Given the wealth of evidence about differences between schools on a wide range of factors (see, for example, Mortimore *et al.*, 1988; Reynolds, 1985a; Rutter *et al.*, 1979; Smith and Tomlinson, 1989), it would be surprising indeed if there were not also variations between schools' rates of exclusion. However, consensus that such differences exist (see, for example, DfE, 1992a, 1993; Galloway *et al.*, 1982; Imich, 1994; NUT, 1992; SHA, 1992) conceals conflicting explanations for them. The claim by the Secondary Heads Association that 'much, if not most, of this difference ... relates to the nature of the intake to the school'

(SHA, 1992, p. 2) is at odds with the findings of the Elton Committee (DES, 1989) and the government's contention that the variation between schools is 'too great to be explained by the socio-economic nature of schools' catchment areas' (DfE, 1992a, p. 3). Without denying the impact of factors relating to the social and economic environment in which schools operate, the view of the government in this respect tends to be supported by the vast majority of academic researchers who have produced increasing evidence that headteachers' attitudes, school status, policies and practices may exert a greater effect on the probability of exclusion than actual pupil behaviour (see, for example, Galloway *et al.*, 1982, 1985; Imich, 1994; McLean, 1987; McManus, 1987, 1995).

McManus (1995) notes that differences in school policies could account for about half of the difference between high and low excluding schools:

> In those [schools] where few pupils are excluded there is a greater degree of shared responsibility, a willingness to face up to and prepare for difficulties that arise, and a determination to accommodate and cope with the vagaries of adolescent demeanour.
>
> (McManus, 1995, p. 42; see also
> Searle, and Benson in this volume)

Notably, official studies fail to take account of the perceptions of excluded pupils and their families. In his research Garner (1994, and in this volume) observes that those pupils who are most vulnerable to exclusion are unlikely to be active participants in or contributors to managing their own behaviour. On the rare occasions the views of excluded pupils and their families have been ascertained, evidence emerges of serious misperceptions and miscommunications between pupils, teachers and parents.

EXPLAINING INCREASES IN THE RATES OF EXCLUSIONS

Explanations for the rise in exclusion rates differ according to who is providing them. Educational professionals and teachers themselves have located their explanatory framework within the wider context of educational reform and the changing nature of public service provision in Britain (Blyth and Milner, 1993, 1994).

The emergence of the education market has also been recognised as contributing to a reduced willingness of headteachers to cope with 'difficult' pupils: 'Heads who had previously been sympathetic to offering extra support to difficult and under-achieving pupils were now seeing them as a liability. They were looking for ways of transferring them to other schools or units' (Stirling, 1992b, p. 128).

Elsewhere, a headteacher interviewed by the BBC (1993) noted that pupils identified as a drain on school resources were perceived as 'passengers ... dragging back' the school and likely to be excluded.

Such implications of the education reforms of the late 1980s were not entirely unexpected, the two professional associations for education social work fearing that these would encourage less flexibility and responsiveness to pupils who are experiencing emotional difficulties or who are not orientated to achievement – with consequent adverse effects on attendance, achievement and behaviour (ACESW and NASWE, 1991).

From our own work we know of one headteacher who had been lobbied by a group of parents threatening to remove their children from the school if he didn't 'do something' about a particularly troublesome pupil.

An evident factor appears to be increasing independence of schools from local authority control, especially the selectivity of Grant Maintained schools, reluctance to admit a previously-excluded pupil appearing to be more evident, the more independent the school is from LEA control (BBC, 1993; Stirling, 1992a, b): 'The rate of admission of excluded pupils [to other schools] declines steeply as ties with LEAs become weaker' (SHA, 1992, p. 4).

The publication of specific performance data may have served to encourage exclusion by other means, through changes in the way in which schools have been required to categorise absences since 1992 as either *authorised* or *unauthorised* (DES, 1991) although until 1994–5 schools have been required to publish details of unauthorised absence only. Given the pressure on schools to minimise the rates of unauthorised absence in order to provide a 'good' public image, the formal categorisation of exclusion as *authorised* absence (and hence schools' exclusion rates withheld from public scrutiny) is clearly helpful as is the tactic of excluding a pupil for truancy (which would otherwise be formally recorded as *unauthorised* absence). Despite the government's disapproval of exclusion as a sanction against truancy (DfE, 1994a) the authors' research indicates that schools are continuing to exclude truanting pupils.

Similarly, informal exclusion, which has the additional 'advantage' of not requiring a report to either the governing body or the LEA, can also be recorded as *authorised* absence (Stirling, 1992a, b). A further bonus for schools is that not only have they been able to get rid of an unwanted pupil without adversely affecting their published attendance record, they have also been able to retain funding for a pupil for whom they no longer provide an education. However, the general concept of 'the money following the pupil' was extended to the excluded pupil from the beginning of the 1994–5 academic year under provisions of the Education Act 1993, bringing to an end this additional incentive to exclude troublesome pupils. Even so, some headteachers will consider the lost revenue a small price to pay to be rid of pupils 'past their sell-by date' (a reference made by a headteacher about a 7-year-old boy she considered at risk of exclusion).

Changed financial arrangements under local management of schools (LMS) – enabling schools to purchase specialist services from the LEA or elsewhere – rather than being provided with them by the LEA as required, may also have played a part. Given the positive financial advantage of getting rid of troublesome pupils, there is an evident financial disincentive for schools to *purchase* specialist help for pupils with behavioural disturbances which might result in the need to provide further expensive facilities which may not be adequately funded through the special educational needs statementing process (Stirling, 1992b). More generally, several commentators have indicted the implications of reduced resources in schools and in LEA support services (NUT, 1992; SHA, 1992; Stirling, 1992a, b). Such deterioration in resources, alongside increased administrative workloads associated with the introduction of the National Curriculum, is claimed to have resulted in an increase in teachers' workloads – imposing more stress on teachers themselves and reducing the time available to spend with individual children (NUT, 1992). And, if teachers are now less successful in maintaining classroom control, might this not itself be testament to the success of explicit

Thatcherite policies to undermine the power and autonomy of the teaching profession (Davies, 1986)?

Some teachers have also argued that the children's rights movement itself, as it affects education and teacher/pupil relationships, may have increased the risks of exclusion. As teachers may be more apprehensive about physically restraining children who are themselves violent or present behaviour problems so exclusion may come to be seen as the *only* option available to them (Dineen, 1993; O'Leary, 1995; Preston, 1993a; Stirling, 1992b).

Finally, research has indicated certain factors external to the school which have been held at least partially responsible for disruptive behaviour within school. The NUT cites deteriorating home circumstances and lack of parental discipline (NUT, 1992), whilst Rutter and Smith (1995) argue that there is evidence of a post-war increase in many forms of child psychiatric disorder which are influenced by prevailing social conditions. McManus (1995) suggests that about 20 per cent of a school's level of exclusions can be attributed to catchment area poverty (see also Hayden in this volume).

REFORM OF THE EXCLUSION PROCESS

The DfE exclusions survey revealed that existing 'legal procedures are not always operated correctly, and certainly not very promptly' (DfE, 1992a, p. 8). In addition, the appeal provisions seemed rarely to operate in favour of pupils and parents. Neither governing bodies nor LEAs made much use of their powers to review exclusions and in the very few instances where parents exercised their right of appeal their chances of success seemed slim indeed. Parents appealed in just over 3 per cent of permanent exclusions and of these just over 17 per cent were successful. Successful parental appeals *and* governing bodies' and LEAs' reviews combined resulted in the reversal of only 5 per cent of all permanent exclusion decisions (DfE, 1993).

Even on the rare occasion where an exclusion is overturned, the intent of such decisions may be thwarted in practice. For example, teaching unions have authorised members not to teach reinstated excludees – sometimes reinforced by a threat of a strike ballot (Kingston, 1995; *Yorkshire Post*, 1993; see also Searle in this volume). Reinforcing the practical importance of school processes, Kingston cites the experience of one pupil, returning to school after a long absence, who was told by the headteacher at assembly to stand up because 'we've all forgotten what you look like'. Not surprisingly the boy failed to reappear the following or on subsequent days (Kingston, 1995, p. 3; see also Cullingford and Morrison in this volume).

Legal changes to the system of exclusion, primarily designed to prevent 'drift' and indecision and to reduce the adverse educational impact of exclusion, have been made under provisions of the Education Act 1993 while more specific guidance on policy and practice is contained in accompanying departmental circulars on 'Pupils with Problems' (DfE, 1994a–c; DfE and DoH, 1994a–c). The main procedural changes have been to limit fixed-period exclusions to a maximum of fifteen days in any single school term and to abolish indefinite exclusions while the guidance is designed to clarify both the circumstances warranting exclusion from school and the powers, rights and duties of head-teachers, governing bodies, local education authorities, pupils and their parents/guardians. As indicated previously the principle of funding following a pupil has been extended to excluded pupils. The LEA's former *powers* to provide education 'otherwise than at school' for excluded pupils have been replaced by a *duty* to do so, which can include providing education in a specialist Pupil Referral Unit. Potentially innovative arrangements for excluded pupils are encouraged, such as the pupil's dual registration at both a mainstream school and a PRU, and the provision of educational programmes in sixth form colleges and technical colleges for older excluded pupils (see also Normington, and Stevenson in this volume).

Early indications of the effect of these changes have been conflicting. During the first term following introduction of the new system in September 1994, the National Association of Head Teachers produced evidence indicating that the rate of permanent exclusions continued to rise drastically, suggesting that pupils who would formerly have been excluded indefinitely were now more likely to be excluded permanently and that the legislative changes had adversely affected previous informal arrangements between schools to find places for excluded pupils (NAHT, 1994). This is supported by the findings of a study conducted by Parsons *et al.*, which show not only that the number of permanent exclusions had tripled between 1991–2 and 1993–4 but also that, for the autumn term 1994, most (70 out of 101) LEAs reported a continuing upward trend. Indeed for five LEAs the number of permanent exclusions recorded for the autumn term 1994 alone exceeded the total number of permanent exclusions for the whole of the previous academic year whilst, nationally, more permanent exclusions were recorded in the autumn term 1994 than in the whole of the 1991–2 academic year (Parsons *et al.*, 1995).

On the other hand, pressures to exclude may be mitigated by the prospect (and reality) of an increasing willingness amongst governing bodies and LEAs to rescind exclusions and of parents becoming more prepared to exercise their rights of appeal and to take legal action. The secretary of the Headmasters' Conference (an organisation of private schools where the concept of parent-as-consumer might be expected to have greater currency than in the state sector) is quoted by Cohen (1995): 'It has been held until now that exclusions or expulsion is something the parents have to accept. How would the headteachers maintain discipline if pupils could force schools to accept them back?' Preston (1994b) cites (the so far unique) instance of the High Court reinstating an excluded 15-year-old.

As yet it is not possible to judge the impact of the Code of Practice on the Identification and Assessment of Special Educational Needs (DfE, 1994d) on exclusion practices. The expectation that schools will exercise a major role in the provision of services for pupils up to and including Stage 3 – including pupils with emotional and behavioural difficulties – may result in the development of more cooperative packages (such as those described by Normington in this volume and by Parsons *et al.*, 1995). However, Parsons *et al.* (1995) have already detected considerable variation in LEA practices regarding the implementation of guidance contained in Circulars 8/94 (DfE, 1994a) and 10/94 (DfE, 1994b) and the Code of Practice. For example, only 'a small number' of LEAs would expect a pupil at risk of exclusion to have been assessed at Stage 3 for emotional and behavioural difficulty. Similarly 'a minority' of LEAs considered the behaviour of excluded pupils as evidence of special educational need while only eight regarded *all* pupils out of school to be at Stage 3 (although a further fourteen LEAs were said to have expressed some association between exclusion and special educational needs by reference to 'observation with a view to formal assessment').

LEGISLATIVE TENSIONS

Provisions to reform arrangements for managing pupil behaviour in schools and for exclusions cannot be considered in a vacuum. As we have previously noted, many commentators are agreed (although not the government itself) that the introduction of education reforms begun in the late 1980s is at least partially responsible for the increase in exclusions. It needs to be recognised, therefore, that the legislation heralding the exclusion reforms and which strives to introduce a new deal for a wide range of pupils with problems has, as its main purpose, the *expansion* of the education market. There is also an internal conflict, highlighted by the work of the Audit Commission on the operation of the Education Act 1981 and by the Association of Metropolitan Authorities, between the pressures to delegate and decentralise resources, placing centralised support at risk, and the recognition of the contribution of those same services to increasingly class-based assessments of individual pupil need (AMA, 1995a; Audit Commission, 1994). Furthermore, as the exclusion of pupils with statements of special needs illustrates, integrationist and market ideologies make uncomfortable bedfellows.

Legislative tensions are particularly evident between education legislation and the Children Act 1989. The central tenet of the Children Act 1989 is the paramountcy of the welfare of the child. It emphasises parental responsibility, requiring professionals to work in partnership with families and to ascertain the wishes of children and young people in any decision affecting their welfare. The Act *increased* the duties of local authorities to 'safeguard and promote the welfare of children, within their area who are in need by providing a range and level of services appropriate to meet those children's needs' (Children Act 1989, Section 17). In contrast, both the Education Reform Act and the Education Act 1993 *restrict* the role of the local authority in the provision of education (and therefore in the lives of children and young people) and neither recognised the rights of the child or young person in relation to education, the government explicitly resisting the opportunity to ensure that educational decisions be informed by consideration of the welfare of the child (Rabinowicz, 1993). So, while the government recognises that many children and young people 'looked after' by local authorities 'feel that they are not meaningfully involved in the decisions being taken about them, including those relating to moves of home or school', and that 'the older ones, are entitled to take part as far as possible in decisions that affect their lives and at least to have their views taken into account' (DfE and DoH, 1994c, p. 9), such a courtesy is not afforded to those children and young people for whom the provisions of the Children Act do *not* apply. Ironically, the only group of pupils whose wishes and feelings about their education must be given 'due consideration' are those subject to an Education Supervision Order for not attending school (Children Act 1989, Section 36 [5]).

At the policy and practice level, the series of circulars accompanying the 1993 Act concerning 'Pupils with Problems' set out a framework designed to promote inter-organisational and inter-professional cooperation and partnership in providing services for school children. These identify critical areas where inter-agency cooperation should occur (DfE, 1994a–c; DfE and DoH, 1994a–c), supplementing the recommendations of the Utting Committee that joint education and social services sub-committees should include strategies to meet the educational needs of children and young people in care (DoH, 1991; see also Firth and Horrocks in this volume). The Social Services Inspectorate and OFSTED have subsequently reaffirmed the need for more effective inter-agency cooperation to ensure the provision of adequate education for 'looked after' children and young people who, whether because of their own failure to attend school regularly or because of exclusion, have no regular educational placement (SSI and OFSTED, 1995).

However, while both the Children Act 1989 (Section 27) and the Education Act 1993 (Section 166) broadly impose a duty of inter-agency cooperation in the provision of services for children 'in need' and with 'special educational needs' respectively, the duty to cooperate is not absolute. Furthermore, a child or young person with special educational needs will not necessarily be 'in need' as defined in the Children Act nor will a child 'in need' necessarily have special educational needs, although the practice of combined assessment (including assessment under disability legislation) is encouraged. Under the Children Act individual local authorities have discretion to define 'need' – the key to eligibility for services under the Act. So, although Sinclair *et al.* (1994) argue that a child not receiving education, whether because of non-attendance or because of exclusion, is a child in need, early research into the implementation of the Children Act indicated that only a quarter of Social Services Departments had included children excluded from school within the category of children 'in need'; 40 per cent had included children with 'special educational needs', and 15 per cent had included truants (DoH, 1993).

The failure of inter-agency cooperation between education and social services departments is more in evidence than its effectiveness (Audit Commission, 1994; SSI and DoH, 1995). Sinclair, for one, is not surprised at this, given increasing pressures on local authority budgets, tensions in legislative changes and the creation of competition between public services and between public and private services:

> there is evidence of a growing tension between professionals in education and Social Services Departments, often despite feelings of goodwill and shared aims, but the ability to work together effectively is being hampered by arguments over budgets and the growing practice of having to contract or buy in services once freely exchanged.
>
> (Sinclair, 1994)

In relation to excluded pupils, Parsons *et al.* (1994) note the lack of inter-agency cooperation at all stages of the exclusion process.

CONCLUSION

In this chapter we have reviewed the emerging body of information and comment concerning exclusion from school in England. It provides a framework for the various contributions to this book and, in particular, Tony Booth's following chapter, which reminds us of the narrowness of any debate which concentrates exclusively on official definitions and processes.

Chapter 2

Stories of exclusion
Natural and unnatural selection

Tony Booth

INTRODUCTION

Whenever an aspect of education achieves public media prominence, discussion of it soon takes on the status of received wisdom.
Even if it is not utterly distorted in the telling and re-telling,
initial progress in explaining a complex set of processes may be
frozen with the repetition of the first accounts. Stories about the
'rise' in disciplinary exclusions in the 1990s in England have taken
on this quality.

Attempts to understand exclusion have often concentrated
narrowly on the use and misuse of the official procedures for
disciplinary exclusion set out in the Education (No. 2) Act 1986
and revised by the Education Act 1993. Important changes in
the education system which affect the numbers officially excluded
on disciplinary grounds have been missed. The relationship
between disciplinary and other forms of exclusion, particularly
of students categorised as having 'special needs', has been left
largely unexplored. By yielding the definition of a complex social
phenomenon to those who frame legislation we limit our scope
for understanding and responding to it.

Attention has been focused on two features of the 'rise' in
disciplinary exclusion; its relationship to competitive pressures in
the education system and the over-preponderance of black, male,
African–Caribbean pupils in the exclusion statistics. Both of these
issues draw attention away from the details of exclusion *events*
at the point of breakdown in the relationship between school and
pupil towards the *processes* of devaluation which may precede it.
This understanding of exclusionary processes could provide
an opportunity for redefining and reinterpreting the nature of

exclusion and the way we should respond to it but it has not been exploited fully. An increase in competition and selection within the system which leads to a greater number of 'disciplinary' exclusions will also lead to more students being excluded on the basis of other undesired characteristics such as low attainments. 'Poor behaviour' and 'low attainment' may be treated within schools as alternative justifications for the exclusion of the same pupils.

The over-representation of African–Caribbean boys in the exclusion statistics has been related to the wider exclusionary processes involved in racism. Yet a while ago it was the 'special needs' statistics that were under scrutiny and racism was said to be at the root of the disproportionate number of black students sent to special schools on the basis of low attainment and presumed 'ability' (Coard, 1971; Tomlinson, 1981). Relatively little attention is given to the disproportionate numbers of black African–Caribbean pupils currently categorised as having 'emotional and behavioural difficulties' and sent to special schools (Cooper *et al.*, 1991).

In both the disciplinary exclusions and exclusions by 'emotional and behavioural difficulty' there is a large under-representation of girls. This is an extremely significant imbalance and cries out for attention, not least because it will be reflected in any special provision for 'excluded' pupils which may thereby be unsatisfactory and unsafe for girls. I will argue that some of the imbalance in the statistics is redressed if we include groups of girls informally excluded because of pregnancy.

One might have thought that the very use of the word 'exclusion' to replace the words 'suspension' and 'expulsion' in describing pupils sent home from school for breaches of discipline, since the Education (No. 2) Act 1986, would push us to connect 'disciplinary exclusion' and other exclusionary events and processes in schools. Exclusion also has an interesting opposite: 'inclusion'. In the 1990s 'inclusion' or 'inclusive education' has begun to replace 'integration' in describing the processes of increasing the participation of students who experience difficulties in learning, disaffection, or have disabilities, within the cultures and curricula of mainstream schools. I have written elsewhere about the dangers of the internationalisation of concepts such as 'inclusion' which detach our understanding from local cultures and histories but I have recognised the advantage offered by the semantic invitation to reflect simultaneously on inclusion and exclusion (Booth, 1995). Yet it is uncommon either for those who work on 'disciplinary exclusions' or for those who work on exclusion by 'special need' to put their heads together or reflect on the way these sets of processes are compartmentalised in their minds.

In this chapter I will attempt to contribute to our understanding of exclusion by drawing together the variety of exclusionary events and processes that occur in schools. I will ask: who is included in and excluded from the exclusion statistics? I will examine, in some detail, the separation of 'disciplinary' and 'special needs exclusions' in the minds of practitioners and academics and reflect on why this happens. I will ask in the light of these discussions how exclusion might be productively defined, and at the consequences this might have for the way exclusion is measured. I will conclude the chapter by asking what difference my change in emphasis makes to research and practice on exclusions.

WHO IS INCLUDED IN AND EXCLUDED FROM EXCLUSION STATISTICS?

To make an appropriate, practical and theoretical, response to 'disciplinary' exclusions we have to relate these to other exclusionary processes which operate in schools. Failure to do this may result in misconceived action based on spurious statistics. Without detailed surveys of local education authorities which look at where all pupils in an area receive their education it is very difficult to begin to piece together accurate statistics on exclusion events. Table 2.1 provides a list of categories of exclusion from school. My justification for linking them together should become clear as the chapter progresses. It is a mixed list, containing both official pigeonholes and reasons for exclusion. Table 2.2 contains an alternative way of viewing some of these categories by highlighting *groups* who are vulnerable to exclusion from mainstream schools. Both ways of thinking about exclusion will be apparent in this section.

Exclusions 1: disciplinary

In the area of disciplinary exclusions attention has been given to both the official exclusions and informal exclusions and these

Table 2.1 Categories of exclusion beyond the mainstream

Exclusions	Categories
1	Disciplinary
	(a) According to official procedures in Education Act 1993.
	(b) Informally without alternative provision.
	(c) Sent to 'Disruptive' or Pupil Referral Units without formal exclusion.
2	'Special need' or 'Learning difficulty'
	(a) Categorised as having 'emotional and behavioural difficulties'.
	(b) Categorised as having low attainment or low 'ability' and (informally) categorised as having 'moderate' or 'severe' learning difficulties.
	(c) Categorised as having a physical or sensory disability.
3	Education otherwise than at school.
4	Truancy.
5	Exclusion by default: active and passive.
6	School-age pregnancy and motherhood.
7	English as an additional language.

Table 2.2 Groups vulnerable to exclusion from mainstream schools

Exclusions	Groups
1	Boys
2	African–Caribbean boys
3	School-age mothers
4	Students with low attainment
5	Disabled students
6	Travellers
7	Children and young people in care

have informed debates about the statistics. Less attention has been paid to pupils in off-site disruptive units established by the Education Act 1944 and reformed as 'pupil referral units' under the Education Act 1993. Such pupils may remain on a mainstream school roll and may not be officially 'excluded'. They may arrive at such provision following an informal exclusion. Such units had a heyday between the mid 1970s and 1980s and then numbers declined though they remained relatively widespread (Lovey *et al.*, 1993; OFSTED, 1993a). Their golden age may return as pressure to contain exclusions mounts. However, the fall in numbers of a whole variety of units, including community homes with education, must have affected exclusionary pressures and the exclusion statistics. In separate chapters in their book, *Exclusion from School*, Lovey *et al.*, (1993) chart the rapid rise in exclusions invoking the disciplinary procedures of the Education (No. 2) Act 1986 and the equally rapid reduction in the use of off-site units for pupils seen as difficult in behaviour without noticing the connection between these two trends.

I listed 'boys' as the first group vulnerable to exclusion in Table 2.2, because of their massive over-representation amongst pupils seen to be difficult in behaviour and subject to exclusion procedures. The way some boys and their teachers engage in battles of classroom control which reduce the attention teachers give to others, particularly girls, is a continuing observation of life in mixed schools (see also Marshall in this volume). The persistence of this phenomenon and its attendant ideologies about male aggression may make the imbalance towards boys in the exclusion statistics seem natural and, therefore, not requiring examination. However, an effective response to disciplinary exclusions as well as discipline problems in general requires a close scrutiny of the behaviour of boys and girls and of teacher perceptions of it and reactions to it.

Exclusions 2: 'special needs'

About 89,000 pupils are categorised as having 'special needs' and excluded from mainstream schools in England, representing 1.49 per cent of all 5–15 year olds (Norwich, 1994). For a large number of these pupils, possibly a majority, difficulties over discipline is a precursor of their exclusion. The separation of disciplinary and 'special needs' exclusions is only part of a pervasive and unproductive separation of difficulties of behaviour and learning in schools. Whilst the interconnections between them are recognised even in official reports (DES, 1989), this has little influence on legislation or school policies. Particularly in secondary schools, divisions have been created and have persisted between pastoral care and learning support staff (Best, 1994) and these are commonly divided from those with a responsibility for pupils whose difficulties are officially recorded on a 'statement of special educational need'.

In practice, it may be a matter of chance whether a pupil is subject to a formal disciplinary exclusion, sent to an off-site disruptive unit, categorised as having 'emotional and behavioural difficulties' or 'learning difficulties', and sent to day or residential special schools (see also Stephenson in this volume). Circular 11/94 refers to the vagaries of assigning pupils to 'pupil referral units' (in the past): 'How and why pupils are referred to units currently varies between LEAs and between units and rarely seems to be determined by clear and consistent LEA policy' (DfE, 1994c, para. 28). Much the same could be said about schools for pupils categorised as having 'emotional and behavioural difficulties' or 'learning difficulties'. Armstrong and Galloway (1992) have portrayed the processes whereby pupils seen to be difficult in behaviour in school who also have difficulties at home may be categorised as having emotional and behavioural difficulties and pushed towards residential special provision (see also Galloway *et al.*, 1994).

The definition of emotional and behavioural difficulties leaves plenty of scope for differences in practice. According to Circular 9/94:

> Emotional and behavioural difficulties lie on the continuum between behaviour which challenges teachers but is within normal, albeit unacceptable, bounds and that which is indicative of serious mental illness. They are persistent (if not necessarily permanent) and constitute learning difficulties.
>
> (DfE and DOH, 1994a, p. 7)

The way in which they constitute learning difficulties is unclear too, since officially a learning difficulty can either be a 'greater difficulty in learning' than others or a 'disability'. Most pupils categorised as having 'emotional and behavioural difficulties' do not have a disability and some do not find learning difficult.

Overall, the group of pupils categorised as having emotional and behavioural difficulties shows many of the characteristics of Education Act 1993 exclusions; there is an overwhelming preponderance of boys (around 6:1), and a considerable over-representation of 'British–Afro–Caribbean boys' (Cooper *et al.*, 1991).

The largest group of pupils excluded from the mainstream on the grounds of their 'special need' are those categorised as having 'learning difficulties' and assigned an additional informal label of 'moderate' or 'severe'. Anyone associated with provision for pupils categorised as having 'moderate learning difficulties' will be aware that in practice pupils, probably the majority, arrive there because they are seen to be difficult in behaviour. One criterion for such learning difficulties set out in the Code of Practice on 'the identification and assessment of special educational needs', is that 'there is evidence of significant emotional or behavioural difficulties, as indicated by ... withdrawn or disruptive behaviour' (DfE, 1994d, para. 3:57). In the early 1970s, it was this provision which gained notoriety for the over-representation of African–Caribbean pupils. No overview of the ethnic composition of pupils in such provision is available.

I have selected three examples to illuminate current attitudes to differences between 'disciplinary' and 'special needs' exclusions in writers about exclusion. The authors of the Family Service Units/Barnados report wrote about both disciplinary and 'special needs' exclusions in the following way:

> Exclusion from school affects two groups of children ... firstly those who have learning disabilities, including those whose ability to learn is impaired by emotional or behavioural difficulties; secondly those whose behaviour is considered disruptive, and where the school system is unable to maintain them. ... In many instances both descriptions apply to a child. However, the causative and associative factors may be different, and to a point the two issues must be treated separately.
>
> (Cohen and Hughes, 1994 p. 1)

The use of the medical terminology of learning 'disability' and 'impairment', more prevalent in the USA than the UK to describe difficulties in learning, reinforces a view that 'special needs' defines a group of pupils whose assessment and categorisation is rational and the province of specialised experts. I take a different view to these authors. The overlap between pupils subject to disciplinary exclusions and those categorised as having 'special needs' is so great that to consider them separately is to misunderstand practice and the policies required to minimise exclusion.

I explored the theoretical sense of differentiating such pupils with a researcher working under the 1993 Act exclusions. He argued that 'special needs' exclusions were a separate issue. They were 'benign' – 'benign exclusions for good kids':

> I'm not an expert on that ... presumably when children were divided off into special schools or separate units it wasn't because they were cast out, it wasn't to their disadvantage. People had good intentions when they set up special schools.

However, exclusions under the 1986 Act were not intended for the good of the pupils themselves, but 'to prevent them from harming others'. They were also exclusions concerning kids 'who were not seen to have something wrong with them, a disability, or a learning difficulty or whatever', they were exclusions of 'normal, in inverted commas, kids, that schools wanted to be rid of'. Again, there is the suggestion that there are some pupils who are abnormal and are dealt with by a rational and benign system of assessment, categorisation and placement.

My third example comes from the Institute of Race Relations report on the disciplinary exclusion of black pupils (Bourne *et al.*, 1994). In his chapter Chris Searle provides an eloquent argument for minimising exclusion: 'The exclusions issue affects thousands of young people and their parents on a daily basis, cutting them off from their human right and entitlement to the best in education' (Searle, 1994, p. 27). Yet he also provides a pertinent example where the exclusion of a British–Asian pupil was 'expedient' because he was said to have 'special needs'. The shifting of categories allowed Chris Searle to see the exclusion of Ahmed as natural and desirable.

> Sometimes such a course of action seems to be the only expedient. Take the case of Ahmed, a 13 year old boy recently arrived from Pakistan, who was having serious problems in learning English in his mainstream school. He was clearly in need of specialised English as a second language and learning difficulties support beyond that which the school was able to offer and his teachers found that they could benefit him little in the mainstream context. His language learning was not progressing, he very quickly became distressed and disruptive in classes, and he was eventually adjudged a safety risk both to himself and his classmates. Appeals to the LEA for him to

be placed in a special school where he could get much closer skilled attention were getting nowhere because of the squeeze on special education resources – and because, as far as the 'system' was concerned, he was still in mainstream education and attending regularly ... the only step a school can take in such a situation, when it considers it absolutely essential for a pupil to have a special school place, is to try to *make* that pupil a priority by excluding him or her from the mainstream school and putting the responsibility for his or her special education back with the LEA. In this case, Ahmed was indefinitely excluded with parental agreement but it took several months to get him regular home tuition and over a year for an assessment by an educational psychologist. Finally, after much internal campaigning and the intervention by the local council for racial equality, a place in a special school was secured for Ahmed.

(Searle, 1994, pp. 20–1)

The information that we have about Ahmed is limited, but, judging by the text, it would seem that Ahmed required support with the difficulties in learning that he was experiencing, including support with acquiring English as an additional language. Why was it not considered natural for this support to be provided in the mainstream and for his mainstream school to continue to take responsibility for him? Instead, it seems, time and effort were expended in segregating him from the mainstream, resulting, for several months, in an education consisting of a few hours a week of home tuition. The 'unnatural' disciplinary exclusion procedures were used to force the LEA into taking responsibility for the pupil because he was seen to require 'special education'. In the absence of a challenge to it, there is an implication here that segregation is also acceptable for pupils who need support because English is an additional language for them.

The notion that there are natural candidates for exclusion – pupils who are not 'normal', who are seen to have 'something wrong with them' – provides a constant opportunity for categorising pupils who 'schools want to be rid of'. The notion in itself fuels the exclusion of pupils on the grounds of their low attainment and presumed ability, their bodily impairment or *their behaviour*.

The notion that 'disciplinary exclusions' are in the interests of others while the exclusion of pupils categorised as having 'special needs' is 'for their own good' cannot be sustained. One legal justification of a child's exclusion on the grounds of 'special needs' is incompatibility 'with the provision of efficient education' for mainstream pupils (Education Act 1993, Clause 160). The possibility has to be considered that the categories which legitimate life outside mainstream schools represent disposal options for unwanted pupils. As one option closes another is chosen.

The over-representation of African–Caribbean boys is a concern because exclusion of any type is disruptive of education and stigmatising. There is a long-standing debate about whether the establishment of special schools or their continuation for any pupils can be considered as benign. While a variety of groups in society may choose to meet and learn together, *compulsory segregation* is never benign; it is always associated with devaluation. Segregation in special schools on the basis of low attainment can be seen as part of a selective system based on reward for success and stigmatisation for failure. Nor is it possible to draw a line between the working class groups who make up the vast majority of pupils in special schools for 'moderate learning difficulties' and 'emotional and behavioural difficulties' and groups of disabled students. As organisations of disabled people and others have made clear, the compulsory segregation of people with disabilities is a denial of basic human rights. The notion that it is done 'for their own good' is seen as patronising and unacceptable (Mason and Rieser, 1990; Oliver, 1990).

There is a further legal oddity about the distinction between 'special need' and 'excluded' or 'disruptive' pupils. Under the terms of the 1993 Act 'special educational provision' is education that is 'additional to, or otherwise different from, the educational provision made generally for children' (DfE, 1993, clause 156). On this definition it would seem that 'pupil referral units' are forms of 'special provision' and that pupils sent to them should be the subject of statementing procedures. The non-special status of the provision has not been challenged legally but this might be more difficult to sustain under the terms of the 1993 Act. Pupil referral units are schools in their own right, under the direct control of LEAs, and for all intents and purposes are a new form of special school. Or perhaps, as argued by Bowers (1994), they should be seen as a return to the old form of special school that existed before the 1981 Act and the statementing procedure, unencumbered by the requirement to follow the

National Curriculum. The avoidance of statementing procedures for pupils excluded from schools retains a fast disposal route out of mainstream schools.

Exclusions 3: education otherwise than at school

There is a group which receives some limited education outside school and which is included with pupils sent to pupil referral units in the government advice on the 'Education by LEAs of children otherwise than at school' (DfE, 1994c). In 1993, 6,600 pupils of compulsory school age and 500 over-16s were said to be receiving some teaching from 2,600 full-time equivalent teachers 'by home tuition, education in hospital or placement in a unit' (DfE, 1994c, para. 16). Some of these pupils would also come under my version of disciplinary exclusions but some are additional exclusions which need to be included in any comprehensive statistics.

Exclusions 4: truancy

There is a clear overlap between the 'voluntary', 'unauthorised absence' of pupils and those formally or informally subject to discipline procedures. I used to think that stories of the exclusion of pupils for truancy were apocryphal until I was told by education social workers that this was a growing problem in the area in which I live. The Elton report (DES, 1989) acknowledged the practice of excluding pupils for truancy and it is asserted in Circular 10/94 that exclusion 'is ... an inappropriate response to non-attendance' (DfE, 1994b, para. 31). There are also cases of truancy which involve a jump before a push and some of these may be the 'voluntary' withdrawals that 'some headteachers' using 'heavy pressure' encourage 'as a way of dealing with troublesome behaviour' (DfE, 1994d, para. 34; see also Cullingford and Morrison in this volume).

The publishing of truancy tables pushed the balance towards greater exclusion of the same pupils even though some schools are taking a very liberal view of what constitutes authorised and unauthorised absence. One class group was told that as long as they brought a note their teacher did not care what it said or who wrote it! At the other end of the school, self-presentation continuum definitions of truancy have been interpreted by some schools to include pupils excluded for disciplinary reasons (Munro, 1993).

Exclusions 5: exclusion by default – active and passive

I have included this category since there are many pupils whose circumstances make it unlikely that they will continue at school or attend school at all unless school and teachers make special attempts to draw them in. Pupils who truant from school may fall into this category if little effort is expended to persuade them to return and this may involve more or less conscious effort. It may apply if nothing is done about racism in schools which exerts a pressure on pupils to become disaffected and act on it. It is evident too for other groups of pupils particularly vulnerable to exclusion as set out in Table 2.2.

Traveller children are subject to particularly high levels of prejudice and there are low rates of school attendance among them, especially at secondary level (Binns, 1990). With the disengagement of schools from their communities encouraged by the legislation of the 1980s and 1990s, as well as the cuts in a variety of support services, schools may be less likely to seek the attendance of traveller children who arrive in their catchment area.

Particular difficulties have been identified with the informal exclusion of children looked after by local authorities (Stirling, 1992a, b; Firth and Horrocks in this volume). The Social Services Inspectorate and Office for Standards in Education report (SSI and OFSTED, 1995) note that 4 per cent of students looked after by local authorities in their sample received no education although 81 per cent of such students had 'no attendance problem'. The report emphasised the need for much greater collaboration between social services and education. A lack of support over education amounting to exclusion by default has been a long-standing theme of the testimony of young people 'in care' (Kahan, 1979).

Exclusions 6: school-age pregnancy and motherhood

In Circular 10/94, on exclusions, it is argued that pregnancy should not be a reason for disciplinary exclusion yet Circular 11/94, on education otherwise than at school, notes that pregnant schoolgirls commonly attend 'pupil referral units' (DfE, 1994b, c). No advice is given about the inclusion or exclusion of teenage fathers. Survey data indicate that the majority of school-age girls who become pregnant and wish to keep their babies, about 4,000 a year, leave mainstream schooling and this represents a significant form of exclusion by default (Dawson, 1994). Concern over exclusionary pressures in mainstream schooling may also be a factor in some girls choosing to have abortions. The stigmatisation of young women and their children in the strictures of some Members of Parliament against single parenthood may have a greater exclusionary effect than the government advice to keep school-age mothers in mainstream schooling.

Exclusions 7: pupils who have English as an additional language

The researcher I interviewed included special language classes for students for whom English is an additional language under the notion of 'benign' exclusions. British–Asian pupils are under-represented in the statistics for 1993 Act exclusions and it would be easy to ignore the exclusionary processes which affect them. Classes for such pupils were common in language centres outside the mainstream in the early 1970s and then withdrawal support increasingly gave way to in-class support (Williamson, 1991). This change was partly fuelled by the view of the Commission for Racial Equality that specialist language units involved 'unfair discrimination' as argued in the 'formal investigation' into Calderdale LEA (CRE, 1986). However, change in practice has been slow (Bourne, 1989).

But even without transfer out of the mainstream there is evidence from an examination of setting and banding policies in secondary schools that some British–Asian pupils are excluded from parts of the curriculum, including public examinations, because of their categorisation as being in need of language support (CRE, 1992). Troyna and Siraj-Blatchford (1993) further analysed the figures on setting produced for one school by the Commission for Racial Equality. They argued that pupils were still defined as in need of language support after several years at secondary school even when they had attended local primary schools. On the basis of their categorisation they were placed in 'low sets' and their chance of mobility between sets was more restricted than for pupils categorised as having 'special needs'. Again there is an implication in this article that the stigmatisation in 'low sets' of the education of pupils categorised as having 'special needs' is a natural part of the organisation of schools, whereas the devaluation of British–Asian children represents unnatural discrimination. Discrimination on the basis of attainment or 'presumed ability' provides an unchallenged screen on to which other forms of devaluation can be projected and then their origins obscured.

DEFINING AND MEASURING EXCLUSION

So, how should exclusion be defined? We cannot allow our definition of the problem of 'exclusion' to be constrained because it is given an official definition in terms of breaches of discipline in the Education Acts 1986 and 1993. Legislators have their own agenda for dividing up the world of education and they accomplish their tasks with varying degrees of coherence. The Education Act 1993, for example, has retained the limited, discriminatory and in some respects nonsensical, definitions of learning difficulty, whatever its effect on learning is, from the 1981 Act. In that Act, a disability is a kind of learning difficulty, an 'emotional and behavioural difficulty'. Just as we are free to define difficulties in learning for ourselves in a way that contributes best to understanding and responding to them, we can reconceptualise exclusion in the way that seems most productive. Yet, in either case, we have to retain a degree of doublethink since in applying official procedures we have to use the legal definitions. The art is to retain some consciousness of what we are doing.

The Education Act 1993 conceives of exclusion as *an event*, which is an extreme breach of an authority relationship set up in the Education (No. 2) Act 1986, which requires headteachers to instil in their pupils 'a proper regard for authority'. I suggest that for most purposes it is more useful to think of exclusion as *a process*. I now think of integration or inclusion in education as involving two processes; the process of increasing the participation of pupils within the cultures and curricula of mainstream schools and the process of decreasing exclusionary pressures. To attempt the first without the second is self-defeating. Pupils included under one category may be excluded under a different label. Exclusion, like segregation, can be conceived of as *the process of decreasing the participation of pupils in the cultures and curricula of mainstream schools.* Exclusion affects all pupils who are devalued by, and in, mainstream school.

Aspects of the process of exclusion are well documented by some writers. Gillborn has provided close observations of the way pupils at secondary school were treated differently for the same activity according to preconceived stereotypes. In particular, African–Caribbean pupils were frequently criticised for behaviour which other pupils shared in but for which white and Asian pupils were not criticised (Gillborn, 1992, p. 6). Such incidents are remembered and contribute not only towards the case for the eventual exclusion of pupils but also to the disaffection of pupils themselves. All devaluations operate in this way as a hidden motive for exclusion and as a source of disaffection which, in producing a reaction in pupils, can then be conveyed as the cause of the problem.

Schools reflect and may attempt to counter devaluations prevalent in society related to 'race', class, gender, sexuality, lifestyle, appearance, behaviour, bodily impairment, low attainment and low presumed 'ability'. Exclusionary processes are created around these issues within and outside schools. At different times and in different contexts some exclusions feel more 'natural' than others. And the naturalness of exclusion may be used in different ways. The attention given to the rights of disabled people has done little to counteract or even call into question the assignment of value according to pupil attainment. There are many examples of the conditional inclusion of pupils with disabilities from special schools provided they have a particular level of attainment (see, for example, Swann, 1987). Devaluations of pupils according to their relative attainment are the most prevalent exclusionary processes in schools. Some people argue that schools and societies should not or could not be run without them. But devaluation leads to disaffection which may in turn lead to disruption in schools. Hence the structuring of attitudes to attainment, for example by setting and streaming policies as well as the more subtle notion of the 'good pupil', is a principle contributor to exclusionary processes as well as to disciplinary exclusions.

MEASURING EXCLUSION

If we look seriously at exclusion events then the measurement of exclusion is far more complex than the examination of 'disciplinary' exclusions. We need to build up a picture of what is happening to all pupils in a variety of LEAs and this needs to be done by intensive ground work rather than surveys which are notoriously unreliable, particularly when they concern politically sensitive data. But, the measurement of exclusion events supplies only a small part of the picture. It may even encourage us to believe that we are grasping the phenomenon of exclusion when we do so. However, to do that we have to be prepared to engage in the complex, messy task of documenting and analysing all the processes of devaluation in schools.

CONCLUSION

In this chapter I have provided a critical review of exclusionary events and processes in an attempt to enhance our understanding and ability to respond to exclusion from school. I have suggested that this understanding has been fragmented and no doubt there are pieces that I have omitted from the picture. I have looked in particular at the separation of 'disciplinary' and 'special needs' exclusions and argue that such a separation requires analysis and explanation. I think the separation lies in divisions in academic careers, school structures, official definitions and subservience to them and is fundamental to some aspirations for society. It involves a sense that there are some exclusions which are natural and hence beyond critical scrutiny. Most importantly its mainten-ance serves to reproduce the devaluation of groups of pupils and to undermine attempts to reduce exclusionary processes in schools.

Chapter 3

The signal of failure
School exclusions and the market system of education

Chris Searle

INTRODUCTION

This commentary around the question of school exclusion is a further development of points I set out in a publication to which I contributed (Bourne *et al.*, 1994), which provoked reaction in many quarters – from OFSTED to the Commission for Racial Equality and an editorial in the *Times Educational Supplement* (June 1994). I was reminded of two other seminal pamphlets with over a hundred years between their publications.

In the late nineteenth century Andrew Mearns wrote passionately about the hundreds of thousands of unemployed, the lumpenproletariat of casual labourers camped at the gates of the City of London, huge numbers of them from the East London Irish immigrant community, a virtual army of the oppressed bottom layer of British urban society (Mearns, cited in Stedman Jones, 1971). In the language of the Christian liberal reformers of the Victorian era, he expounded upon 'the moral corruption, the heartbreaking misery' around him. There, 'in the very centre of our great cities, concealed by the thinnest crust of civilisation and decency' was this 'vast mass' of those excluded from society's opportunities and benefits, those wandering the streets of cities with no future, no prospects, in bitterness, frustration and thoughts of desperation. Inner-city parents and teachers in contemporary Britain will realise that little has changed in this new era of Victorianism and coarse revival of educational elitism. Many excluded children and young people are either sitting at home, doing very little to enhance their education, or wandering the city centres, shopping malls or local streets of inner city neighbourhoods, tempted towards shoplifting, housebreaking, vandalism and other forms of crime, drug abuse and gang conflict. They are also acting as magnets for thousands of other potential truants (BBC, 1993). In a country that boasts that it pioneered the concept and practice of universal education, here are tens of thousands who have been dropped from the school system, many receiving no formal education at all (SHA, 1992). What would this outcast youth of our own times have made of the words of the man at the head of the 'new' state education system – the creation of the 1988 Conservative government which he, John Patten, the Secretary of State for Education, was continuing and expanding – who on one hand dismissed inner-city schools as 'duff schools, debauching their communities', and on the other proclaimed universities as 'the pinnacles of excellence, the ivory silos fit for the toils of scholarly elites' (*Guardian*, 1994)? Such extremes, the forebears of which were excoriated in Mearns' pamphlet of 1893, are proudly vindicated and expressed through the reality of state education structure and provision in 1994, six years after the passage of the Thatcher/Baker Education Reform Act 1988.

There are also striking similarities between the plights of excluded children in British inner-city areas and those in rapidly emerging economies (Dimenstein, 1992). If we can put aside the soccer adulation and names such as Romario and Bebeto just for a moment and consider the reality of the lives of the urban children of Brazil, we can see the effects upon them of this erstwhile showpiece of neo-liberal economics, the home of the so-called 'economic miracle' based upon the same financial systems that Thatcherite politicians so admired. In the midst of this 'miracle' there are 31 million Brazilian street children out of education. Some of these have never been to school, some have rejected it or have been rejected by the education system. In huge cities such as São Paulo, Rio de Janeiro, Recife or Salvador the result is that these children have been turned to violent crime, prostitution and drug trafficking. These attitudes expose them to police violence and health risks of the most serious sort, including death from AIDS. For example, during a six-month period in 1990, 500 children were murdered by death gangs, vigilante shopkeepers and disaffected maverick police officers. Dimenstein (1992, p. 29) writes that the attitude of the Brazilian school system towards these children is to refuse 'to accept responsibility for schooling, especially if they have been in trouble'. Does that, in everyday school parlance, ring a bell in London – in Brent, Newham or Lambeth – or in Birmingham, Manchester, Nottingham or Sheffield? How close to the British inner-city reality is that statement – and Dimenstein's Brazilian story – for those 66,000 ex-pupils, the most pertinent human evidence of the colossal failure of the Education Reform Act 1988?

As increasing numbers of excluded pupils become enmeshed in crime – with angry shopkeepers and private security firms telephoning schools with alarming frequency, informing them that their excluded or truanting pupils have been caught shoplifting – and as direct involvement with local police over crimes of street violence, drugs possession or theft becomes almost a daily occurrence, the comparisons with situations such as those in Brazilian cities become less and less far-fetched. This is all the more true as growing number of inner-city schools are themselves falling into a Brazilian-type economic situation with chronic underfunding and fast-increasing class sizes, deficit budgets, underdeveloped resources and a 'peripheral' financial identity, often comparing starkly with the more prosperous and solvent schools in the 'centre' of the wealthier suburbs.

In March 1995 an article in the *Sheffield Telegraph* (Draper, 1995), headlined 'Huge leap in school exclusions', told the grim story of an expected doubling of permanent exclusions from the school year 1993–4 to 1994–5. It was only halfway through the year and already the number of exclusions had overtaken the total for the entire previous year. In an honest and open statement from Sheffield Education Department, Education Officer Lynda Taylor commented: 'We're no different from any other area, it's a national phenomenon. The shortage of resources in schools means less staff, therefore less adults are available to support and counsel and control difficult adolescents' (Taylor, cited in Draper, 1995).

She continued by pointing out that despite the high exclusion rate, many more young people were falling into the 'at risk' category; that expulsion and exclusion were symptoms of potentially far worse predicaments:

> We shouldn't be looking at the number of children excluded from schools, but the number of children who are known to have potential problems.

There has been a rapid increase in other indicators too – the exclusion figures are very much lower than recorded statistics of juveniles known to the justice system and the numbers known to use and abuse substances.

(Taylor, cited in Draper, 1995)

Such is the context in which many inner-city secondary schools, such as Earl Marshal, find themselves. Such is the challenge, with the ever-decreasing resources being allotted to them, they must to take up on a daily basis.

EXCLUSION AND REJECTION

An all-too-common situation is illustrated by the following instance. A 14-year-old Pakistani boy was brought to me by his father and an Asian community worker. The family lived in a part of Sheffield some distance away from the community of our school. The boy had spent the previous two-and-a-half years out of school. He had been excluded from his secondary school halfway through his first year there (Year 7), subsequently missing all of Year 8 and Year 9. His father was asking if he could join our school from the beginning of Year 10. The boy's frustration and nervousness at the prospect of a return to school after such a long absence was accentuated by a serious stammer which clearly needed the attention of a speech therapist. He had been excluded originally for threatening a teacher and the other schools nearer to his home had refused to accept him. One had given as its reason for not admitting him that too many of his friends were already pupils there. Implicit in this statement was the notion that the school did not want to be overloaded with black pupils. Now he was to start his Year 10 GCSE coursework, having had just four months of secondary school education some three years earlier.

There are thousands of black young people in similar predicaments in British inner cities. Sometimes they are outside the school system because of outright racism within it. Frequently they have right on their side, if they are right to be, as they very often are, the first to reject, resist and rebel against the demotivating and often narrow and racist National Curriculum now institutionalised across the British state-school system. It has so little within it about black history and achievement, and it provokes much of the disruption, rebellion and defiance of large numbers of black young people at school.

According to our LEA, Earl Marshal school is at the top of the list of disadvantaged schools in the city by eight full points on their Index of Disadvantage. Therefore, I believe that we must resist the idea and practice of *expulsion* (the people of Britain know it by that single word, not the more confusing and mystifying 'permanent exclusion' coined by the educational bureaucracy) as much as it is possible to do so. We should do this in the same spirit and with the same resolve that we generated when we campaigned against and saw the end of that other sanction – corporal punishment in schools – despite the anxiety this creates for teachers. For example, a senior colleague, who was clearly agitated, remarked to me: 'How can we continue to do away with the sanction of expelling the worst-behaved students? None of the children in the school now are frightened of anyone in authority any more.'

In saying that, she was very worried. I disagreed with her, saying that the removal of fear was a part of my approach to the development of school life but I added that exactly the same comment as hers was commonly made by many teachers before the abolition of corporal punishment, two decades earlier. Of course, the truth is that teachers themselves, when encouraged, are among the most creative of professionals and can always find solutions and creative answers to the most complex problems of school life. The abolition of corporal punishment gave teachers the opportunity to develop skills in alternative approaches and strategies of counselling and community liaison that they had not thought possible hitherto. An end to 'permanent exclusion' (except in the most dire and unavoidable circumstances) would have the same positive effect. Hence a part of our school's policy on exclusions reads thus:

> The policy of the school is not to use exclusion as a routine disciplinary approach in any area of school life. Exclusions from lessons as well as exclusions from school will be discouraged. The approach of the school is to *resolve* its problems internally, to find creative and lasting situations to any behaviour that interferes with the normal operation of school life.
>
> Permanent exclusion from school will only be invoked in an extreme or unresolvable situation, after every other possible

expedient or sanction has been exhausted. The school will always seek to use the invaluable resources of the community through parental involvement, governor involvement and the support of community groups and associations to seek solutions to problems of student indiscipline.

(Earl Marshal School, 1993a)

EXCLUSION AND THE EDUCATION REFORM ACT

However, in spite of the enormous range of skills and potential that teachers have to be imaginative in finding solutions for difficult situations involving their pupils, the system devised and introduced through the Thatcher enterprise of the Education Act 1988 is a huge disincentive to teacher creativity. Two dominant themes of this legislation have proved to be particularly pernicious to the lives of inner-city schools and have been central to inflaming the 'exclusions' issue. The first is the barbarism behind the concept of the 'education market place' and its management through the Act of the abolition of formal school 'catchment areas' (which linked 'feeder' primary schools to specific secondary schools in particular local neighbourhoods). In its place is the system of 'open enrolment', which is designed to destroy community-based comprehensive education. A scramble for pupil heads has been provoked, which allows the so-called 'popular' schools (usually the more richly-resourced, larger suburban schools) to choose who they want as their pupils, and reject those whom they do not find compatible. This has made the proclaimed Thatcherite shibboleth of 'parental choice' into a masquerade and also revealed its true meaning. In fact, its reverse is true: it is these richer, suburban schools who select their pupils from oversubscribed numbers, and de-select those whom they do not want, either by refusing to admit them in the first place, or, in the cases of many (particularly black pupils from inner-city areas), by expelling them in the midst of their secondary education if they require too much extra energy, pastoral attention or pose a pedagogical challenge – often passing them back to their local thinly-resourced and already hard-pressed schools in the communities where they had their primary school education.

This 'market' system is fundamentally inimicable to the comprehensive system, breaking up catchment areas and disrupting locally-based secondary education – especially in working class neighbourhoods. Pupils from these are continuously lured towards the richer suburban schools, with their own local community comprehensives at constant risk of closure through the fabricated 'surplus places' argument (that they have too few pupils, too many spare places and are therefore not cost-effective), or the 'non-viability' argument (that they are too small, with too few resources to be able to offer the full range of National Curriculum subjects). Yet more and more often, the long-distance education of inner-city young people in suburban schools is brusquely interrupted by a compulsory move caused by 'permanent exclusion'. Thus they are forced to move back to schooling in their own neighbourhood at critical times in their coursework when they may be in the middle of preparing for GCSE examinations.

CURRICULUM OF DISAFFECTION

The second aspect of legislation to have a pernicious effect is the National Curriculum itself. Its central concept – that of a state-licensed corpus of knowledge handed down through government 'orders' to teachers for 'delivery' in the classroom – is effectively de-skilling teachers, attacking their instinct to be creative and original at the point of sharing and imparting knowledge. Such a concept is a daily disincentive to imaginative and stimulating teaching. Of course, teachers are conductors of knowledge but they are also its constructors and interpreters in the process of the teaching and learning in the classroom between their pupils and themselves. To make them subject to 'orders' from a command curriculum is to force on to them a system of formulaic and dead knowledge being passed on by a teacher who is a reluctant servant of government to a pupil who may or may not be a willing receptacle. This is the distortion of the education process which lies at the centre of the National Curriculum and it is the children and young people of the inner city, particularly those from the black communities, who are the first to rebel against it – sometimes with the consequence of the pupil's final removal from his or her school.

In staff rooms across the country the concerns of thousands of teachers have been forced towards the issues around *workload* (how much we have to assess and test and deal with National Curriculum paraphernalia) rather than with the *content* and *process* of teaching (the true pedagogy of what and how we teach) which was at the forefront of teachers' minds in the 1970s and early 1980s. The National Curriculum has undermined the essential tasks and priorities of teaching as a creative act and replaced them with a routine of prefabricated activity. On staff room union and in-service notice boards we read the proof of this, dominated as they are by literature around 'workload' or the National Curriculum and its 'delivery'. Party to this emphasis too is the creation of OFSTED whose inspectors have usurped the former LEA advisory services, which, despite their limitations and frequent detachment from the classroom, did offer genuine curriculum and teacher support to schools. Now the fundamental questions of how, why and what we teach have been overlaid by OFSTED preoccupations and relentless in-service sessions on 'How to prepare for inspection' or 'How to deliver National Curriculum Key Stage Three or Four'. The education support services now no longer support the teachers and schools but support instead the uncritical imparting of the National Curriculum and its 'orders', with OFSTED acting as its police officers, even ensuring that there is proper adherence to Christian assemblies although the majority of pupils may have no living connection with Christianity. Across the country's schools there is a deadening new conformity, with OFSTED inspectors insisting upon the same formula and criteria for all schools in their inspections, as if every one were a predominantly white, monolingual, Christian and homogenous institution. Even the conservative *Times Educational Supplement* had this to report about OFSTED activity in a predominantly black comprehensive school in Birmingham:

> Elaine Foster, headteacher of Handsworth Wood Girls in Birmingham, was unhappy about the new inspection system. Before their OFSTED inspection, the school had specifically requested that the team include people sympathetic to the needs of inner cities and issues of race and gender. There had been three black members of the team – but they were systematically marginalised. Inspectors needed to be made aware of racism and stereotyping, she said.
>
> Ms Foster added: 'I know eight or nine black heads and six of us were inspected in the first round of inspection. Some of my colleagues have been totally devastated by the experience.'
>
> (Young, 1994, p. 11)

The implementation of the National Curriculum is forcing boredom and irrelevance into the heart of our schools despite the best efforts of conscientious teachers. Pupil rebellion and disruption becomes not only explicable but also, to its protagonists, justifiable and in the ballooning exclusion figures are to be found the true shape of its consequences.

THE DE-SKILLING OF TEACHERS

The workload burden forced upon teachers by the much-increased amount of non-classroom work has squeezed and restricted the amount of time and energy that teachers have to spend upon their pupils and their individual learning and behavioural needs. Form teachers and personal tutors now cannot spend their time on the counselling that many of their pupils need in order to affect positively their general attitude to school and the quality of their learning. Time and energy previously devoted to young people's welfare, which might before have made a significant difference in turning around disaffected behaviour or changing negative attitudes and therefore have prevented conduct leading to exclusion, is being usurped and lost at a time when it is needed more than ever. The frustration and stress that many teachers experience because of this squeeze on the time which they can devote to pastoral issues has sometimes reinforced a 'culture of exclusion' in schools, whose managements turn prematurely to exclusion as a response to their hard-pressed colleagues and as an expedient to relieve them of the pressure and responsibility of dealing with their disaffected pupils. Some teachers and their organisations, sometimes out of desperation and the urge to find scapegoats, sometimes out of a refusal to face up to the central government forces that are crushing inner-city education specifically and pressurising state education generally, are turning on the pupils and blaming *them* as the easiest and most vulnerable of targets. In *The Times* (Preston, 1994a, p. 1), the General Secretary of the National Association of Schoolmasters and Union of Women Teachers (NAS/UWT), Nigel de Gruchy, reminding us of some of the sentiments to be found within the pages of Dimenstein's (1992) Brazilian testimony, was quoted as saying that 'disruptive pupils were the biggest barrier to raising standards' in schools, following an OFSTED survey which revealed a record number of 'disruptive pupils' being excluded. The report was released in the wake of a John Major prime ministerial pronouncement lamenting the growth of a 'yob culture' amongst urban young people.

The position taken by the second-largest teachers' union in England is an indication of the seriousness of the 'exclusions' debate in staffrooms and in the heart of state education – and how it is influencing teachers' perceptions. At Earl Marshal School there remain stark divisions over this question which have resulted in NAS/UWT members targeting individual pupils and refusing to teach them – with full support from their regional and national executives. In one case the union told its member not to meet with a helpful black parent who had willingly come to school to try to resolve the behaviour problem between his son and the teacher. Such treatment of a parent and discriminatory action against individual pupils is an attempt to force school managements and governing bodies into making exclusions at the demand of teachers. It can only worsen the situation, degrade teacher trade unionism and foster mistrust between communities and schools – as well as put out on the streets more and more pupils, endangering both their futures and the social health of their communities.

MEETING THE CHALLENGE

> Exclusion is seldom the measure of a child's capacity to learn; it is an indication, instead, of the teacher's refusal to be challenged.
>
> (Sivanandan, 1994)

Adding this assertion to the damage being done to inner city education by the market economics guiding the Education Act 1988 results in 'an education system which puts a premium not on the educability of the child but on the price of the education', with 'the challenge to the teacher the financial cost of keeping him or her in school, not the human cost of keeping him/her out' (Sivanandan, 1994, p. v). That financial cost is growing more and more threatening to inner-city children as the consequence of financial restraints. Announcements of large-scale losses from educational budgets from October 1993 showed London losing as much as £120 million, with Birmingham and Bradford also suffering particularly badly. As the *Observer*

(Hugill, 1993) reported: 'Local authorities with a large proportion of single-parent families and substantial ethnic minority populations will be the main losers. Affluent shire counties will gain the most.' Even OFSTED broke ranks with the government following these cuts, declaring that 'pupils in the poorest areas were not getting enough help in schools to break out of deprivation and underprivileged family backgrounds'. Three days earlier their own report, *Access and Achievement in Urban Education*, had shown that the 1988 'Reforms' had done little to improve or raise standards in inner-city schools, recognising that they needed much greater resources to help to realise opportunities for their pupils. And in a strange maritime image, they wrote: 'Most schools in these disadvantaged areas do not have the capacity for sustainable renewal. The rising tide of national educational change is not lifting these boats' (cited in Preston, 1993b).

So how can standards in inner-city schools be improved within both the current legal and political context and without resorting to exclusion? Our school's attempts to keep faith with our policy on exclusions has not resulted in disaster or a disintegration of school life. After four years without a single permanent exclusion we found an improvement in our GCSE results at the three top grades (150 per cent improvement in 1993); a significantly reduced truancy rate; a big increase in the post-16 staying-on rate and a growth in overall school numbers from 400 in September 1990 to just over 600 in July 1994. We still exclude pupils temporarily like most other schools but this is used more as an overnight action; as an immediate response to fighting, bullying, racism, sexism or aggression to teachers in order to trigger the involvement of parents in school the very next day. If the parent does not come to school promptly, we follow up with a telephone call or a visit by either a community liaison teacher, a head of year or an education welfare officer.

We have adopted a three-strand response to pupil disaffection and disruption. The first involves increasing motivation by broadening the curriculum and making it more pertinent to the real lives of our pupils and their communities. This may seem obvious but, at a time when the narrowness and irrelevance of so much of National Curriculum material and prescription is being imposed across multilingual and internationalist inner-city schools, it becomes a vital theme. We teach Urdu and Arabic to GCSE level as modern languages alongside French and German at the heart of our mainstream curriculum. In our context, greater motivation is powerfully generated by developing fields of study closely connected to the lives, languages and cultures of our pupils. Their internationalism is emphasised by research into the histories of their families who may have arrived in England from Pakistan, Kashmir, Yemen, Somalia or the Caribbean. Our book of 'herstories', *Lives of Love and Hope* (Earl Marshal School, 1993b), telling of mothers' life-stories from interviews conducted, translated and transcribed by their daughters, was short-listed for the Arts Council Raymond Williams Prize in 1994. Pupils' lives are linked to young people from similar communities in other British cities, while fundraising and solidarity projects are creating to support the prospects and struggles of the peoples in their nations of origin and other peoples such as the Kurds, Palestinians or Bosnians. All of this becomes the stuff of the school curriculum; it increases connection, diminishes alienation and enhances the enthusiasm and motivation to learn. However, it is not contained within the 'orders' of the National Curriculum.

The second strand is the emphasis upon counselling. Recently we established a senior post with responsibility for extending 'Counselling, Community Liaison and Democratic Development'. This is an essential post for us, with the postholder developing a counselling mode of pastoral work across the school, coordinating links with community groups and organisations and involving them in school life – while also developing democratic structures and pupil fora. The strengthening of these areas of school life is crucial if we are to reduce pupil alienation and thus the behaviour that can lead directly to exclusions. The objective is that all teachers will gradually become attuned to a counselling mode of approaching problems with pupils rather than resorting to the provocative and largely ineffectual approach of direct confrontation and the consequent polarisation between teacher and pupil. This way of working needs to be accompanied by a general democratisation of school life, to put back to the pupils the responsibility for their behaviour and personal growth in a co-operative setting. Concurrently there needs to be democratic and participatory fora and structures within the school to enable pupils to express that growth and maturing process and teachers to acknowledge and also learn through it. This does not simply mean a tokenistic school council but an active tutorial system which puts responsibility and power to the pupils on a day-to-day basis. We certainly have a very long way to go in applying these ideas but such are our objectives.

The third strand recognises that, as has already been emphasised, the strengths of local communities and their organisation must be harnessed. This primarily means ensuring that the *governance* of the school is genuinely in the hands of those who use it and are served by it. Thus our governing body has strong and authentic representation, not only from teachers and parents from all its constituent communities but also from the *organisations* of these communities. In our case this includes the Somali Community Association of Sheffield, the Yemeni Community Association, Sheffield and District African–Caribbean Association and local Pakistani mosque associations. When we find that a pupil or groups of pupils from these communities are behaving badly and appear to be becoming intractable we involve our governors both individually and through their organisations. For example, one of our Somali pupils, fresh from a violent situation in his home city following the civil war in Northern Somalia where he was on the fringe of military activity, brandished a knife at another pupil. It was difficult for us as senior managers of the school, completely outside of the boy's cultural context, to deal effectively with him so we took him to the Somali Community Centre. The Secretary kept him there with him for the day and he and his colleagues spent some invaluable time counselling the pupil, persuading him to consider and change his behaviour. His aggression mellowed and he was never again found to be in a similar situation. This proved to be a most successful strategy and one we have adopted on other occasions. We also convene panels of governors to interview pupils, in the presence of their parents, if they have broken their 'Contract of Conduct', made when they have returned from a temporary exclusion, before giving them 'A Final Opportunity' contract to sign, to be monitored by a particular governor. We have also invited parents of pupils displaying disruptive behaviour into school to spend a day going from lesson to lesson with their son or daughter. This strategy had a particularly sobering effect on one very volatile and disruptive boy whose father, an elder at the local mosque, exerted considerable influence over the conduct of many of his son's peers too! Such visits have often had very fruitful consequences in settling down these pupils to their work and calming their behaviour for a period long beyond the parental visit.

The school has become the venue for a number of extra-curricular initiatives arranged by community organisations. Their influence over the life of the school and influence on the behaviour of pupils has been positive, giving a greater self-discipline and commitment to school-time activities of participating pupils, as well as empowering local parents and familiarising them with the school. These include a Koranic and Urdu class organised by the local mosque which is held every evening and on Saturdays, a Saturday Somali community class and the largest Arabic supplementary school in the country. This is administered and staffed by volunteers from the Yemeni community and regularly attracts upwards of 150 pupils to its Saturday and Sunday sessions. Also there is a National Curriculum enrichment class run by the Yemeni community in collaboration with the school. In addition, the Devon Malcolm Cricket Centre (named after the England cricketer of Jamaican origin who lived and played his early cricket in the neighbourhood of the school) is organised by cricket enthusiasts from the Caribbean and Pakistani communities. All these projects work towards their own objectives but they also act as genuine motivators and forces to decrease pupil alienation from the daily run of school life. They are all strands of the school's most essential theme: to use to the full the rich resource of the community as a fundamental support strategy to transform alienated attitudes and check disruptive behaviour as part of a continuing drive to find new, imaginative and effective solutions as constructive alternatives to exclusion.

Yet, along with these efforts to make the school and community as one, there must be tackled the attitudes that some teachers have about the assumed superiority of their own background and culture compared to those of the young people they are teaching and the parents in the communities that they serve. Schools need to confront many dimensions of ignorance, including those within their own culture. These attitudes have been reinforced by the narrow and prejudiced foundation of the National Curriculum itself. This bolsters white cultural values at the expense of those of the pupil and in doing so creates a one-way curriculum rather than a shared concept of knowledge between teacher and pupil. This is the reality of inner-city education. The curriculum on the doorstep of the inner-city school may embrace the world in its

languages, family histories, national cultures and religions. Its
living knowledge will certainly always be broader, more sophisticated and complex, wiser and more imaginative in concept and
range than the narrow chauvinism of the National Curriculum.
It is that combined culture of our international communities,
fused with everything positive, generous and human in the British
culture, that needs to be at the centre of the inner-city school's
concept of knowledge and curriculum. That is what will motivate
our pupils, hold them on to learning and enable them to see
their purpose in the school purpose.

The rich achievement of bilingualism, for example, of thousands
of black young people, which is employed so skilfully in their
family and community contexts – helping senior and non-English
speaking members of their families in difficult social predicaments
– still remains largely unrecognised and non-accredited by the
education system and university entry boards. This situation
compares starkly and unjustly with the way in which monolingual
English-speaking pupils learn French or German at GCSE or 'A'
level in much more purely academic and much less life-orientated
situations and then use the formal qualifications that they gain to
secure further progress in the education system and university
entry. Meanwhile, the pupils who are completely bilingual in
English and Arabic, or English and Hindi, or English and Punjabi,
or English and Somali find their bilingual achievement marginalised or ignored by the structures outside their own communities.
Now we see increasing numbers of bilingual inner-city young
people being excluded from school with their most invaluable
educational asset – their ability and facility to move in and out of
two languages – devalued and treated with indifference by the state
education system.

Teachers, local education authority workers, curriculum
developers and all those who are a part of the organisation
of education, both locally and nationally, must also work with a
new respect and sense of humility in their relationships with inner-
city communities and their young people, learning, internalising
and appreciating the cultural strength that they bring to the fabric
of our schools. Only in this way will there be the construction of trust and the renewal of motivation which will bring
the opportunities to reverse this tragic process of the systematic
exclusion of thousands of young people from British schools, and
the restoration of their right not only to be educated but also to

look upon education with credibility and trust as their pathway into life.

The pioneer public school headmaster and patriarch of *Tom Brown's Schooldays*, Thomas Arnold of Rugby, wrote as one of his founding principles that: 'Till a man learns that the first, second and third duty of a schoolmaster is to get rid of unpromising subjects, a great public school will never be what it might be, and what it ought to be' (James, 1994, p. 163). Such is the way of elitism. As practitioners of community comprehensive schools and opponents of all such supremacist notions of education – in this case coming from the very top end of the first Victorian market in education – we should examine Arnold's statement carefully, for it is at the base of the 'exclusion culture' which still rules in very many state schools. If comprehensive schools are to be truly what they aspire to be, then there is room for all the young people of a particular community in them: the advanced and less advanced but also the motivated and the disaffected. It is the school's purpose to provide for all and to undo disaffection and demotivation in the process. At the heart of the local community, the school's mission is to be able to work with all for the betterment of community life. This is bound to mean that disaffection from school can be tackled only by skilled and committed teachers with a strong counselling emphasis and an instinctive practice of involving parents and community as closely as possible.

Chapter 4

Government policy and disadvantaged children

Margaret Stirling

INTRODUCTION

This chapter is based on ethnographic research I undertook in a metropolitan borough and a rural county authority on the effect of government policy and legislation on the education of disadvantaged children.

Initially, I considered the effect of the Education Reform Act 1988 on emotionally and behaviourally disturbed pupils, concluding that they were being increasingly educationally marginalised. Research presently under way explores the relationship between government policy and school exclusions; the thesis considering those excluded as comprising a policy generated group, and exclusion as a process of marginalisation.

As the composition of this group is ultimately dependent upon decisions taken by schools, I argue that changes in the number and nature of school exclusions can be particularly informative as to the practical effects of prevailing policy.

The effects of policy can be examined in terms of whom it empowers, whose interests it serves, and whom it disempowers, illustrating the divisiveness of an education system which reinforces and exacerbates social hierarchical differences rather than maximising educational potential and creating opportunities for social mobility.

The central argument presented in this chapter is the concept of *exclusion as a process of disempowerment.*

RESEARCH METHODS

The research draws on 76 in-depth, semi-structured, 40-minute interviews with *key* professionals in the field, conducted over a period of six years. It also draws on extensive background data from referrals to the Social Services in one metropolitan authority, including 300 detailed case files.

Whilst the method of research has been based essentially within an ethnographic tradition, there are certain distinct features. Woods (1986) argues that ethnography is particularly well suited to helping to close the gulf between researcher and teacher, educational research and educational practice. Burgess (1989, p. 60) states that 'ethnographic data are based on close relationships in the field'.

As one of four advisory teachers employed by the Social Services Department in a large metropolitan authority, my daily work entailed acting on behalf of children and young people excluded from school, those at risk of exclusion and those involved in the exclusion process. This required attending meetings, case conferences, undertaking school and home visits, and involved inter-agency working with other professionals. From a research point of view, this provided a wealth of data and enabled me to become accepted. However, the obvious danger in relying heavily on such sources would be that of 'over-rapport'. Hammersley (1984) comments that the social setting to be studied 'however familiar to the researcher, must be treated as anthropologically strange'.

Those interviewed included: headteachers, deputy headteachers and heads of special needs departments in mainstream schools; education social workers; principal educational psychologists and educational psychologists; heads of support services, heads or deputies of off-site units; unit managers in social services children's homes, a principal at a community home with education, an area office team manager (children), and a representative of staff involved with the juvenile courts; a senior education officer (Special Educational Needs, SEN), education officers (SEN), and an LEA adviser (SEN); and a community relations officer and Section 11 teachers.

The sequence of research interviews was intended to co-ordinate differing professional viewpoints in order to understand and illustrate the exclusion process. Hammersley (1984) referring to the work of Denzin (1978), notes that 'The use of multiple sources of data offers the possibility of triangulation as a means of assessing the construct validity of various data items.'

RESEARCH FINDINGS

Despite the multiplicity of professional perspectives, the picture presented was consistent. This is perhaps best illustrated by two interviews conducted in mainstream schools. The head of a school aspiring to grant maintained status, while discussing educational reforms, concluded that the more 'difficult' pupils would need to be educated in small units; clearly viewing this as both good and appropriate:

> It's the best place for them, where they can be with their own kind ... and get more help. They'll not want to do proper work, for exams that is, they'll just disrupt the lessons.

The head of a school with a strong reputation in special needs integration described similar developments in response to educational reforms but, in contrast, viewed these with alarm:

> We don't have a separate 'Special Needs' group in our school, we do the best we can for *all* our pupils. All those with statements are fully integrated, I mean they're supported in the class.
>
> But we're getting more requests for transfers of statemented children from other schools who say they don't have the resources and recommend us to the parents. It's 'cause they just don't want these kids. ... The Education Reform Act is having a disastrous effect on integration.

Despite the wide range of vested professional interests inherent in the sample, and differing views on developments, there was no disagreement as to the practical effect of government education reforms. Schools have become less tolerant of children who are difficult to teach.

SHORT-TERM EXCLUSIONS AND ABSENCE FROM SCHOOL

A significant feature of the research was how unofficial exclusions from schools within one authority greatly outweighed official,

that is, formally processed, exclusions. Children were found to be
sent home from school for a wide variety of reasons which schools
did not regard as 'formal' exclusion. Frequently, children were sent
home until an informal meeting with parents or carers could be
arranged. Pupils were sent home in order to modify their dress to
conform with school uniform requirements. African–Caribbean
boys had been sent home until patterns cut into their hair grew out
– consequently missing school for several weeks. Respondents
within Social Services Departments complained that, once a
pattern of being out of school was introduced, this predisposed
the youngster to long-term non-attendance, particularly where the
peer group within a children's home was largely out of school.
Concern was expressed as to the opportunity this created for
becoming involved in offending behaviour. (See also Searle,
Cullingford and Morrison, and Normington in this volume.)

Whilst the sample described below may not be representative
of other local authorities, the factors to which respondents mainly
drew attention, reforms within schools, are nationally applicable.
Consequently, I consider that recorded exclusion figures could
well present just 'the tip of the iceberg'.

Within the metropolitan authority, seven Social Services
Children's Home unit managers were interviewed. Out of a
total of 60 children in residence in these homes, 32 were not
attending school on a regular basis. But what was particularly
disturbing was that of these 32 children only two could be
identified by the unit managers as permanently excluded from
school. The rest constituted an unknown or unofficial category
(Stirling, 1992b). Follow up research revealed that the majority of these constituted a category of pupils who ceased to
attend school after repeated short-term exclusions. Although for
the most part these were secondary pupils, some were of primary-
school age. Given the degree of consternation that a recognised national increase in exclusions has prompted, concern
based largely on officially given figures, the above ratio of
recorded exclusion to those *in reality* out of school is particularly worrying. Later samples, within different children's homes,
have confirmed this broad proportional relationship which in
the initial sample was just 6.25 per cent formally recorded, the
remainder of those out of school being unknown or 'hidden'.
Other research has indicated similar findings (Garnett 1994;
Sinclair *et al.*, 1994).

Unit managers, referring to their registers and case file documentation, pointed out the link between repeated short-term exclusions and long-term chronic truancy. In view of the obligation upon schools to record attendance figures, it could be anticipated that this would be 'picked up' by the school. However, following through these long-term non-attenders showed this not to be the case. An entry of 'authorised absence' in the register can unwittingly conceal prolonged periods out of school.

For example, a girl whose parental note (sent prior to her accommodation by the local authority) explained that she was absent owing to period pains was entered as being absent on medical grounds for over one term. Another child, whose initial note informed the school that he had 'flu, was entered as absent for this reason for several months. Similarly pupils offered just two hours a week teaching at a unit were entered as in receipt of 'education otherwise', even though in some cases they failed to attend the unit.

When I queried why the school's education social worker had not become involved, the response was that the child had failed to come to the attention of appropriate staff.

Given public criticism of increasing officially recorded exclusion numbers, schools providing official figures and their LEAs may be reluctant to represent themselves as either having a high truancy or a high exclusion rate. Consequently I consider research based on the perceptions of *key* professionals in the field, practitioners working daily and directly with children out of school, is likely to present a fuller picture.

CONSEQUENCES: THE EFFECT ON BLACK BOYS

I contend that the government's education policy exacerbates inequality in education; that it is fundamentally inconsistent with equal educational opportunities. Children comprising traditionally disadvantaged minority groups are further disadvantaged within the present competitive education system; children in Social Services accommodation, children with special educational needs, particularly those with emotional and behavioural difficulties, and also children from ethnic minorities. (For a fuller discussion, see Booth in this volume; also Blyth and Milner, and Firth and Horrocks).

In the metropolitan authority studied, African–Caribbean and Asian children and young people constituted over 40 per cent of recorded exclusions while comprising less than 10 per cent of the total school population. African–Caribbean boys constitute the great majority of these.

In cases where a black pupil has been excluded from school, the race of the pupil very often features as an issue in the *background* to the exclusion, most frequently in the form of complaints by the pupil that the school is racist. While most schools immediately deny this, when they are presented with evidence of past complaints by pupils and their parents the schools often acknowledge pupils' past grievances but evidently feel that there is little they are able to do about racist behaviour (see also Blyth and Milner in this volume).

For example, an African–Caribbean pupil who was subject to persistent insidious racial abuse by his white peer group was subsequently permanently excluded from a school for fighting in the playground. The school pointed out, quite rightly, that they could not accept violent behaviour and would exclude a white boy for the same offence. White boys were involved in the fight but the black boy was held responsible since he had initiated the *physical* incident as a response to persistent racial taunts which the school recognised as merely *verbal* provocation. A significant factor in the school's decision to exclude was their perception of the pupil's 'negative attitude'. However, the pupil's relationship with staff had been influenced by their past unwillingness, or inability, to address the racial taunts to which (they confirmed) he had been subjected.

There was evidence that some teachers' perceptions of black pupils as a group differed from their perception of white pupils. When I questioned a deputy headteacher on the reasons for the high number of African–Caribbean boys excluded from the school, he concluded that 'We expect the same basic standards of discipline of all boys but we find these [African–Caribbean] boys are more badly behaved'. This respondent expressed the concern that black boys resort to physical violence more readily. Other teachers interviewed complained of finding black boys more difficult to teach than other children.

A white secondary school teacher described to me the degree of physical intimidation she felt when confronted by a particular black boy. She explained that she experienced physical symptoms of anxiety on seeing him. She admitted that when shopping in the city centre she would avoid underpasses in case she should be followed by 'a group of them'. This response had been generated by the unpleasant experience she had had in working with an extremely aggressive black boy and his associates. Regrettably, she had limited contact with and knowledge of the environment in which black pupils live and perceived this as negative, as she had not taken the opportunity to avail herself of a more balanced experience of the black community. This teacher finds black children 'difficult to teach', although evidently the difficulty lies as much with the teacher as with her pupils.

The following case illustrates the persistence of the view that black children are 'unreasonably' or 'naturally' violent. A 3-year-old black boy was excluded on his first day from nursery school. The school was in a predominantly white area and the other children attending had limited contact with black children. The little boy was subject to much interest by the others which eventually led to a few of them licking their fingers and wiping his skin, asking, 'Does it wash off?'. The ensuing distressed behaviour on the part of the small black child led to staff attention. In struggling to pick him up the headteacher lost her spectacles which were damaged. She decided that he was a violent and disturbed child and excluded him.

Schools frequently respond to accusations of racism by protesting that they 'treat all children the same' and expect equal standards of behaviour from all children. In this they fail to allow that not all children are the same and some have the disadvantage of being subject to additional pressures on account of discrimination levelled against ethnic minority groups (Stirling, 1993).

In the exclusion of black pupils, attention is focused on the child's misbehaviour, that is, the symptoms of the problem, rather than on the common cause of such presenting misbehaviour which is specific to black pupils. In practice it is quicker and far easier for the school to 'solve' the problem by removing the recalcitrant victim of racism rather than to address the issue itself.

SOCIAL CONSEQUENCES

Pupils whose behaviour schools have found difficult to manage are then in the hands of carers twenty-four hours a day. This may exacerbate stress within the family that can result in the breakdown in relationships and precipitate the need for the pupil to be accommodated by the local authority (see, additionally, Cohen and Hughes, 1994).

Social Services respondents commented on the number of children received into care with no record of offending who quickly established a pattern of offending once accommodated; becoming involved in solvent abuse, addiction to arcade games, shoplifting, street robberies, taking and driving away, burglaries, arson and prostitution (see also Searle in this volume).

In my research I found that there was generally a gap of several weeks and in some cases many months before alternative provision was offered excluded pupils (see also Firth and Horrocks, and Mitchell in this volume). A few, mainly the older ones, were lost to the system and never returned to school. Off-site alternative educational provision for excluded pupils was found invariably inadequate in both quality and quantity (see Blyth and Milner in this volume) and was rarely purpose built.

Despite working under extremely difficult physical conditions, staff in such units are often committed and can develop good relationships with young people. However, in the authority studied, the degree of success they were able to achieve was limited by the fact that they offered only part-time teaching, the most difficult youngsters receiving just a few hours a week. Pupils undergoing an assessment of special educational needs were often found to receive as little as five hours a week for at least fifteen months and in some cases for as long as three years.

CONCLUSIONS

In the language of the Citizens' Charter, parents have a right to a greater choice of schools, pupils have a right to a broad and balanced curriculum, and schools have a right to manage their own budget (DfE, 1994e), all of which will raise the standard of education: 'The overriding aim of government policy is continuously to raise the standards achieved in schools' (DfE, 1992b, 2.1).

Inherent within the idea, that above all else *standards* must be raised, is the beginning of the problem of increasing school exclusions. National assessment has become a yardstick against which standards can be measured and which schools can use to evaluate how individual pupils measure up. There will of course be those who 'fall below the mark' using these criteria.

In the operation of market forces, *disparity* is what drives competition; we have to have losers in order to sustain the winners. Rather than promoting equality of opportunities through education, *inequality* is a necessary driving force within a competitive system. Consequently I consider the resulting disadvantaged group, identified as 'Pupils with Problems', not as an inadvertent or unfortunate side effect of government education policy but as an integral and necessary feature of a competitive education system.

Not only are academic standards to be improved, so too are moral standards (DfE, 1992b, 1: 29–1, p.32). 'The idea that children can't be punished is no longer feasible ... we can no longer afford to tolerate bad behaviour in schools' (Grice and Hymas, 1994). This is consistent with the view expressed by Prime Minister John Major in a party political broadcast: 'We need to condemn a little more and understand a little less' (Major, 1993).

Schools are encouraged not to tolerate bad behaviour. The sanction system exercised by schools allows for the child to be excluded. Therefore, the government's education policy gives schools the ideological rationale to exclude difficult pupils. The increased population of excluded children and young people is policy generated. I question the sincerity of government concern on school exclusions because diversity (or disparity) is *necessary* in the competitive operation of market forces which control access to a hierarchical system of schooling. As the Secretary of State for Education commented, 'There will be schools that are suitable for certain pupils, and others that are suitable for others . .. there will *inevitably* be the others' (DfE, 1992b). In establishing Pupil Referral Units, the government is determining a place for pupils deemed to be below 'improved standards in schools'. One respondent in my study referred to this as a new 'lowerarchy'.

Chapter 5

Black boys excluded from school
Race or masculinity issues?

Eric Blyth and Judith Milner

INTRODUCTION

This chapter reviews the evidence concerning the exclusion from school of young black people. Some possible reasons for the disproportionate number of exclusions of African–Caribbean males are outlined and one school's efforts to address the problem are described.

LEAs usually exercise the greatest care in their categorisation of minority ethnic pupils and it is common to find sophisticated systems of such categorisation in official school records. It has been our experience during the research reported here that these categories do not extend to a school's daily experiences of racial differences. Teachers, in our experience, seem to view pupils as 'black', 'white' or 'Asian' although there is some evidence that they make distinctions between various categories of non-English white pupils. Pupils, similarly, do not make distinctions between black British and African–Caribbean and they especially show different distinctions regarding mixed-race status to those of their teachers. As headteachers hold the power to exclude or otherwise, we use the categories here which have most meaning for them. For a teacher in the middle of a confrontation with a pupil the subtle meanings of different Asian origins and culture or degrees of 'blackness' have little significance – pupils are perceived as *black*, *Asian*, or *white*.

Should accurate statistics be available (see Chapter 1 in this volume), there remains the problem that some pupils are vulnerable to a range of educational disadvantage and it is difficult to disentangle the overlapping effects of multiple disadvantage in order to study the possible effects of race on school exclusion practices. For example, Sinclair *et al.*'s (1994) study of 'looked after' children found that these children were also more likely to be involved in truancy, have special educational needs and be excluded from school. Although a majority of the children studied were from minority ethnic groups, they were not predominantly black children. This supports previous research which indicates that children of mixed race, both boys and girls, are more likely to be 'looked after' than are black and white children (Department of Health, 1992a). A study of the educational experiences of 'looked after' children (Garnett, 1994) noted a link between exclusion and being 'looked after' but did not make links with ethnicity.

Similarly, Cooper *et al.*, (1991) report an over-representation of black children in units for children with emotional and behaviour difficulties but comment that both black and white *boys* are over-represented, making it difficult to separate gender from race effects. And many of the studies which focus particularly on the exclusion rates of black children fail to distinguish between girls and boys. For example, the Commission for Racial Equality (1985) found that black pupils in Birmingham were not only four times more likely to ·be excluded from school than white pupils but also were excluded at an earlier age and after fewer incidents of disruptive behaviour. By 1992, Mayet had established that although black pupils make up only 9 per cent of the school population in Birmingham, they constitute 30 per cent of exclusions. This represents similar numbers to the incomplete DfE study (1992a) which estimated that, nationally, whilst black pupils make up 2 per cent of the school population, they account for more than 8 per cent of permanent exclusions.

Subsequent small-scale research studies (see Stirling, Hayden in this volume) suggest that black excluded pupils are almost exclusively *male* and *African–Caribbean*. Whilst the whole picture is complicated by the multi-relationship of vulnerabilities in the education system and the lack of precise numbers, it can be confidently asserted that not only are African–Caribbean boys more likely to be excluded from school than any other ethnic group of pupils but also that schools and parents view this with serious concern (Channel 4, 1994).

WHY ARE AFRICAN–CARIBBEAN BOYS SO VULNERABLE TO SCHOOL EXCLUSION?

One argument for the reasons for the disproportionate exclusion rates of African–Caribbean boys is that they might be more violent and difficult to handle in schools. This argument is difficult to sustain in face of the facts about exclusions, the reasons given for excluding pupils having more to do with a cluster of negative behaviours than with overt violence. Neither does this accord with research into African–Caribbean attitudes to education. Whilst black boys may be as *anti-school* as many of their white peers, they are much less likely to be *anti-education* (Duncan, 1988; Tizard *et al.*, 1988). They are only too aware of the need for educational qualifications if they are to counter the effects of racism in the world of work.

Another, equally simplistic, argument is that teachers are racist. This argument does not in itself explain why boys from other minority ethnic groups are not equally over-represented in exclusion rates. For example, there is no hard evidence of widespread exclusion rates among Asian boys. Neither would this argument explain the differing exclusion rates of black boys and girls. What does seem very much more likely is that teachers are influenced by the same stereotypes of African–Caribbean males that exist within the wider society we live in and which views black *masculinity* as problematic and potentially threatening. There is substantial support for this in the research literature. Brandt (1986) found that teachers tended to be more likely to perceive African–Caribbean pupils as *truculent* and Asian pupils as *conformist*. Mac an Ghaill (1988) found that teachers extend the stereotype of conformist, middle-class Asian pupils – who are also academically successful (Broom, 1988; Kelly, 1988) – to *all* Asian pupils. At the same time, they are unable readily to identify groups of conformist African–Caribbean pupils who tend to band together for solidarity in schools (Duncan, 1988; Mac an Ghaill, 1988). This promotes the emergence of a construction of African–Caribbean pupils as potentially 'dangerous', with Asian pupils being subject to a different stereotype (see, for example, Pitman, 1995).

The complicated and largely unconscious ways in which a racial stereotype manifests itself is illustrated by two studies of social workers' assessments of pupil behaviour problems using vignettes in which the only significant difference between the pupils was race. The first study (Osuwu–Bempah, 1994) found that social workers were more likely to ascribe identity problems to 'black' pupils and to prescribe the need for a 'strong male model' than they did to 'white' pupils. The second study (Blyth and Milner, 1995) found that social workers constructed quite different family situations for 'black' and 'white' pupils. The 'white' pupil was assumed to be 'on the verge' of trouble because of the pressures of single parenthood on his 'unsupported' mother who was probably experiencing acute social and financial problems, with all that this might imply in terms of a restricted diet. Conversely, the 'black' pupil was viewed as an 'out of control' boy with a non-coping mother. Despite the lack of any evidence in the vignette, his behaviour was described as 'violent'. In the vignette, the pupil had brought a note to school requesting a four-week absence for a family holiday. In the case of the 'black' boy, social workers suggested that he might have forged the note whereas in the case of the 'white' pupil, this holiday was construed in positive terms – probably a trip abroad to visit relatives and a 'chance in a lifetime'.

BLACK MASCULINITY

Sivanandan observes that:

> The exclusion of the black child ... is once again being regarded as another element in the social pathology of the black family, rather than as an indicator of a *differentially structured racism* that works against the poorest sections of the black community in particular.
>
> (Sivanandan, 1994, p. v.; our emphasis)

And it is the differential structuring that is of particular relevance in understanding attitudes towards African–Caribbean male pupils; working-class children of all ethnic backgrounds are more likely to be underrated by teachers who fail to stretch them to their full potential (Smith and Tomlinson, 1989). Westwood (1990) has demonstrated how African–Caribbean masculinity is exoticised; with youths falling into either the sporting hero (Frank Bruno/Daley Thompson) or feckless and irresponsible categories – but with both categories supporting stereotypes about black physical vigour. At the same time, widely held views of black single parenting hint at possibly emasculated black male youth – again with potential for physical dangerousness. This view of black manhood is somehow dislocated from 'the family' and, within a white perspective that ignores the history of racism, fails to acknowledge that family stability remains the overriding norm among black families in this country. For example, Mirza (1992) argues that a comparison between young black and white single-parent families shows black single parenting as more common than white single parenting but an analysis of black/black families looks quite different. Her study showed that 78 per cent of black families had two parents and that a significant number of the single-parent families were headed by a male – a factor not found in white single-parent families. She maintains that the *comparatively* high incidence of single parenthood among black women is explained by the relative autonomy and equality between the sexes in the black community and that there is no evidence that black men are considered marginal in the lives of black women. Similarly, Phoenix (1991) considers that black single-parent families are not an indicator of emasculation of black males or weakened family structures but rather a positive and strategic lifestyle; as, indeed, it is to some extent in terms of white single-parent families. The general pathologisation of single-parent families with its emphasis on the problems of deliberate welfare motherhood has been overdone to the extent that it marginalises fathers who may not be married to mothers or live with them but who are, nevertheless, influential in the lives of the children. Phares (1992) showed that a substantial proportion of children under 18 years of age have contact with their biological fathers, regardless of whether or not they live with them.

However, it is probably fruitless to list counter-arguments to stereotyping or exhort teachers to undergo race awareness training as the processes of stereotype construction run deep. Although usually well intentioned and totally committed to pupil welfare, the belief structures held by professionals are deeply influenced by their training. Many of the set texts encourage spurious justifications for the exoticisation of black masculinity. For example, Erikson's (1977) widely used text *Childhood and Society* talks about the psychological factors in the development of differing forms of 'nigger' identity. Incredibly, this text is so embedded in professional discourses that it forms the basis for much of Maxime's (1984) work on psychological 'nigrescence' (the development of positive black identity) and there is a hint of expected physical vigour in her workbooks, which depict black girls as tall netball players.

It seems much more useful to us to concentrate on the precise behaviours where misunderstandings commonly occur which feed teacher perceptions of black dangerousness and pupil perspectives of teacher racism. We suggest that many of these misunderstandings occur around different expression of verbal and non-verbal communication.

WHITE TEACHER–BLACK PUPIL COMMUNICATIONS

Gibson and Barrow (1986) suggest that one of the major issues in black/white communications is an assumption that both African–Caribbean pupils and teachers speak the same language. Whilst teachers can readily appreciate pupils' potential communication problems when they speak English as a second language and are, therefore, alert to potential misunderstandings, they consistently assume a mutual understanding with African–Caribbean pupils.

Gibson and Barrow (1986) suggest that this is a two-way process, with black pupils similarly thinking that their language is the same, despite subtle and significant differences. The two groups are also in agreement about non-verbal communication, both assuming that this is a problematic area although here they define it differently. Teachers, for example, find much non-verbal communication on the part of African–Caribbean pupils simply offensive and insolent. Pupils, on the other hand, complain bitterly that their teachers misinterpret their body language. For example, pupils on the BBC 2 programme *All Black* maintained that 'the way we are, swaggering, laid back, just the way we are' (BBC 2, 13 August 1993) leads to their being perceived negatively and picked on. On the same programme Carlton Douglas, a black headteacher of a comprehensive school, commented that these perceptions meant that teachers 'home in on [black] pupils'. As a constellation of negative behaviours is a constant factor in school exclusions, it seems central to begin with this issue in any attempt to reduce the numbers of black male exclusions. But, where schools have attempted to do just this, there have been complications of the effects of wider stereotyping effects. This is particularly true in instances where schools have sought confrontation training to tackle this issue. This again assumes that black youths are inherently dangerous. Although (mis)communication constitutes a more useful starting point than rhetoric about the effects of Local Management of Schools and institutional racism, how potential 'violence' is processed and handled in schools requires a more detailed and sophisticated analysis. We report on one such attempt below.

Research in one local authority area

It was within this context that we were initially invited to evaluate a project which had been initiated in one local authority area – an area which serves a predominantly urban community with recognised areas of high socio-economic deprivation – and which has a socially, culturally and racially diverse population. The local authority itself had already recognised that male African–Caribbeans were considerably over-represented amongst its population of excluded pupils, and that parents of excluded pupils believed that home–school communication and mutual support concerning behavioural issues could be improved. The local authority had identified as a priority for action not only the reduction in the overall numbers of excluded pupils but also the reduction of the disproportionate exposure to exclusion of male African–Caribbeans. Specifically it proposed to develop a project which aimed:

1   To reduce the number and proportion of African–Caribbean pupils excluded from school and reduce behaviour problems in school which might be a precursor to exclusion.
2   To increase parental involvement and reduce dissatisfaction with the school's response to children presenting behaviour problems.
3   To improve monitoring of pupils believed to be at risk of exclusion.
4   To obtain increased knowledge about the process of exclusion of African–Caribbean pupils.
5   To develop and implement a range of strategies (individual to 'whole school') designed to prevent exclusion.

In the event one high school serving an inner-city area and with a large minority ethnic group population agreed to participate in the project. Additional funding was secured to provide additional input from an education welfare officer and an educational psychologist. The school had already developed a positive behaviour policy which was prominently brought to the attention of both staff and pupils. The main activities undertaken by the project at the time we were invited to become involved had been the establishment of:

1   A computerised database drawing on information from Pupil Referral Forms which identify incidents of disruptive behaviour.
2   An 'exclusion group' (consisting of school staff and other professionals) meeting termly.
3   A programme of groupwork (social skills) sessions with pupils with identified behavioural problems and considered to be at risk of exclusion.

Further activities planned included the implementation of a mentor system for pupils facing difficulties, increasing staff awareness of behaviour issues, and the development of teachers' skills in handling confrontation through in-service training provision.

Although both the local education authority and the school formally used a detailed classification system for indicating pupils' ethnic background, in practice we found that teachers used the much broader ethnic categorisations: 'White', 'Black' and 'Asian' described earlier. These three groups made up 92.5 per cent of the student population and their distribution is indicated in Table 5.1.

Table 5.1 Student population: gender and ethnicity (percentages)

	Male	Female	Total
White	26.1	23.8	49.9
Black	9.7	6.8	16.5
Asian	14.4	11.7	26.1
Total	50.2	42.3	92.5

The findings

Preliminary results show that there are a number of vulnerabilities in the school system which may exacerbate the potential for black/white miscommunications. These vulnerabilities include very small numbers of identifiable pupils and staff and larger numbers of vulnerable situations – particular lessons, years, groups and times of day. A combination of a vulnerable pupil and vulnerable member of staff in a specific lesson at a certain time of day was very much more likely to lead to miscommunications spilling over into unacceptable pupil behaviour and a resulting teacher response leading to disciplinary referral 'up' the system.

Distribution by pupil age/year group

Pupils in Year 9 (13–14-year-olds) were disproportionately represented, accounting for 41 per cent of the total number of Pupil Referral Forms issued. This age group is generally recognised as a problem year for discipline (see, for example, Gillham, 1981). However, even with this one-year group there was a noticeable variation between individual forms, with 2 forms (out of 6) accounting for just under half of all Year 9 referrals. What was also apparent was the exceptionally few Year 8 students who were the subject of a Pupil Referral Form, accounting for only 3 per cent of the total number of Pupil Referral Forms issued. (So far it has not been possible to provide a plausible explanation for the apparent insularity of Year 8 pupils to disciplinary proceedings.)

Distribution by period

The school day was divided into seven periods, the fifth and sixth (afternoon) periods presenting most discipline problems, accounting for 46 per cent of the total number of Pupil Referral Forms issued. It was noticeable that morning and afternoon breaks and lunch time generated the issue of few forms. However, these times were supervised by senior staff who, it was thought by staff contacts, might be more likely to resort to informal and unrecorded sanctions than more junior staff. (This was a salutary reminder of the limits which can be placed on research based on official sources and documentation!)

Analysis by day

There appeared to be a slight reduction in the issue of Pupil Referral Forms towards the end of the week. However, as the school was introducing a computerised system of attendance registration it was not possible to compare this data with attendance records. It remains possible that those pupils at particular risk of being issued with a Referral Form may well be absent later in the week.

Distribution by date

There appears to be no consistent pattern other than the expected reduction during incomplete weeks, although this is consistent with both local and national patterns (Badger, 1992).

Distribution by teacher

As might have been expected there were variations between individual teachers concerning the issue of Pupil Referral Forms (see, for example, McManus, 1995). Eleven teachers were responsible for issuing 60 per cent of all Pupil Referral Forms, each issuing more than ten referral forms during the term. The majority of these teachers were female and included one temporary and two part-time teachers. In the main, this group comprised the most 'vulnerable' members of the teaching staff.

Of the eleven teachers, one white female and two white males issued Pupil Referral Forms to significantly more black than white pupils. Distinct patterns were evident with each of these, the female teacher referring black students in Year 10 (14–15-year-olds) predominantly in morning lessons whilst the two male teachers referred black Year 9 and Year 10 boys across the school day.

Distribution by pupil

The nine boys (five black and four white) and the one (black) girl who between them account for almost a quarter of all Pupil Referral Forms issued, each receiving five or more referrals during the term, were not over-represented in any of the other 'vulnerable' groupings. This suggests that they were pupils for whom an individualised programme might be appropriate. The differences in their displays of disruptive behaviour were quite marked. For example, the boy who had received the most Pupil Referral Forms appears to have started the term as a cheeky boy who played up in one particular lesson with one particular teacher and then 'branched out'. At the time of writing it is not possible to suggest whether his behaviour deteriorated or whether he simply gained a name for himself amongst other teachers (and students) and was exposed to the risk of scapegoating. The pupil in this group with the least number of referrals displayed a potentially more worrying pattern of behaviour, details on the referral forms indicating a problem of violent incidents with male teachers during afternoons. (In the subsequent term this pupil was excluded for a fixed term.)

Distribution by gender and ethnicity

Overall, boys were three times more likely than girls to be issued with a Pupil Referral Form. African–Caribbean boys were twice as likely as their white and Asian peers to be issued with a Pupil Referral Form, although Asian boys in Year 9 were over-represented in comparison to their numbers in the pupil group as a whole. African–Caribbean girls were over-represented compared to their white and Asian peers and, indeed, were slightly more likely to be issued with a Pupil Referral Form than white boys. However, as illustrated in the previous paragraph, black pupils were even more disproportionately represented amongst the most frequently referred students.

Distribution by type of incident

The Pupil Referral Forms included a means for categorisation of the type of incident or behaviour resulting in the issue of the form. Final categorisation of incident was made by a senior member of staff to whom the pupil was referred, so was highly dependent on the information provided on the form and subject to interpretation by the senior staff member. Two categories were most frequently used: 'constant irritant to class and teacher' and 'persistent refusal to follow reasonable instruction'. Both of these suggest 'last straw' type incidents and this is consistent with other research showing that pupils are most frequently excluded for a constellation of negative behaviours rather than overt violence (see, for example, DfE, 1992a; SHA, 1992). Research into pupil perceptions of disciplinary events (see Cullingford and Morrison, and de Pear and Garner in this volume) shows that they do not view their behaviour in terms of a gradual build up of frustration for the teacher, viewing each incident separately. Understandably, both pupils and teachers are frustrated by these 'last straw' incidents, with neither party being much in the mood for increased tolerance over misunderstandings.

Exclusions

There was no obvious link between the issue of Pupil Referral Forms and exclusions during the same period, although there may well be a time lag between the types of event. The fixed-term exclusions for this duration included a disproportionate number of Asian boys, especially noticeable because of their generally low referral rate.

Discussion

This modest analysis does not claim to have unearthed any universal truths about discipline in schools. It is merely a tool by which the school in question can begin to examine its own practices in a way that has relevance and meaning for all members of staff. To date it has highlighted two main issues for the school.

First, resources can be targeted efficiently to vulnerable areas of school life. For example, an on-going analysis of this sort helps to identify pupils who will benefit from individual programmes but also staff who need support. One simple measure which has resulted from a discussion of the findings to date has been some small timetabling changes to enable vulnerable members of staff and pupils to have a break from each other at vulnerable times of the day. Training interventions with respect to confrontation training can also be targeted more effectively.

Second, there has been lengthy discussion amongst senior staff about their own low referral rate. At first this was assumed to indicate greater confidence among senior staff over their authority with pupils but a tentative hypothesis has emerged which may have more bearing on the exclusion process. It may be that the exclusion process in this school takes place outside the official disciplinary agenda. For example, a pupil who misbehaves with a vulnerable member of staff is likely to figure in the referral-form league table whilst a pupil who misbehaves at lunch time with a senior member of staff may find himself/herself on the receiving end of unrecorded sanctions (McManus, 1995). Staff are undecided as to the precise workings of this possible process. It could be due to a low tolerance of challenges to their authority or it could reflect support for more junior staff who are perceived as being 'played up' unfairly by some pupils. At present staff are considering that there may be more gender effects operating rather than racial ones: that senior teachers (who are mostly male) may find particular difficulties in tolerating masculine assertiveness on the part of older male pupils – in terms of this being a challenge to themselves or their more junior female colleagues. It is also tentatively suggested that white male teachers may find the masculine assertiveness of black pupils to female teachers more difficult to tolerate than that of white pupils. At the moment, this leads to the school considering anti-sexist policies and practice as much as anti-racist policies and practice.

FURTHER ISSUES

Any school with a disproportionate rate of exclusions for black male pupils could usefully remember that while white pupils are negotiating with teachers as (un)equal but similar members of a socialisation process, the situation for black pupils is much more complicated. These pupils must negotiate three different social contexts – the *mainstream* (white) socialisation process in schools in which they constitute a *minority* (racist) and, within that minority context, they have to negotiate black *cultural* agendas, which can be as diverse as Rastafarianism or black religious cultures. Their strategies will not always be appropriately displayed: 'The mainstream socialisation agenda has to be negotiated *in lieu* of the minority and black cultural agendas. These agendas clearly conflict with the mainstream one; and, for that matter with each other as well' (Boykim and Toms, 1985; our emphasis).

In order to explore how these difficulties manifest themselves in teacher–pupil communication, we would suggest that an analysis such as that described above could be usefully considered. It is particularly important that such an analysis should be a non-observational one (Badger, 1992), so that schools are faced with making sense of their own 'bald' facts. We further suggest that school support staff might well consider it their role to set up such a project. This would constitute an integral part of their role if they are to identify the urgent problems schools face and to provide approximately targeted assistance. This form of 'assessment of the whole' before assessment of individuals might well assist pastoral staff in developing a clear and coherent role for themselves in a rapidly changing world.

Chapter 6

No home, no school, no future
Exclusions and children who are 'looked after'

Howard Firth and Christine Horrocks

INTRODUCTION

School in an open society is seen as a place to obtain social justice and to achieve equality of opportunity. Indeed, for children and young people who are 'looked after', school may prove to be the only constant source of stability in a fragmented and troubled life. Unfortunately, it seems that, within the current political climate in education, such prevailing expectations regarding educational entitlement may not be taken as absolute for all children. A joint report by the Department of Health Social Services Inspectorate and OFSTED highlighted grave concern regarding the education of children and young people 'looked after'; at least 25 per cent of children at Key Stage 4 were facing 'acute difficulties'. These children were often not attending school and, 'many have been excluded and have no regular educational placement' (SSI and OFSTED, 1995, p. 43). A regional survey (Maginnis, 1993) calculated that a child living in a children's home is eighty times more likely to be excluded from school than a child living with his or her family. Such figures give a bleak prognosis regarding equality of opportunity and indeed social justice for the 60,000 children and young people who are currently 'looked after' by local authorities. On an average day, many of these young people will be without education; either excluded, awaiting placements or refusing to attend – drifting in a vacuum of failure.

Those 'looked after' children and young people who remain in school appear to experience very little in the way of successful educational attainment (Biehal *et al.*, 1992; Garnett, 1992, 1994). A study by Firth (1992) recording the academic achievements of 'looked after' children and young people found of the 146 year 11 pupils studied, only 39 gained one or more GCSE passes. Of the 39, no more than 15 gained a pass at levels A–C. Garnett, (1992) in her research into the educational attainments and destinations of children and young people 'looked after', found that 'less than half of the Looked After group, 48 per cent, obtained at lease one GCSE at grade A–G compared with 98 per cent of the County's year 11s'.

Furthermore, only a quarter of her sample of young people, who had experience of the care system for five years or longer, left school with any formal qualifications whatsoever. In one-third of the cases studied, social workers had no idea if exams had been taken or had no actual record on file. These dismal findings are further supported in the SSI and OFSTED investigation into the education of 'looked after' children and young people: 'children in secondary schools seldom reach standards close to those expected. None of the children featured were judged by teachers as likely to achieve 5 subjects at grade A–C in GCSE' (SSI and OFSTED, 1995, p. 11).

This compares very unfavourably with the general school population where 38.3 per cent of pupils in year 11 achieved 5 or more A–Cs in 1993. To embrace any recommendations made to address such issues, and incidentally gain a local authority 'feel good' factor, apparently appealing and costly projects are initiated. Many of these projects reinforce to 'looked after' children and young people that their educational needs differ from those of the general population. National Curriculum and full-time schooling is often replaced with unacceptable alternatives – motor biking, outdoor education, crime prevention, and work experience. As parents, we should pose the question – would such activities fulfil the educational requirements of *our* children? The answer to such a question would be a resounding 'no'. We would demand full-time education in a 'proper' school, with recognised educational aims and objectives.

WHAT DOES THE FUTURE HOLD FOR A CARE LEAVER?

Jackson (1994) points out that it is only through school that children earn a passport to a different kind of future. This is one of the reasons why parents care so passionately: why they move house, take out insurance, and even risk political censure to send their children to the school of their choice. Are local authorities prepared to make comparable sacrifices in their role as parents? Are they inspired to secure a 'different kind of future' for 'their' children?

It has consistently been found that between 25 per cent and 40 per cent of all young homeless people aged under-21 have a care background (DoH, 1980; *Times Educational Supplement*, 13.10.95, 1995). A survey of young people leaving care considered that 15 per cent of young people studied were homeless within three to nine months of either moving to independence or being legally discharged from care (Biehal *et al.*, 1992). Research has shown the inability of care leavers to find and sustain employment (Biehal *et al.*, 1992; Stein and Carey, 1986). 'Eighty per cent of young care leavers were unemployed, two and a half years after leaving care' (NCB, 1993). Young people who fail to secure an adequate education will find it extremely difficult to progress towards permanent employment and financial security in today's economic climate.

Studies of care leavers show that many young women were either pregnant or had children at the point of legal discharge from care (Biehal *et al.*, 1992; Garnett, 1992). Also, an alarming 38 per cent of young prisoners had spent a period in local authority care (NCB, 1992). A picture is emerging of the corporate parent failing to shape successfully the futures of children and young people who are 'looked after'. Education, as previously suggested, may be a means to procuring more positive outcomes for children and young people who are 'looked after'. However, in order to attempt to assure a more optimistic future, evident failings within the prevailing system must first be recognised and addressed.

DISPROPORTIONATE EXCLUSIONS: WHY?

Care history

It is assumed that 'looked after' children and young people have the weight and support of the local authority to secure their rights to equality and opportunity within the education system. If this is the case, why is it that these children are found to be so disadvantaged educationally? Surely it is not unreasonable to suggest that the absence of a sound education may have a substantial part to play in their distressing outcomes. Nevertheless, the most popular explanation given for 'looked after' children and young people's lack of achievement focuses around a familiar excuse. These young people are deemed to be the products of their early childhood experience and, indeed, what should we expect from children who come from such a disadvantaged background? Research has shown that children and young people who require local authority placements have experienced various levels of deprivation (Bebbington and Miles, 1989), therefore it would be naive to disregard completely the impact of past experience on a young person's ability and attitude toward education. But past experience is an extremely lame and convenient excuse for the care system's failure to meet often complex and diverse needs. The Utting review of residential child care clearly rejected such assumptions: 'Care authorities should act to remedy the educational disadvantage of children in their care, and do all that a good parent would do to ensure that children's needs are met' (DoH, 1991, p. 10, para. 29).

The competence to bring about a positive change in the educational experience of children and young people who are 'looked after' requires those who care for children to act on their behalf. This may prove to be an unrealised recommendation. Walker (1994) emphasised that local authorities view significant improvements to the care system independently of strategies addressing the educational disadvantage of their children. Education is viewed outside the remit of social services: 'Education is seen exclusively as a matter of entitlement, opportunity and attainment and, therefore, outside the remit and jurisdiction of social services authorities' (Walker, 1994, p. 340).

It is obviously not acceptable to set rigid departmental boundaries when dealing with children's futures. Repeatedly, the call is for inter-agency collaboration in the provision of services for children (DoH, 1991; Jones and Bilton, 1994; SSI and OFSTED, 1995). The Audit Commission report, *Seen But Not Heard* (1994) stressed the necessity to accept shared responsibility when responding to the educational needs of 'looked after' children and young people: 'Social services and education need to accept joint ownership of the problem of disrupted education of children "looked after" and work together to find solutions' (Audit Commission, 1994, p. 25).

Regrettably such recommendations are seldom realised. As a consequence the education of 'looked after' children and young people becomes a tenuous issue, relying on undelivered inter-departmental co-operation rather than direct and specific service provision. A natural development of the failure to be specific and to transcend departmental boundaries is a progression to-wards a blame culture, with social services complaining that the education authority is frustrating the educational opportunities of children and young people who are 'looked after' and the LEA emphasising poor social work and care practice which mitigates against any form of educational advancement – both departments feeling safe in the knowledge that responsibility lies elsewhere.

Legislation

A critical factor in the failure to improve on the educational achievements of children in local authority care is to be found within three recent legislative measures: the Children Act 1989, the Education Reform Act 1988 and the Education Act 1993. These measures dealing with essential services for children operate on different principles (Sinclair, 1994). The Children Act legislated for the child and, indeed, made all agents of care collectively responsible for service delivery. It clearly identifies statutory requirements to safeguard and promote the welfare of all children, with specific reference for the provision of services for children 'who are in need'.

(10)   For the purpose of this Part a child shall be taken to be in need if:

(a) he is unlikely to achieve or maintain, or to have the opportunity of achieving or maintaining, a reasonable standard of health or development without the provision for him of services by a local authority under this part;

(b) his health or development is likely to be significantly impaired, or further impaired, without the provision for him of such services ...

(11)   ... 'development' means physical, intellectual, emotional, social or behavioural development.

(Children Act 1989, Part III, S. 17)

Evidently, children and young people who are 'looked after' are to be included within the framework of this statute. Those who are not 'achieving or maintaining a reasonable standard' have the right to support and assistance in their educational endeavours.

The Education Reform Act 1988 and the Education Act 1993 had a totally different agenda; establishing schools in the market place and competing for the patronage of parents, with quite resounding consequences for many children. Such differing interpretations work in a way that is detrimental to the most vulnerable children in society. These legislative measures make schools less willing to tolerate those children who may have difficulty adjusting to changes in their lives. Difficulties experienced outside school will obviously, at times, overspill into school, and as a consequence children may need extra support. There is, according to Walker (1994), an expectation from schools and the social services department that both can look towards the local authority for extra support. This is an impossible request when the majority of local education authority resources have been effectively removed from local authority control through the implementation of local management of schools (LMS) and delegated budgets.

In an arena where the LEA's powers of persuasion and control are diminished and schools' independence enhanced, there has been a natural movement to adopt an increasingly narrow view, with little incentive to act collectively in the interests of 'looked after' children and young people. With crude performance indicators becoming a major priority in schools it is prudent to consider how a pupil who is 'looked after' might affect a school's performance and thereafter its competitive position. Children who find difficulty conforming to the expectations of the school regime, regarding behaviour and attainment, project a negative image to parents. Such pupils rarely enhance the schools' performance or attendance levels. Within a market system where parental support and patronage is clearly linked to funding, these are elements which can not be disregarded. In order to maximise both attendance and attainment there may be a desire for the school to relieve itself of those pupils who would adversely affect such goals: 'exclusion policies can be used to rid schools of challenging pupils who may be seen as threats to the schools' performance and reputation' (Jones and Bilton, 1994, p. 25).

Subsequently, children most in need of safeguarding and welfare promotions, as highlighted in the Children Act 1989, may be the least likely to receive such support from our present education system. Contrasting legislation has apparently laid down a framework for indifference and inactivity regarding vulnerable children's needs, both within schools and the local authority.

Stability

Research has repeatedly shown that an overriding theme for children and young people 'looked after' is the lack of stability in child care placements (Biehal *et al.*, 1992; Fletcher-Campbell and Hall, 1990). Stein and Carey (1986) found that 40 per cent of care leavers had experienced five or more placements while in 'care'. This level of instability has enormous consequences for children in determining school achievement (Heath *et al.*, 1989). Evidently, one of the most debilitating factors endured by a child in local authority care is the rarity of a consistent and continuous person to overview progress. Even relatively untroubled childhoods include bad patches which are steered through by a parent with an eye to the future. Most parents carry an education plan in their head to which they consistently refer. The goals and expectations are long term, and, although the way forward may be fraught with hiccups and adjustments, a shared destination with their children is usually achieved. This kind of stable relationship and shared aims and objectives is rarely present for a child in care, whose life is a succession of residential and foster placements punctuated by brief periods at home. In such circumstances plans are changed frequently and the parental principles social workers hold dear are abandoned for the expediency of meeting immediate needs such as a roof over their head or other demands for a 'quick fix'.

Schools do not help to diminish the consequences of constant change, often failing fully to appreciate the changes that are taking place and effectively to assess the appropriate needs of children and young people who are 'looked after'. Assessment and systematic recording of children's progress has been found to be lamentably inadequate, thus providing only partial information for both the present education placement and

Table 6.1 Care placement change and permanent exclusion

Number of children	Number of moves	Number permanently excluded	Percentage permanently excluded
1	7	1	100
3	6	3	100
5	5	4	80
12	4	5	42
26	3	10	38
39	2	15	38
70	1	26	37
202	0	41	20

Source: Firth, 1995

any successive school: 'Commonly, school records were too disorganised to give a full account of the child to the next school or new teacher' (SSI and OFSTED, 1995, p. 18).

As a consequence it would not seem unrealistic to suggest that fragmented information, inconsistency and lack of continuity has an impact on both achievement and behaviour in school. Pupils who are unable, or viewed as unwilling, to conform to specific school criteria may find that they become potential candidates for exclusion. In a study of placement changes (Firth, 1995a) a close association was established between care placement change and permanent exclusion (Table 6.1).

It would be irresponsible to imply that placement change was the only mitigating factor involved when a pupil became permanently excluded from school. However, clearly suggested is a relationship between stability of placement and school exclusion; pupils with five or more moves can supposedly expect little from the present education system. It is also regrettable to note that, even with consistency of placement, 'looked after' children and young people have a 20 per cent chance of being permanently excluded. From such results it is evident that social service departments should carefully consider the effect placement changes can have on the educational careers of young people. Jackson (1987) called for social services departments to consider education as a high priority in care placement changes. From her research she noted that this was 'rarely given much significance' with evidently quite profound consequences for young people.

Low priority – low expectations

A common theme for many children and young people who are 'looked after' by their local authority is how children often underestimate their own potential and do not expect to do well at school. Children do not acquire such views in isolation but it would be difficult to determine precisely the origins of their low expectations. However, there is evidence to suggest that such attitudes are not ameliorated once a child enters the care system. Further mitigating factors for educational deficits and disproportionate exclusions are the low priority afforded to education and the low educational expectations of social workers, carers and teachers: 'social workers, teachers and carers did not give the children's educational progress and standards of achievement sufficient priority compared with the attention given to such matters as care, relationships and contact with parents' (SSI and OFSTED, 1995, p. 3).

Highlighting the disparity in attention given to education, as opposed to other concerns, does not aim to diminish attention given to other matters. Rather, the aim is to emphasise the need to raise the profile of education as a crucial factor in planning and subsequent 'looked after' placements. Maintaining stability of school placement should be a priority when making care plans. Unfortunately, for many children, school disruption has been found to be a consequence of placement change (Farmer and Parker, 1991). Jackson (1994) identified (as one of the most important findings in her research) the low priority given by social workers to education when making assessments. When low priority is aligned with low expectations it is hardly surprising that children and young people who are 'looked after' fail to recognise their own potential.

Carers can provide a vital link between school and the care placement. However, evidence indicates that, notably in residential care, this vital link is not made (SSI and OFSTED, 1995, p. 30). Millham et al. (1986) suggest that care staff may have attitudes to school and education which would be unhelpful to a child in care. In their study they found 'only 32 per cent enjoyed their own school days, 62 per cent failed the 11+ exam, 57 per cent left at the earliest opportunity' (Millham et al., 1986, p. 65). This research also inferred that contact with schools may remind residential workers of previous personal humiliations in the educational arena. Evidence of this nature does not engender confidence in the ability of residential staff to support and promote positive educational achievement for 'looked after' children and young people. Further research (Fletcher-Campbell and Hall, 1990) found that residential workers often have a sense of professional marginality. They may reduce this anxiety by avoiding contact with teachers, preferring the telephone to face-to-face encounters and visiting schools only when it becomes unavoidable. Based on such evidence it could be assumed that staff in residential homes would reinforce a child's own indifference to education.

Failure to meet the educational needs of 'looked after' children and young people does not rest only within the social work domain; teachers are also guilty of failing to make real demands and address needs (Fletcher, 1993; SSI and OFSTED, 1995). Pupils attending school may feel different and in some cases ashamed – stigmatised (Stein and Carey, 1986). Providing them with the confidence to recognise their potential and take chances in order to realise positive outcomes is both a time-consuming and skilful operation, requiring a great deal of sensitivity. Teachers may recognise children who are facing 'acute problems'; however, 'while sympathetic, they express diffidence about their ability to help older children recognising that the children often require more skilled support' (SSI and OFSTED, 1995, p. 20). Recognising problems is not enough; teachers should be enabled to appreciate the necessity to access or acquire the skills that meet the needs of children with 'acute problems'. This would entail resources being made available for support services and training. As children and young people who are 'looked after' are already disadvantaged, they need positive and appropriate support in order to redress their existing disadvantage. This cannot be achieved by an alternative syllabus or the lowering of expectations albeit often due to well-meant sympathetic responses. 'Looked after' children and young people consistently say they want somebody to expect and demand a lot more. They need to be stimulated and motivated in order that their school experiences will be more favourable. This motivation can only be brought about via a change in attitudes; social workers, teachers and carers all need to recognise and realise the potential of children and young people who are 'looked after'. Such a change in attitudes might work towards alleviating problems in schools rather than maintaining the present levels of inertia which ultimately leads to exclusion not only from school but also from society for many 'looked after' children and young people.

THE WAY FORWARD: PRACTICAL SOLUTIONS

How can escalating exclusion rates of 'looked after' children and young people be prevented and reduced? At a national conference organised by the Who Cares? Trust (1995) overwhelming evidence was provided by delegates and speakers regarding the progress being made in a number of local authorities, especially Manchester, Hampshire, Cambridgeshire, Humberside, Salford and Derbyshire, where a number of unique innovations are reducing the number of exclusions. The starting point for these authorities is the young person; listening to those who are directly affected by any action taken, pointing the way toward practical solutions (Garner, 1994; de Pear and Garner, and John in this volume). This factor was highlighted in one authority's 'Listening to Children' project (Firth, 1993) in which all young people present emphasised the importance they placed on 'proper' schooling and their need to be fully involved.

If I were the Director of Social Services, I would make sure all the kids were in school.

I would like to be normal and go to school.

Let young people in care have the opportunity to pass GCSEs.

These thought-provoking comments all referred to normality and equal entitlement. Children and young people in care were not requesting home tuition, a Pupil Referral Unit, or a work experience project, but a 'proper' school. What are the critical steps we need to take in order to resolve current escalating difficulties in school for 'looked after' children? Of paramount importance is for social services departments to prioritise education within any future strategic planning regarding children 'looked after'.

Education: a social work task

Although Firth (1995b) has identified education as the second largest problem facing social workers after child protection, most local authority social services departments maintain an ambivalence towards the issue, assuming that securing equal access is totally within the remit of the LEA. Yet as SSI and OFSTED (1995) points out, with the delegation of management and financial responsibilities to schools and their governing bodies social services departments can no longer look to this lead. Social services departments, *alongside* the LEA, must assume this mantle and make access to education a strategic issue for all social services' staff. Utting (DoH, 1991) in the special review of residential care endorsed the recommendations of the Pindown Enquiry (Levy and Kahan, 1991), stating that there should be a named person at senior manager level with responsibility for:

1 ensuring care and attention is given to education, career development and the working of children and young people in care;
2 the consideration of any policy or practice issue.

All too often these recommendations have either been ignored or added to the existing remit of a manager who has given it little priority. There is a definite necessity to be specific regarding managerial responsibilities and accountability. Successful authorities have embraced recommendations through the appointment of a senior manager with a primary objective to address the educational issues of 'looked after' children and young people. In Hampshire this post includes the management of a team of sixteen support teachers skilled in education and social work practice. Their task is to make sure children and young people who are 'looked after' have the same educational opportunities as those living at home. Jackson (1995) endorses this strategy, emphasising: 'A specialised support service is needed on the lines of those already existing in Manchester/Hampshire. It needs to be staffed by teachers who carry credibility with schools and know their way around both the education and care system.'

SPECIALISED SUPPORT SERVICES: REDUCING EXCLUSIONS

In care means high expectations

Natural parents talk about further, higher education and career development and the family support necessary for this while care system professionals talk about jobs, claiming benefit and independent living. These latter expectations need to be raised and realised. If exclusions of 'looked after' children and young people are to be reduced, specialised education support services need to establish a firm and effective working partnership between social service departments, LEAs and schools. All must realistically work towards ensuring that education is a priority in all departmental care planning. Time must be taken to create and maintain effective links with schools by providing time-limited in-school support, based on clear and jointly owned support plans. Work must be undertaken with staff in residential homes in establishing and maintaining high levels of school attendance. This undertaking would mean ensuring that all social work teams and staff of children's homes have working education policies aiming to improve the academic achievements of children and young people in the care system. In order to capitalise on educational advancement, education support services should encourage and develop practical support systems for helping young people to continue into further and higher education. The aim of such specialised support services is to advocate on all the educational issues which affect children and young people who are 'looked after'. To support the rhetoric, core tasks must include:

1 Consistency in school and care placement.
2 Where necessary, provision of practical support in a new school placement.
3 Maintenance of high standards of attendance.
4 Challenging schools on unnecessary exclusions.
5 Challenging delays in school admissions.
6 Ensuring that there is effective communication and a working partnership with all schools.
7 Negotiation and design of individual programmes with the school.
8 Long term education plans with achievable targets for all children and young people 'looked after'.
9 Celebration of individual success and achievement.
10 Support for the ethos and standards of the young person's school.
11 Establishment of compacts with local colleges and universities.
12 Inclusion of educational issues within the core Social Services Department training calendar.

13 Provision of appropriate resources and work areas in all children's homes.
14 Maintenance of a database on all 'looked after' children and young people and their educational records.

Hampshire County Council has experienced relative success after adopting this approach. What is most heartening is that permanent exclusions are a rarity in the majority of the authority's residential establishments, a factor directly attributable to the relationship between the children's home and the local schools (Table 6.2).

Reducing costs and redirecting resources

The key question to be asked is: are such extensive education support services affordable in the prevailing economic climate? In reality it has been found that by supporting the educational component of care plans, considerable overall reductions in departmental spending have been made by:

1 Preventing 'family breakdown' and the subsequent necessity for a residential or foster placement.
2 Increasing the possibility of a young person already in local authority care to return home.

Table 6.2 Comparison of educational experience between the general population and 'looked after' children (percentages)

	General population	Looked 'after'	Southern county 1993–4	Southern county 1994–5
Leaving school with qualifications	95.0	25.0	36.0	46.0
Out of education for over one year	1.0	25.0	4.3	2.9
Continued into Further Education	65.0	9.0	27.0	34.7
Permanently excluded	0.5	25.0	8.3	6.6

Source: Firth, 1995

3   Enhancing foster placement opportunities for children and young people in residential care.
4   Reducing the stress placed on vulnerable foster placements that may be in danger of unplanned endings.
5   Providing appropriate local schooling, thus eliminating the need for out of area placements.
6   Enabling children and young people to return from expensive out-of-area provision.

When payoffs of such magnitude are achieved an education support service presents as a wise and beneficial investment. However, cooperation and consistency are the vital factors required to realise the outcome of a positive educational experience for children and young people who are 'looked after'.

Multi-agency action a practical partnership

The Children Act 1989 clearly places the responsibility for safeguarding the development of children at risk on the entire local authority, not specific departments. Section 17(11) of the Act states that development means physical, intellectual, social or behavioural, effectively making the social services department, LEA and school partners in the process. Any collaboration must be at a practical as well as at a strategic level; promoting a new kind of relationship built on a shared action plan between the local authority and schools. Raising awareness and acknowledging difficulties is only the starting point of any solution. Joint working practices must become an expectation with build-in accountability. Joint reporting should be undertaken, reviewing shared difficulties and joint progress and setting achievable targets for the coming year. The basis of this relationship is 'practical problem-solving' on items that are high on the agenda for 'looked after' children and young people.

To promote this more unified approach, a pilot training workshop took place the purpose of which was to create an effective working partnership between schools, LEAs and social services departments for children in critical need. As a direct result of this inter-agency workshop, a working group consisting of headteachers, social work managers, LEA representatives and the social services department education managers are developing a service level agreement. The key action points in this agreement are:

1   To substantially improve communication at all levels.
2   To identify roles and responsibilities and characteristic depart-
    mental procedures.
3   To promote a collective understanding and appreciation of
    current policies regarding the education of children in local
    authority care.
4   To identify named persons in particular local authority depart-
    ments, who will have specific responsibility for the services
    that support 'looked after' children in school.
5   To arrange joint training opportunities and induction pro-
    grammes that increase the recognition of shared objectives
    and mutual solutions to complex problems.

The outcome of this initiative will hopefully be to reduce inter-
departmental bureaucratic tangles in order to explore flexible
ways of working together in the interest of all children and young
people. This reduction would prevent unnecessary exclusions
through jointly-planned early intervention.

The Audit Commission Report, *Seen but not Heard* (1994) criticised local authorities for the disappointing lack of coordination.
In only one-quarter of authorities did a cross-departmental
approach to planning for children exist. The report called for
Health Authorities, social services departments, LEAs and voluntary agencies to publish joint plans for improving services.
The report highlights that although £2 billion is spent each year
on services for children, little joint planning was evident. If young
people in the care system are to be seen, heard, educated and
employed, and therefore able to take their rightful place in
society, each local authority must provide multi-agency children's
service plans in which addressing the educational needs of 'looked
after' children and young people is a discrete section, with joint
accountability. Through these plans, realistic improvements can
be made regarding the educational opportunities of children in
the care of their local authority. The critical factor in this strategic
vision is a corporate partnership. This partnership should be based
on a practical commitment and the belief that children in the
care system have the right to expect the backing of the corporate might of the entire local authority.

Chapter 7

Professionals, children and power

Wendy Marshall

INTRODUCTION

Concepts of power inform discussions of exclusions and the aim of this chapter is to bring this more explicitly into focus. The main reason for exclusion given by schools to parents, children and LEAs is 'disobedience in various forms' (DfE, 1993) which consists primarily of insolence, disruption and uncooperative behaviour rather than violence. This evokes an expectation of children as normally obedient to the 'natural' authority of teachers and schools and in which children may be understood as actors only when disobedient. A naturalised and institutionalised adult expectation of authority and associated ideas of the nature of the child are thus in need of some analysis and exploration.

This chapter examines the powerful myths of liberal authority as this continues to inform ideas of appropriate child–adult relations and has been the focus of critical theorising. It explores competing frameworks for understanding adult–child power relations and argues that there are profound tensions and contradictions in contemporary relations of authority with children which need to be located in a context of uncertainty.

LIBERAL MYTHS AND THE ABSENTING OF CHILDREN'S POWER

The authority of teachers may draw upon different metaphors of power which relate to both understandings of authority in *loco parentis* and metaphors of contractual authority delegated from the sovereign power of the state.

In the liberal tradition of political theorising the social body is understood as having been established via a social contract. Hobbes, the seventeenth-century English political theorist, suggested that to ensure a minimum political order within which to pursue their individual desires, people should be understood as having rationally agreed to give up their power to a sovereign authority (for a fuller discussion see, for example, Clegg, 1989). The establishment of the state and a framework of law continues to be seen as that which enables the individual to pursue his or her own desires without infringing the rights of others. The liberal emphasis on individual free will, within the context of a social contract, enables the modern family to be private, largely self-regulating and autonomous. Actions initiated by sovereign subjects should not step outside authorisation; if individual wills do not conform then the sovereign power uses its 'reserve powers' to prevent these actions. In the nineteenth century, fears of urban disorder in the context of industrialisation can be understood to have produced a focus on the child as a key point of reform and progress via education (Ehrenreich and English, 1979). Schooling is the first major institutionalised form of the new modern western childhood where children are excluded from full participation in the adult world of work on the grounds that they are seen both as in need of protection and as 'incompetent' (Hendrick, 1990). Parents are legally obliged to ensure their children receive education. Thus, when they exclude children from school, teachers are underlining the responsibility of the parents for ensuring their children behave appropriately. A key concern of the government is that proper procedures are followed by schools and LEAs so that parents have not been unjustly restricted (DfE, 1994b).

This classical model of authority by prior consent, which is binding on everyone, does not apply to children who, by virtue of their status as not yet rational, cannot be assumed to have taken part in the social contract and cannot be entrusted with the obligations of citizenship. Children are not regarded as autonomous but engaged in a process of becoming independent. Hence the partnership in education is understood to be with the parent and not with the child. This absence of the child in the educational partnership has been identified as problematic (Blyth and Milner, 1996).

As education is understood as a partnership with parents in the socialisation of children into the adult world, teachers also incorporate notions of *loco parentis*. Although the pre-liberal political concepts of divine right with an absolute patriarch receiving unquestioning obedience from passive subjects were reconstructed in liberal theorising, Elshtain (1981) suggests that these earlier terms have remained influential and that this may be particularly true in relation to ideas about the family. She cites Rousseau, for whom the family predated civil society, who understood paternal authority as established by nature and Locke who suggested that the father's power and authority is natural until the child reaches the age of adulthood (Elshtain, 1981). The child is thus in a special relationship to both the state and the family in that the child is understood as not yet having acquired rationality. Both educational and parental philosophies in the twentieth century have drawn on Rousseau's notions, set out in *Emile* in 1762 (Rousseau, 1956), of the child as natural. In opposition to the earlier more authoritarian views of the child, child-centred parenting and child-centred education are understood as more democratic, producing a subject with emerging rational capacities rather than mere obedience. The child is expected to flourish within a controlled but enabling environment where choice is significant and where the child's immanent rationality will unfold through exploration and self expression. Strain (1995), for instance, suggests that the classical liberal notions of positive and negative freedom are used by teachers to distinguish for children the 'licence' they may be seeking from the freedom which comes from obeying the rules which enable them to grow. This implies the possibility of a greater inclusion for children now in the mythical 'liberal' contract.

However, the Newsons' (1976) study shows that the taken for granted quality of the obedience principle still remains in evidence. Similarly Hood-Williams (1990) discusses the continued salience of natural authority in adult–child relations in which adults demand respect and punish children accordingly. Whilst an emerging state concern with children's rights has in some ways restricted the form of authority and punishment, teacher authority continues to be imbued with wider social legitimacy through its mythical relation to a deferred sovereign power. It is imagined symbolically as a rational order imposed on the raw natural material of the child. Children themselves are not understood as sharing in adult authority and issues of power do not figure in the discussions unless an abuse of adult power is thought to have occurred. Thus, the child's relationship to adults at home and at school is expected to be one of legitimate and natural subordination.

COMPETING STRUCTURES OF POWER

Bardy (1994) and Mayall (1994a) suggest that whilst adults largely avoid the issue of power between children and adults, children themselves talk clearly in these terms about their own experiences of adults, both at home and at school, as restrictive and controlling. Ideas of authority in relation to children have been intricately linked to notions of qualitative differences between adults and children: 'The crucial distinction that makes children children is that they are not adults; as individuals and as a social group they lack adulthood' (Mayall, 1994a, p. 118).

The evaluation of the relevance, fairness or legitimacy of adults' use of power in relation to children only arises where this is detached from an assumed basis in naturalised relations. Qvortrup suggests that: 'Questioning the principal of ontological differences between adults and children is a challenge to the ideological foundation for adults' "natural" right to exert power over children' (Qvortrup, 1994, p. 3).

The emergence of a sociology of childhood as a distinct area of study marks an interest in reconceptualising children as caught up in a structure of childhood (see, Prout and James, 1990 for a discussion of this as an emerging paradigm). The conditions of childhood, though related to children's actual dependence, are seen as largely serving adult interests rather than those of children. Qvortrup comments on the lack of data on children's social conditions in official and academic accounts, suggesting that they are 'the invisible group *par excellence* in our society' (Qvortrup, 1990). He contrasts the paucity of systematic study of childhood as a social dynamic with the many studies of the dynamics of children's development and socialisation. Sociologists of childhood have been concerned to demonstrate the socially constructed and thus changeable nature of the institution of childhood in opposition to the erstwhile dominant view of childhood as natural, thereby rendering children and childhood visible as areas of study in their own right. Qvortrup (1990) makes connections with women and workers as social groups who have demanded the right to be heard and have challenged their oppression. Other writers have suggested parallels between the emergence of women's studies and 'child studies' and explicitly argued for links with feminist theorising (Alanen, 1994; Oakley, 1994). Dominant social ideas of children and childhood are questioned within this new sociological approach where developmental psychology and socialisation theory are understood as implicated in maintaining an ideological presumption of children's incapability. Woodhead (1990) discusses how children's 'needs' have been contextualised within a scientifically knowable course of natural development rather than being identified as issues of cultural or personal values.

Although the structure of childhood is not as yet well elaborated, writers generally indicate a framework which relates to existing critical theorising on structure within Marxism and feminism with the common central elements of oppression, ideology and resistance related to a structurally produced opposition of interests. Whilst the explicit theorising of the structure of generation remains loose, the connections with wider structural theorising suggests a particular formulation of power. Power is held by adults and is largely repressive. Oldman (1994) proposes a more explicit analysis which identifies adults involved in 'childwork' (such as child care and schooling) as a specific class in relations of exploitation with children. He argues that 'childwork' provides many jobs in the public sector and that resources are orchestrated to support adult rather than child interests. Oldman outlines a three-system model of stratification: gender, employment and generation, but this model is complex with limited discussion as to how the different dimensions may be articulated. It is noticeable that throughout his work children are referred to as if they were undifferentiated and there is no mention of 'race' as a fourth structure. Prout and James (1990) recognise the relevance of other structural features (class, gender or ethnicity) as variables for children but, again, this is not well detailed.

Whilst the sociology of childhood is in the early stages of attempting to elaborate a theoretical understanding of childhood as a structural feature, writers have emphasised the extent to which children need to be understood as actors. The new area of study has an expressed interest in putting children at the centre of analysis within the constraints of the structural conditions of childhood. Prout and James (1990) locate their discussion within existing sociological debates about the differential emphasis on structure or agency. Similarly Mayall suggests the analysis of children as actors can form 'part of the larger enterprise of teasing out the interrelationships of agency and structure' (Mayall, 1994b). A key role is given to the authentic voice of children as a resource for criticism of the existing conditions of childhood. The child is understood as active by virtue of humanist assumptions of children's intrinsic, natural capacities that are obscured by adult defined conditions and beliefs. Children's subjectivity is framed largely in oppositional terms to the identified ideology. This could be seen as involving a romanticisation of the child as naturally competent and reasonable rather than incompetent and irrational.

Qvortrup, discussing the status of children's everyday conflicts with adults, suggests that children who challenge teachers or parents may be exercising the only way available to them of 'airing their dissatisfactions' (Qvortrup, 1990). Mayall similarly states that children not only question adult constructions of childhood 'but act to resist, oppose, or find ways through gaps in adult ideologies, institutions and structures' (Mayall, 1994b, p. 5). This indicates a political sympathy with children and an analysis of micro interactions between children and adults as set in a macro context of childhood as an institution. Thus this tends to encapsulate children's conflicts with adults within a dynamic of oppression. Exclusion from school in these terms would necessarily be located within a political process of children's general resistance to the oppressive authority of the teacher. Although not specifically examining exclusions, Mayall (1994a) outlines differences between home and school pointing out the different opportunities for children's assertion in the two contexts, suggesting that children are less able to negotiate as individuals within school-based authority systems. Adult ideologies are portrayed as organised in predictable ways which produce a consistency to the meaning of children's responses. However, research on exclusions reveals differences within school practices and implies a variation in forms of authority: 'Differing schools exclude children for different reasons and to widely differing degrees' (Cohen and Hughes, 1994, p. 14). Excluded children also offer a variety of explanations of the meaning of their behaviour in school (see also Cullingford and Morrison, de Pear and Garner, and John in this volume). With a structural model come theoretical difficulties which are particularly pertinent in relation to exclusions where boys, whether white working-class or black, are over represented. In delineating a structure of childhood, differences between children become minimised. The general imagery of adults, portrayed within the sociology of childhood as a constraining force, also limits the possibility of considering children's capacity to initiate strategies that are aimed at controlling rather than resisting others.

In contrast with liberal theorising, the existing critical tradition (such as Marxism and feminism on which the sociology of childhood draws) has attempted to denaturalise social categories and conditions. The analysis of naturalised hierarchies between categories of people as an ideological process usefully unties existing power relations from the issue of legitimacy. Whilst the focus of the critical frameworks is distinct, reflecting disparate moral, political and conceptual analyses, as theories of power they, in parallel with theorising on generation as a structure, similarly deconstruct ideas of legitimate authority. Structural theories also highlight the effects of the wider social organisation on the conditions within which individuals operate and challenge individual models of power. These stress the importance of material constraints and the problem becomes one 'where the opportunities for action and therefore the exercise of power are unequally distributed before the interaction begins' (Oldersma and Davis, 1991, p. 7).

In general terms, writers have sought to raise issues of illegitimate power relations through concepts of oppression. Children's relations with adults, by being located within a wider project of denaturalising gender or class relations, are implicitly considered in more problematic terms. In contrast with the liberal frame, where education is seen as the site of equal opportunities and the reward of merit, the education system is understood as crucially biased in favour of dominant groups. This is conceptualised through an analysis of education as an arena where knowledge, though claimed as neutral, is culturally loaded and clearly ideological. Writers such as Barrett (1980), Lees (1986) and Willis (1977) have focused on the hidden curriculum of cultural representation and the reproduction of gender and class ideologies. In this sense power operates invisibly before any particular child enters the school. The focus is on identifying divisions between children and linking these with divisions between adults demonstrating a commonality of systematic repression and disadvantage within the particular structure in focus. Children are seen as the privileged site for observing the formation of class and gender identities.

The problem of domination is not therefore defined as specifically a children's issue. It is not as children that authority becomes relevant but as members of class and gender categories which may be articulated in specific terms in relation to children. The school can be understood not as separate from the adult world but as linked with other parts of the state and social structure. In these terms critical theories tend to reduce questions of children's relations with authority to that of the oppressive axis under consideration which tends to obscure the complexity of power. Accounts of resistance in early work on male pupils (Willis, 1977) imbued particular anti-school behaviour with wider political meaning in which conflicts in the micro are seen as representing wider class relations. These frameworks have located the teacher/pupil relationship as riven with tensions produced by the wider social purposes of education as a site of the reproduction of inequalities and in which the school is characterised by its use of a power that is distorting, repressive, and divisive. While this structural emphasis may capture some of the aspects of social control involved in a system for large-scale processing of children, this may be overly deterministic. It may explain large-scale structural patterns but does not explain how individual interactions can be theorised within it, thereby reducing the role of subjectivity for teachers and children alike, and minimising the textured nature of their relationship. Whichever structure is being considered all structurally-based accounts of power suggest that power is largely prohibitive and that oppression is systematic.

NEW POSSIBILITIES OF POWER

Within the frameworks discussed above, teachers' authority is seen as a repressive power held over children where recourse to exclusion is a final sanction. It is assumed that adult and child always stand in stark contrast to each other whether in terms of rationality or power. Foucault questions the relevance of ideas of power as primarily repressive by counterposing this with an idea of power as productive (Sawicki, 1991). He provides an account of the development of modern technologies of power to control the population (see also Clegg, 1989, for a fuller discussion) which operate in subtle terms through engaging self regulation. Rather than children's obedience being maintained through the constant vigilance of adults, he argues that disciplinary strategies permeate modern education (Foucault, 1977).

Walkerdine (1984, 1989) locates child-centred pedagogy within this general social shift to self regulation. Authority acquired a facilitative role inviting its internalisation as the route to producing a self regulating and autonomous child. Walkerdine and Lucey (1989) discuss the modern ideal for both home and school of a totally regulated environment in which overt conflict and aggression disappeared. They argue that this involves distinct forms of coercion through models of autonomy and choice wherein aggression is suppressed rather than eliminated. Foucault gives discursive practices a central place within new forms of power. Discourses are understood as coherent sets of statements which contain the rules and procedures for defining acceptable truths and are embedded in concrete practices. Power is enmeshed in the practices of creating different meanings and is unstable by virtue of the nature of dynamic and competing regimes of truth. Teacher authority, far from being a clear concept with certain parameters and guaranteed effects, relates to distinct forms of professional knowledge and practice which may involve different ideas and expectations of normal child behaviour, the meaning of disturbance, and the nature of education. Teachers are themselves regulated in discourse and hence do not hold power in any simple way.

If authority has been subject to modernising effects both in school and in parenting practices (Urwin, 1984; Walkerdine and Lucey, 1989), then a repressive account obscures more complex dynamics between children and teachers within a liberal humanist context. Disciplinary power is seen to work via the engagement of the subject through the production of competencies rather than by preventing activity or removing power and via this to harness self regulation: 'Power operates not to stop its targets acting but to control their actions' (Bell, 1993, p. 32).

In these terms children becoming 'out of control' relates closely to what children are being controlled for and what control means within particular discourses and practices. Rather than parents or teachers working within a consensual frame of 'discipline' where 'disobedience' is a simple continuum, issues of control need to be understood as contextualised within distinct practices and expectations. In relation to exclusion, a post-structural framework would allow for an examination of the effect of contemporary policies and practices in education on the micro instances of teacher authority in dynamic terms (Hargreaves, 1994).

This framework also has implications for the part played within schools by children themselves in terms of power and resistance. In repressive accounts of power, children's resistance emerges through their nature as irrational or as a natural response to oppression and is seen as absent of, and set apart, from power. In contrast, Foucault considers resistance and power as interrelated and implicating one another. It is through children's capacity to exercise power that they are also able to resist. The continuity of children's status as powerless can thus be subjected to greater scrutiny. School can be considered as producing children's powers as well as eliciting their subordination and control. Walkerdine suggests that the child-centred discourse, for instance, in valuing self expression rather than repression, and self regulation rather than coercion, itself opened up the possibilities of resistance: 'This helps to produce the space in the practice for children to be powerful' (Walkerdine, 1990, p. 8).

Davies (1990) similarly discusses how teachers invite children's participation as a strategy of control but this also produces possibilities for children's assertion and choices. In these terms a modern context of discipline opens a space where children are legitimately active in ways that cannot be predictably controlled by teachers. Children's resistance can be considered as caught up with their attempt to negotiate available identities produced in discourses operating in school. Discourses are spoken through individuals and are contingent on specific interactions between people. Thus power is always relational and flows through the dynamics of language and practices. Use of certain positions in discourse is constrained by age, gender, class and race identities (see Holloway's 1989 account of gender-differentiated positions in discourses, for instance). Jones (1993) cautions against a view of children as simply choosing identities freely and suggests that they are likely to take up prevailing ones. However, though work exists on the way teachers classify children with relevance to practices of discipline (see, for example, Blyth and Milner in this volume on teachers' production of racial stereotypes), the complex way in which these identities are negotiated and redefined by children themselves has been under-examined. Children can be seen as actively engaged in negotiating the meanings of what it is to be a child, or a girl, or a boy, a 'good' or 'disruptive' pupil, which are subject to various and contradictory ideas. Jordan (1995) uses a discursive analysis which illustrates how children's identities and assertion are implicated in the emergence of conflicts with adults. She proposes a general division within boys in school between the difficult (for the teacher and other children) 'fighting boys' who demonstrate the warrior discourse of masculinity in opposition to school rules and control, and the other boys who conform to school demands and construct their masculinity in other terms. Mac an Ghaill's (1994) discussion of 'anti-school' boys also links a 'macho' stance and confrontational approaches to teachers. He further comments on the 'unintended' effects of teacher responses whereby some female pupils were attracted to 'anti-school' boys because of their effectiveness in being recognised, albeit negatively, as 'powerful' by the teachers (Mac an Ghaill, 1994). This suggests conflicts with teachers acquire different meanings when read through discourses on gender, where this figures as the achieving of masculinity suppressing other ways in which this is seen, such as school failure, within a pedagogic discourse.

Locating children in both a relational and discursive context also counters analysis of children's interaction with teachers as the only focus for children's assertion. It becomes possible to develop more complex ways of understanding how power operates interactively in classroom settings where children's bids for power in relation to each other will affect their interactions with teachers (see also John in this volume).

Connolly (1995) shows how, in the primary school he studied, the group most often identified by the teacher as problematic was African–Caribbean boys who were made more visible as 'bad' within broader racist discourses. This was interrelated with processes within the relationships amongst the children where white boys also drew on racist discourses and opposed black boys, already identified by teachers as naughty and hence more masculine, in the playground. A more aggressive identity for black boys was produced contributing to their further visibility in class (see also Stirling in this volume).

Although these accounts redefine the general nature of children's conflict with teachers they do not explain exclusion *per se*. However, considering the complexity of children's identity in school enables a re-examination of the context in which the meanings of discipline are negotiated. This shifts an understanding of the interactional dynamics within which exclusion occurs as having something to do with children's power as well as their powerlessness. While exclusions evoke for teachers and policy makers varied discourses on authority and the child as natural, the processes of interaction between teacher and child which produce the decision to exclude may be located in more fluid constructions of the child both *qua* child and as a member of race, class and gender groups with variable and contradictory discourses within each of these categories.

A post-structuralist analysis also allows for an examination of teachers' power as variable. If children are active subjects then their behaviour may have specific power effects on teachers. Walkerdine (1990) analyses a classroom incident involving young children and a female primary teacher where two boys temporarily position the teacher as subordinate through the use of sexually explicit language. The teacher is unable to reassert control as the dichotomy between adult and child has been redefined momentarily as one between male and female wherein the males are more powerful. By examining teachers as regulated in discourse it becomes possible to examine not only the effects of particular acts of assertion by children but also how children may acquire power through the way the adult is regulated by ideas of his or her own responsibilities and duties in relation to the control of children. In these terms children's behaviour, for instance creating a noisy classroom, achieves some of its power effects from how it may signify an 'inadequate' teacher within prevailing ideas of professionalism (see also Gill and Monsen in this volume). In research on gender differences in control strategies, male teachers have been linked with an authoritarian position on discipline whereby the maintaining and loosening of control signified the achieving of masculinity or the creation of weakness (Robinson, 1992). Teachers engage in discipline in the context of their own shifting experiences of power and powerlessness in relation to children. This opens up the idea that interactions involving conflict may carry complex and ambivalent signification for teachers as well as children, as they become positioned in different discourses. Some children may become more vulnerable to coercive sanctions, such as exclusion, not simply because of the extent of indiscipline in quantitative terms, but in relation to how teachers have become positioned as temporarily powerless through the effects of particular discourses.

Thus, through some discourses, children are able to enact strategies that gain power for them in relation to adults and can be experienced by adults as powerful. However, in the context of institutionalised adult authority these may produce situations where children are excluded and can be seen as *powerfully* powerless.

Part II

Consequences of exclusions

Chapter 8

The cost of primary school exclusions

Carl Parsons

INTRODUCTION

When exclusions take place it is well established that there is considerable distress to the children, their families and also the schools concerned (see, for example, Blyth and Milner, 1993; Bourne *et al.*, 1994; Cohen and Hughes, 1994). A neglected area of study has been that of financial costs of exclusion. These are considerable for what is a vastly inferior, inadequate educational experience for the child. The 'cost shunting' that results from exclusion means that other parts of the education system and other services, particularly social services, bear the cost of supporting the excluded pupil. The claim explored in this chapter is that the aggregate cost to the totality of services is greater than if the child had been maintained in school. Inter-agency collaboration may be necessary since many excluded children and young people live in families experiencing difficulties. Maintaining children in school may have beneficial long-term consequences for the family as well as the child and it is certainly the case that permanent exclusion is a deeply damaging experience (see Cullingford and Morrison, and de Pear and Garner in this volume).

METHODS

This chapter reports on a project funded by the Joseph Rowntree Foundation which examined eleven cases of exclusion costs in three LEAs in the period April–December 1993 (Parsons *et al.*, 1994).

Eighty-two individuals were interviewed in connection with the eleven cases and documents were analysed where possible. An

attempt was made to cost the alternative provision and the intervention from other services during what is called the 'debris
management' period (Parsons, 1994) and to compare this to the
standard annual cost of educating a primary school child.

Various ways exist of costing the education of a pupil in a
mainstream primary school. The Age Weighted Pupil Unit
(AWPU) is different for different LEAs, varying between £940
and £1,010 in 1991–2 in the three LEAs involved in this study.
The AWPU is the sum the school gets for each pupil and
makes up over 80 per cent of its income. The Chartered Institute
of Public Finance and Accountancy (CIPFA, 1993) figures for the
year 1991–2 allow a calculation that the average cost of a primary
school child in England in 1991–2 was £1,412.23 (£1,679.04
in London and £1,371.61 in English counties). The calculation
involves dividing receipts and expenditure by the number of
pupils.

Costings for provision made for the excluded pupil were
estimated by taking the hourly pay for the person involved in
1992–3, adding the 'on-costs' (national insurance and super-
annuation) and usually doubling this figure to take account of
overheads. An educational psychologist is calculated as costing
£10.80 per hour (with on-costs) and £21.60 when overheads are
included. A general practitioner's hourly rate is calculated at
£23.40 and is doubled to give the full cost. For family support
sessional workers and for home tutors only their salaries are
costed in, though there is an element of overheads involved in
office staff making arrangements, receiving reports, and so on.

This is an uncomplicated, transparent way of calculating the
costs, and while it cannot be entirely accurate – different points
on the salary scales, time spent by the professional given to the
nearest hour – it offers a robust and realistic estimate.

FINDINGS

Eight of the eleven families were facing difficulties of various
kinds with social services already involved with seven of them.
The children's total days of exclusions from schools varied from
17 to 360 with the average being 145 days. Two of the pupils
were first excluded as infants. All were boys.

While the agents involved are still mostly from education and
bear the brunt of the cost, social services particularly are drawn in.

Families in difficulty are placed in even greater difficulties by a child's exclusion. The child, facing problems already, is not being placed in a supportive setting following exclusion. If the best place for a child's care, development and learning during the day time is school, resources are best channelled to help to retain the pupil there. Out of school following exclusion, the child is almost always in an unprepared and unstructured environment and, in many cases, in a family environment already strained, and possibly damaging to the child (see also Cohen and Hughes, 1994). In one case a child was already accommodated by social services and exclusion actually led to a temporary foster arrangement breaking down and considerable expense following from this.

THE COST OF EXCLUSION

Costing public services, and more particularly child care services, is a relatively recent development. The field has been led by one or two specialist research units such as the Personal Social Services Research Unit (PSSRU) at the University of Kent at Canterbury. Few attempts have been made to cost child care services in this country, with fostering and residential care receiving the most attention (Beecham and Knapp, 1993; Kavanagh, 1988; Knapp, 1986). This costing exercise draws on the theoretical costing framework and unit cost work developed by the PSSRU (Netten and Beecham, 1993; Netten and Smart, 1993).

Current cost consciousness may well be a result of increasing awareness of the effect that public policy decisions have on resources. Resources are often scarce in relation to the demands made of them. There is little doubt that decisions made by policy makers, planners, purchasers and providers of public services benefit from examination of the resource implications of any public policy decision. 'We have observed in our work across many public policy programme areas that decision-making informed by *some* costs data is better than decision-making with *no* costs data' (Knapp *et al.*, 1993, p. 1).

By definition, the permanent exclusion of a child from school amounts to the surrender of educational and financial responsibility for that child by that institution. The responsibility, both educational and financial, must be picked up by one or more other agencies. The cost distribution may be borne by many different agencies and the decision by a school to exclude a child may have a large cost effect on another agency. It has been pointed out by other cost studies that 'the distribution of the cost burden need bear no resemblance to the distribution of responsibility for taking decisions' (Knapp *et al.*, 1993, p. 21).

One of the aims of addressing the cost of exclusion is to give an account of where the cost burden falls. The decision by a school to surrender responsibility for a child can affect a wide range of other agencies. Most obviously the responsibility for educating a child will fall to another agent such as a home tuition unit. However, the cumulative effect of a child being excluded, coupled with delay in finding replacement education, may mean the child and his/her family require added support from a range of agencies including the special needs department of the local education authority, social services, health services, social security agencies, as well as the increased possibility that the child may become involved in crime (see, for example, Searle, and Stirling in this volume). In the eleven cases studied here, the costs ranged from minimal, in the case of a child whose mother was content to keep him at home (though the EWO has been called upon to enforce attendance), to the child whose exclusion allied with the suspicion of sexual abuse led to heavy demands on social services.

Cost sharing and shunting may be both inter- and intra-agency. An example of inter-agency shifting of the cost burden might be in the case where a child, given no formal replacement education by the local education authority, attends a social services run family centre which provides some education. In other cases, education provision and the responsibility for finding it is shuffled within different branches of the LEA when 'education otherwise' is provided by a home tuition unit. Perverse incentives are encouraged by individual school/unit budget holding. Further cost-shunting complications can arise if a child in school was supported by provision under a special needs audit before exclusion. Maintaining the additional provision after exclusion became almost impossible for the pupils in this study.

The conclusion is that the provision for child IJ (see Table 8.1) in the course of a year cost well over £2,000 more than the provision in school – even allowing for increased costs of school education from 1991–2.

Table 8.1 Total cost by service sector for out-of-school period
for child IJ

Care package by sector element	Total cost (£) of out of school period (360 days)	Indicative cost (£) for school year equivalent (190 days)
Social services		
Reception	14.96	7.90
Assessment	69.00	36.42
Family therapy	64.40	33.99
Family centre (inc. travel)	443.36	234.00
Total social services cost	591.72	312.31
LEA		
Home tuition in own home	324.00	171.00
Home tuition in home tuition unit (inc. travel)	6,400.00	3,377.78
Total LEA cost	6,724.00	3,548.78
Police		
Police officer	41.58	21.95
Total police cost	41.58	21.95
Total cost all services	7,357.30	3,883.04

Analysing and speculating further on costs, the cases of three
children, AB, QR and ST (see Table 8.2), were examined in a
less detailed way. The costs were much in line with those which
applied with child IJ. Important differences were in the amount
of additional social services support required by child QR.

There were considerable costs to the parents of AB and ST
of two sorts: first they paid for private assessments, took the
child for hospital appointments and actively sought diagnosis
and treatment that was not forthcoming as a matter of course;
second, the parents lost time at work – in AB's case the mother
had to give up her part-time job, and illness, attributed to stress,
led ST's mother to give up her job.

Finally, it is important to consider the long-term recurring
costs that may ensue if substantial intervention is not provided
early. Secondary school is likely to face problems with the child,
child and family health are likely to suffer and require medical

Table 8.2 Total cost by service sector for out-of-school provision for three children AB, QR and ST, and indicative costs for school-year equivalent

Care package element	Child AB (Out-of-school period = 45 days)		Child QR Out-of-school (period = 265 days)		Child ST Out-of-school (period = 152 days)	
	Time (hrs)	Cost (£)	Time (hrs)	Cost (£)	Time (hrs)	Cost (£)
Social services						
Reception	1	14.96	1	14.96	1	14.96
Assessment	3	69.00	3	69.00	3	69.00
Family therapy	28	450.00	30	483.00	26	418.60
Therapy sessions			8	128.80		
Child guidance clinic					12	169.20
Family support sessional workers			24	164.40		
			(travel)	60.00		
Total social services cost		533.96		920.16		671.76
Local Education Authority						
Educational psychologist	10	216.00	28	604.80	30	648.00
EWO	16	209.60	15	196.50	10	131.10
Education officers	6	136.38	9	205.02	24	546.72
Director of Education	1	45.00			2	90.00
Special needs panel			6	720.00		
Traveller education services			9	156.87		
Home tuition (unit)			150	2,700.00	34½	1,242.00
Total LEA cost		606.98		4,583.19		2,657.82
Health						
GP	3	140.40	2	97.60		
Consultant	6	307.20			4	204.80
Child psychology clinic	8	128.80				
Total health cost		576.40		97.60		204.80
Police						
Officer	4	110.08	4	110.08	6	165.12
Total cost all services		1,827.42		5,711.03		3,699.50
Indicative cost for school year equivalent	*			4,166.40		4,624.37

treatment, crime is a distinct probability (Utting *et al.*, 1993) – in three cases an actuality – and longer-term problems of adjustment are likely to continue into adulthood (White *et al.*, 1990). There are strong indications that concerted early intervention pays dividends (Carpenter, 1994).

INTERVENING IN PRIMARY SCHOOL EXCLUSION

The school career of the excluded primary school pupil followed a fairly regular course. Tolerance at the start of the experience of the primary pupil's disruptive behaviour rapidly gave way to concern. Conventionally the concern did not lead to measured adapted strategies to deal with the child. Early intervention usually took the form of removal, sitting the pupil outside the headteacher's office or the provision of a classroom assistant. The classroom assistant's role was often to *insulate* the rest of the class, and the teacher, from the disruptive pupil. Intervention was generally not *designed* as a response to the child's needs and difficulties. Referrals were made to the educational psychological services and while assessments were begun the process was slow. It was evident that the majority of families were in difficulties but support for them was also slow and low key.

This process meant that the point of exclusion became an explosive event. When the child was ejected from school it inevitably led to a degree of trauma for both child and parents because there was no organised transition from one form of institutional provision to another. In two of the eleven cases studied in this research mothers cut down their hours or gave up their job. One father lost paid work time. The effect of this on the child, a child who was usually in the state of being unable to control his own behaviour, was inevitably damaging. The manner in which the exclusion occurred meant that there were increased difficulties for follow-up services to deal with, including, for example, work with stressed families and children whose self-esteem was further damaged.

After exclusion, the child experienced an alienation from ordinary school life accompanied by an unmanaged and unpatterned daily experience, which was a further challenge to be addressed by the follow-up services. This 'debris management' has been evident and made all the more difficult because of insufficient intervention before, or at the point of, exclusion. I would suggest that intervention earlier in the school *and* in the family is required.

CONCLUSION

This chapter argues that the money spent on pupils excluded from primary school would be best spent on maintaining the pupils *in* school. If the argument is about changing to a particular policy *because it is cheaper* it may obscure or block the argument about ultimate rights of children to receive education. It could be that even if a child at risk of exclusion does cost three or four times that required to maintain an 'ordinary' child in a mainstream school, that money should be found. The *finance* argument may work against the *principle* argument. It may get in the way of the development of good public policy.

There is, as Lloyd-Smith (1993) would claim, a policy vacuum. Policy and action in these areas are not driven by sound welfare goals which we wish to achieve but by how much or little there is to spend. In a policy vacuum, agencies are not mobilised to cater for the excluded child who then becomes debris outside the system. Services move slowly to deal with this ejected 'problem' and try to make improvements in a situation which has been made worse by the suddenness of the exclusion into a context where there is no prepared support. The way back for the permanently excluded child is difficult. The problems take place within straitened financial circumstances of under-resourced local agencies having difficulties fulfilling a particular aim of the welfare state, as Hills (1993, p. 6) sees it, of 'stepping in where the family fails'. It is also within a national political culture which is against dependence and requires that individuals and families take responsibility for their own actions.

A decisive change in orientation is needed if the best chances are to be provided for these children to remain integrated or to reintegrate in such a way that they will become, at the very minimum, accepted and accepting members of young adult society. The numbers of children excluded from primary schools have continued to rise in 1993–4 and into the autumn of 1994 (DfE, 1995b) despite the advice contained within *Pupils with Problems* circulars and the *Code of Practice* (DfE, 1994a–c; DfE and DOH, 1994a–c; DfE 1994a). The prospect of what these children might become and what might happen to them, without appropriate provision, is frightening. Finance aside, the principle should be that we do *not* permit such damaging rejection experiences to happen to the developing young.

Chapter 9

The effects of waiting time on excluded children

Lynda Mitchell

INTRODUCTION

There are two sides to the exclusion process; before, and after. Exclusion studies tend to concentrate, by definition, on what follows rather than what precedes exclusion. Exclusion in the main is an event which evolves rather than occurring as a 'one-off' incident and an appropriate opening to such a study would include recognition of the work and effort of many teachers who have given pupils who are eventually excluded tremendous help and support in order to endeavour to keep them within the education system.

The longitudinal study outlined in this chapter was conducted in one municipal local authority, a relatively small metropolitan authority with nineteen secondary schools plus feeder middle, junior, infant and first schools with a total school population of approximately 48,000. The authority is currently undergoing a process of reorganisation in order to standardise the ages of transfer.

RESEARCH METHOD

Data was collected over two academic years, beginning in September 1990 and continuing through until July 1992. Much of the data were obtained from the special services section of the LEA which deals with exclusions and all special educational needs. Some information was also provided by individual schools, the Professional Assistants, the Schools' Psychological Service and the Education Welfare Service.

All exclusions which were notified to the authority are included in the analysis, with particular attention being paid to indefinite and permanent exclusions. Recorded fixed-term exclusions ranged from one day to thirty-one days in duration (though in the latter case, since the authority imposed a limit of twenty days for any fixed-term exclusion, a case conference was called and the child in question was returned to school within twenty days).

The Education (No. 2) Act 1986 was in operation during the period of the study. Accordingly, if the total number of days per pupil per term was less than five, then the school was not required by law to notify the authority. Such exclusions are therefore not included in the data, neither has there been any attempt to quantify the number of illegal exclusions, that is, the exclusions which are not recorded in the school exclusion book or those totalling five days or more per individual per term which are not notified to the authority.

REASONS FOR EXCLUSIONS

The National Union of Teachers (1992) lists five reasons for pupil exclusions. In order of priority these are: disruptive/negative attitude to school (including verbal abuse, defiance, bad language, insolence and refusal to obey instructions); assaults/ bullying; pilfering; malicious damage; absconding from school/ poor attendance. This roughly corresponds to my own research in the LEA which indicates the following reasons for exclusion during the academic year 1991–2 (Figure 9.1).

1 Disruption: including disruption in lessons, refusal to accept punishments given as a result of poor behaviour, breaking contracts and other general poor behaviour which disrupts the smooth running of schools.
2 Physical abuse: including assault on pupils, teachers and other adults.
3 Verbal abuse: including insolence, swearing, disobedience, and abusive language to pupils.
4 Truancy, plus other attendance problems including absconding.
5 Criminal activity: including drug-related activities, vandalism and theft.

From the evidence obtainable it seems that specific reasons for the exclusion of individual pupils did not alter significantly over the two-year period. It would appear that the underlying trend for the increasing numbers of exclusions lay within a

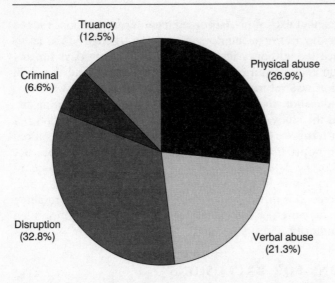

Figure 9.1   Reasons for exclusion (Sept. 1991–July 1992)

context-related rather than a child-related rationale, in line with earlier research findings. For example, the Advisory Centre for Education found that the highest proportion of permanent exclusions reported to them involved children with special educational needs, concluding: 'With increasing pressure on decreasing resources, schools may find it more expedient to regard a child as naughty rather than needy' (ACE, 1991).

OFSTED (1993b) indicated a number of possible hypotheses for the increase in exclusions as follows:

1   Increased stress in families being reflected in difficult behaviour in schools.
2   Reduced levels of teacher tolerance in the face of repeated minor misdemeanours.
3   A form of punishment on a tariff.
4   To bring parents into schools to discuss a child's behaviour.
5   A self-imposed pressure to raise the image of schools by being seen to be tough on discipline issues.
6   A response to those pupils who fail to turn up regularly to school.

7   A consequence of staffing difficulties in inner-city schools.
8   Headteachers no longer willing to make informal arrange-
    ments between each other when they are considering
    indefinite or permanent exclusion.
9   To secure special educational needs placement or additional
    support for individual pupils – reflected in a growing num-
    ber of requests for statementing.

(OFSTED, 1993b, p. 3)

The evidence recorded by the NUT (1992) from information
gathered from schools in fourteen LEAs places a rather different emphasis upon the underlying causes for the increases in
exclusions:

1   Insufficient resources under LMS – A variety of factors
    were identified. ...
2   The impending publication of competitive school test and
    general performance league tables.
3   Deteriorating home circumstances and lack of parental
    discipline.

(NUT, 1992, p. 5)

'Insufficient resources' included a lack of central LEA resources
such as alternative provision, psychological service support and
a reduction in home tuition provision, in addition to poor funding
for pupils with special needs and pressure due to the National
Curriculum, testing and assessment.

DIFFERENCES BETWEEN SCHOOLS

The fact that exclusion rates vary between schools which have
similar catchment areas is well documented in the existing literature (see, for example, Galloway, 1982; McManus, 1990), and
the rate of exclusion may vary according to the internal practices within schools. It has been suggested that: 'Schools with
higher than expected suspension rates tended to have a list of
suspension-worthy offences' (McManus 1990, p. 23). McManus
identified the routes taken by individual pupils through the
pastoral system as an important factor in the exclusion rate; the
faster a pupil reached the deputy or headteacher, the more likely
that pupil was to be excluded.

Findings from my own research, supported by other evidence
(see, for example, Benson in this volume), suggest that exclusion

rates may be influenced by a philosophical belief on the part of senior management either that exclusions are an entirely appropriate way of dealing with difficult pupils as the education of the other pupils in the school is at risk; or that difficult pupils can only be properly educated within the mainstream and that to exclude them is to abdicate the overall responsibility for every pupil which rightfully belongs to the school.

These two opposing philosophical stances are embodied in the following comments made to me by senior teachers from two different high schools in the study:

> I wouldn't remove [Fred] from school ... I've got to think about the individual, and if I take him out of school and put him onto the streets, which is what the authority are saying, the lad hasn't a chance, and I won't do that because we care, and so long as we care we cope.

> How far can the learning and teaching be compromised by the tiny minority?

The majority of pupils were excluded for a series of disruptive incidents followed by a precipitating incident. A minority of pupils were excluded for a particularly serious 'one-off' offence, for instance, carrying and selling cannabis resin in school.

Some schools seemed to use the exclusion system deliberately to remove specific pupils from the school, carefully collecting the necessary 'evidence' which the LEAs, with half an eye on potential appeals by parents, are rightly so keen to have documented as a very good case can usually be made for persistently disruptive pupils.

Schools' patterns of exclusion were also significant. The usual pattern of exclusion for any child, in theory, should include at least one short-term exclusion before permanent exclusion is contemplated by the school, unless there are exceptional circumstances. This should therefore mean that the pattern for each school should include a number of fixed-term exclusions for each registered permanent exclusion. However, schools tended to develop trends over a number of years, some producing many more indefinite or permanent exclusions than fixed term. This may be partially due to undocumented exclusions, the use of such exclusions not notified to the authority giving the individual pupil concerned the necessary increasing intensification of sanctions usually employed in disciplinary systems. It was interesting to observe the changing patterns of exclusion beginning to emerge since the abolition of the indefinite category in 1994, with the resultant increase in permanent exclusions in some schools.

DISRUPTION MANAGEMENT

Lawrence *et al.* (1984) differentiate between three levels of disruption within a school: child, class and school. There has been advice on how teachers might reduce disruption within the classroom, concentrating on various techniques available to the teacher such as behaviour modification, presentation of lessons and other classroom management strategies in order to minimise disruption by individuals or by a group of individuals with a class. School disruption, however, is not within the sole control of the individual teacher, and Lawrence *et al.*, (1984) point to major issues which face teachers in 'difficult' schools. The first feature is that much time is spent by individual teachers in classroom control and in following up incidents and truants. This has implications for preparation and marking time. A school with a high proportion of difficult pupils may have difficulties over vandalism and the upkeep of the general appearance of the school and also with movement of pupils around the school in terms of aggressive behaviour, thefts and lateness to lessons. A negative spiral of low expectations, disaffection, and teacher stress, may develop. Although such schools do exist, it does not necessarily follow that the exclusion rate for such a school will be a high one.

THE NATURE OF THE EXCLUDED POPULATION

The majority of excluded pupils within the LEA studied were white boys (around 88 per cent for the academic year 1991–2). This was also reflected within the national statistics, which additionally indicate that African–Caribbean students are vastly over-represented within the exclusion rates (see, for example, Grunsell, 1980).

Most excluded pupils were of secondary school age (i.e. 11–16), with the peak in rate being at the age of 15 (year 10 pupils). This is reflective of national trends (DfE, 1992a, 1993).

MULTIPLE EXCLUSIONS

Table 9.1 gives details of those pupils who were excluded more than once during the same academic year. It can be seen that although the total number of pupils with more than one exclusion increased over the two-year period, the proportion in relation to the total number of excluded pupils remained roughly the same. Table 9.2 gives more detail of multiple exclusions for those pupils who were *permanently* excluded. The figures include those pupils who were originally excluded indefinitely but had the status of the exclusion altered to permanent (i.e. 6 pupils in 1990–1, 14 pupils in 1991–2). The likelihood of a pupil who has been excluded permanently to have already been excluded during the same academic year therefore rises significantly to 45.7 per cent in 1990–1, and to 46 per cent in 1991–2. Almost half of the pupils excluded permanently over the two-year period had previously been excluded during the same academic year. This indicates that schools may be tolerating difficult pupil behaviour for a longer length of time before excluding particular pupils

Table 9.1 Pupils with multiple exclusions (all types of exclusion)

Total number of pupils	1990–1	1991–2
Excluded	120	185
With multiple exclusions	27	48
As a % of pupils excluded	22.5	25.9

Table 9.2 Previous exclusions of permanently excluded pupils.

Excluded within the academic year	1990–1	1991–2
On 1 other occasion	8	18
On 2 other occasions	7	2
On 3 other occasions	3	4
At no other time	16	23
Permanently twice	2	3
Total	36	50*

* This total exceeds the total of pupils permanently excluded because one child who was permanently excluded twice had also been excluded on two other occasions during the same academic year.

either indefinitely or permanently. Other evidence that this may be so was obtained by case-study information from nine high schools within the LEA. Each high school provided examples of two or three students who were considered to exhibit particularly difficult behaviour within school. Ten out of the nineteen children had exhibited very challenging behaviour since their entry to the school (at either 11 or 13 years of age), with seven children having exhibited such behaviour for a much longer time, either since their middle or first school. One pupil had been difficult for only one year, whilst the teacher of one pupil was not certain when the poor behaviour began.

This situation raises several questions as to the continuity of education prior to exclusion. Exclusion is largely a process which balances disruption within the school against the rights of an individual to an education equal to that of his or her peers. When the balance is tipped in favour of the pupil group, then exclusion is the result. However, there will already have been some loss of education to a greater or lesser degree before the actual exclusion occurs. There may have been disruption to lessons in order to deal with specific incidents; for example, when a pupil is waiting for a member of staff to deal with the situation. Additionally, 'internal exclusion' processes may have been at work, such as isolation from one or more lessons or for a period of time. Part-time attendance may have been a strategy employed by the school in order to prevent the irretrievable breakdown of the school/pupil relationship. The pupil may have been truanting from specific lessons or sessions or the school may have used fixed-term exclusion as a previous strategy. There are many ways in which the education of the pupil may have been lost before the act of exclusion ever takes place. Such 'waiting time' is hidden from view but its effects, such as becoming accustomed to a disrupted education over a period of time, must not be forgotten in the aftermath of the exclusion. This 'waiting time' was an interesting feature of this study.

LENGTH OF TIME OUT OF SCHOOL

For the purposes of this study, the length of time out of school was calculated from the point of exclusion, ending with the pupil's return to school. For a number of the pupils listed, a return to school had not been effected by the time the annual report was

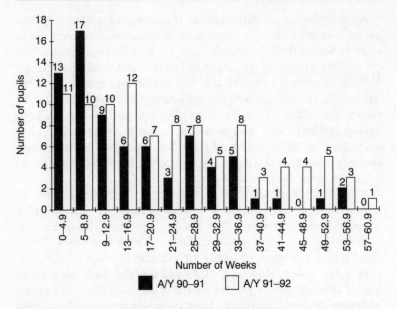

Figure 9.2 Time spent out of school; indefinite/permanent exclusions (Sept. 1990 – July 1992)

written so the length of time spent out of school was calculated up to the dates that the reports were written (i.e. November 1991 and October 1992 respectively).

Estimates of dates were as accurate as was feasible but where an exact date for reinstatement to school was unobtainable, the date of the exclusion conference was taken as the date of re-entry, i.e. within twenty days. Holiday periods were included in the length of time out of school. The length of time was calculated for each of the pupils who were indefinitely or permanently excluded during the period studied.

Figure 9.2 shows a comparison between the academic years 1990–1 and 1991–2. The length of time pupils spent out of school increased over the two-year period. The average times taken for a return to school were: in 1990–1, 16.5 weeks (correct at 14/11/91); in 1991–2, 23.2 weeks (correct at 16/10/92).

The reasons for delays to readmissions included the categories of parent focused, school focused and LEA focused deferments. In practice they usually merged together, sometimes becoming inseparable.

An important question is what happens to the children who are excluded?

OUTCOMES OF EXCLUSIONS

There was a change in the outcomes for fixed term exclusions over the two-year period. In 1990–1, all those pupils who were excluded for a fixed term returned to the excluding school (76 exclusions in total). However, in the academic year 1991–2, of the 123 fixed term exclusions:

  2 pupils transferred to other mainstream schools;
  3 pupils returned to school with extra support;
  2 pupils began to have their educational needs assessed;
  1 exclusion was converted to indefinite status;
115 exclusions resulted in a return to the excluding school.

In 1991–2 there were 113 exclusion case conferences held as a result of indefinite or permanent exclusions. In twelve cases a conference was not called, a variety of reasons being put forward by the LEA, including factors such as the proximity of the pupil to reaching school-leaving age; the pupil being readmitted after an internal case conference at the school; the pupil transferring directly to alternative provision or for home tuition; the pupil being transferred to secure accommodation; the abandonment of the exclusion; or the headteacher finding another school for the pupil.

It was common practice within indefinite exclusion conferences to alter the status of the exclusion to permanent whilst all parties were present and thereby consenting to hold the permanent exclusion conference consecutively, thus saving the need to reconvene at a later date. This happened on six occasions in 1990–1 and on fifteen occasions in 1991–2.

ALTERNATIVE EDUCATION PROVISION

The LEA provides a school for boys aged 7–16 with emotional and behavioural difficulties whose needs cannot be met within mainstream education. It provides boarding facilities on weekdays during term times and a number of day places.

The increase in numbers of both excluded and 'statemented' pupils meant that, in 1990–1, six new pupils were placed in this

LEA resource and four pupils were placed on the waiting list. In 1991–2, one pupil was placed, with six pupils remaining on the waiting list. By the end of the Spring term of 1992, this resource was vastly over-subscribed, with a waiting list which provided only a slim chance of a place at the school being obtained. This contributes to the waiting time of pupils as the chances of obtaining alternative interim education provision were reduced.

During the period of the study there were approximately fifty pupils receiving home tuition for two hours daily. This was originally intended for pupils who were out of school for medical reasons but almost half of the pupils receiving home tuition were excluded from school or exhibited severe behaviour difficulties. For instance, of the pupils excluded indefinitely or permanently during 1991–2, nineteen received home tuition after being excluded, with four on the waiting list.

There was a slight increase over the period of the study in the number of pupils offered places at the LEA off-site unit. The unit caters for pupils who experience difficulties in their last year of schooling although it was originally established in 1979 to cater for pupils 'in care' or those being assessed. It subsequently reduced its age range to year 11 pupils following reduced demand from clients after the implementation of the Children Act 1989 and has since been redesignated as the LEA's Pupil Referral

Table 9.3 Exclusion outcomes for academic years 1990–1 and 1991–2

Outcomes	Year 1990–1		Year 1991–2	
	Indefinite	Permanent	Indefinite	Permanent
Returned to similar school	27	12	32	15
Transferred to local authority special school	2	7	0	1
Transferred to out-of-district special school	0	0	0	0
Home tuition	5	9	6	13
Pupil referral unit	1	1	3	3
Nothing	2	6	17	20
Total	37	35	58	52

Unit. Referrals are from the Education Welfare Service, Schools' Psychological Service, schools and the LEA. In total during 1991–2, fourteen excluded pupils were offered a place or were on the waiting list at the Unit.

Table 9.3 shows comparisons in the outcomes of exclusions between 1990–1 and 1991–2. Outcomes are expressed in terms of the number of excluded pupils, not by the number of exclusions.

LEA PILOT PROJECT FOR EXCLUDED YOUNGSTERS

The LEA introduced a pilot project for youngsters in years 9–11 in 1991 in order to provide an interim form of education for those pupils who were excluded from mainstream school, thereby beginning to address the issue of time spent out of the education system. Its initial aims were as follows:

1 To look at ways of providing out of school support to young people whose behaviour is severely disrupting the normal teaching situation.
2 To offer a range of positive relationship-building experiences.
3 To offer coping skills which will enable reintegration into the mainstream situation.
4 To offer situations which will help the young people to examine their own attitudes and values.
5 To support young people in the transition back to mainstream education.
6 To provide a positive educational environment.

This provision provides short-term, full-time education for around sixteen youngsters.

TIME TAKEN BETWEEN EXCLUSION AND EXCLUSION CONFERENCE

The average time taken to organise an exclusion case conference increased from 5 weeks in 1990–1 to 8.7 weeks in 1991–2 . This increase was due mainly to the increased number of excluded pupils. The time scale ranged from 1.7 weeks to a maximum of 33 weeks. The extra time taken for exclusion case conferences to be arranged was also due to delays caused by schools and by parents.

In the cases where no exclusion conference took place, the time was measured between the pupil being excluded and appropriate provision being organised or the pupil leaving school.

Increasing numbers of pupils on long-term indefinite or permanent exclusions drifted out of education; particularly those pupils aged 14 and over. Such pupils were often difficult to place in other mainstream schools: having begun courses leading to GCSE examinations; being accommodated by Social Services; requiring alternative provision which was not available; or refusing placements which were offered. Some of these factors are illustrated in the case examples below.

John was excluded indefinitely from his middle school because of truancy and refusal to work in lessons. At his case conference five weeks later, the status of the exclusion was altered to permanent. The decision of the conference was that John and his mother should choose another school. The middle school which was chosen initially refused to admit John even though there were vacancies, finally admitting him twenty weeks later. Three weeks after admission John was indefinitely excluded for headbutting another pupil. At his exclusion case conference, three weeks after he was excluded from the second middle school, once more the status was altered to permanent. The LEA was not empowered to direct reinstatement as it was a church-aided school so the boy was given home tuition. At transfer to secondary schooling, the high school refused to admit John because of his exclusion record. Eventually he was readmitted on a part-time basis after October half term, initially with his home tutor. From John's original exclusion date to his entry to high school, a total of fifty-seven weeks elapsed.

Jack was excluded permanently, aged 15, in October for disruption in lessons and serious sexual comments to a teacher. One month later, at his exclusion case conference, the LEA agreed to look at the possibility of providing additional resources and the school agreed to reinstate the pupil. In May, Jack was permanently excluded again, the exclusion conference upholding the permanent exclusion. Jack was subsequently offered a place at a specialist unit, which his mother refused. The consequence of this was that Jack left school almost two years later, still waiting for home tuition.

Mark was excluded from his high school in February for disobedience, truancy and trouble out of school. He was admitted to a pilot project for excluded pupils in November and after Christmas transferred to a placement at another unit where he finished his education. The exclusion conference was held at the beginning of June.

CONCLUSION

It is very difficult and probably a waste of energy trying to apportion blame for the 'waiting time' experienced by pupils. Whilst each individual exclusion is different, delays for readmission can be separated into factors which are parent or child focused, school focused or LEA focused. Often, no one factor is completely the cause of delays although a combination of two or three interwoven reasons was regularly apparent.

What is of major concern is the 'waiting time' between the various *stages* of the exclusion process: the time taken between the exclusion and the exclusion conference or the LEA decision; between the decision and the pupil returning to full-time education. Pupils may be out of the education system for a period of several months and, sometimes, years. What then is their chance of returning successfully into a system which has ignored their needs for so long?

Chapter 10

Who excludes whom?
The personal experience of exclusion

Cedric Cullingford and Jenny Morrison

INTRODUCTION

'Exclusion' might at first appear as a clear and precise term, just as it can be a decisive act. But the more we explore the meaning of the term from the point of view of those who suffer from it, the more complex it becomes. The relationship between the harsh experiences of school, such as bullying, and the subsequent disillusionment that leads to truancy and exclusion is a close one. Indeed, to separate truancy and exclusion is merely to acknowledge that the school has at last reflected and made official the actions taken by the pupil. In the research reported here there are no cases of pupils being suddenly and unwillingly excluded from school. Long before this happens they have been, at least occasionally, playing truant. More importantly they have been psychologically excluding themselves long before the school formally excludes them.

It sometimes appears that exclusion from school, not allowing the habitual truant to come back, is a kind of conspiracy or agreement, made the more urgent because of the way the government proposes to use truancy figures as a means of assessing schools. Exclusion can appear to justify schools' failure to keep their pupils. No-one can doubt the personal relief felt by the teachers facing large classes and difficult pupils when a particular source of disruption is absent. The responsibility is the pupils' but the blame is attached to the school. It is worth bearing in mind through this chapter, which reports on empirical research, that the more we explored the psychological aspects of truancy and the personal feelings and traumas that lead to it, such as being part of a conspiracy of bullying which involves not only the majority of pupils but also teachers (Cullingford and Morrison, 1995), the more difficult it is to define its parameters. Besides, if truancy is voluntary physical exclusion from school, more politely termed absenteeism, how do we describe the way that children mentally turn themselves off from lessons and remain uninvolved, if physically there; that is, the 'invisible children'? (Pye, 1991).

The majority of research studies into truancy and exclusion from school have concentrated on quantifying the number of incidents or on institutional processes. Research that explores pupils' own perceptions as a means of understanding the reason for truanting and the behaviour which leads to exclusion from schools is comparatively recent. Most studies of truancy and exclusion are in fact centred on the social policies and the responsibilities of different agencies. With a few exceptions (Reynolds *et al.*, 1980; Rutter *et al.*, 1979) research into absenteeism has neglected social processes and the relationships that occur within and outside school, concentrating on the formal aspects of schooling such as size, staffing patterns and administration (Fogelman *et al.*, 1980) or aspects of the curriculum.

Stoll and O'Keefe (1989) reported that approximately two-thirds of pupils admitted truanting at some time, during years 4 to 11, the most common form of which was post-registration truancy. They argue that until recently LEAs, teachers unions, the Department for Education and schools have consistently denied that truancy exists on such a large scale. Such denials are supposedly supported by attendance figures obtained from school registers. Attendance figures derived from registers are, however, renowned for their unreliability as they do not include details of post-registration truancy which is by far the most prevalent form.

Blyth and Milner (1993) conclude that the phenomenon of exclusion has obtained the status of a moral panic. As with truancy, there is wide variation in reported incidence with studies indicating that the numbers of exclusions is growing (Imich, 1994). Official data is incomplete as many exclusions are 'unofficial' and thus go unrecorded (Stirling, in this volume).

Although some of the reasons given for excluding a pupil appear trivial, Blyth and Milner demonstrate that they may represent the 'final straw' in a long process of deterioration in relationships between pupils and staff. They argue that in the context of the new education market children are increasingly viewed in terms of attendance, behaviour or attainment rather than having any intrinsic value. Thus, 'school responses to poor attendance by means of exclusion provides a neat (if somewhat illogical) way for schools to get rid of troublesome pupils whilst at the same time improving their published attendance records' (Blyth and Milner, 1993, p. 262).

Whether or not school attendance problems are a recent phenomenon, the research evidence indicates the adverse effects of missing school (Hibbett and Fogelman 1988, 1990; Rodgers, 1990). Being excluded from school may increase the risk of entering local authority care and there is mounting evidence to suggest that this can jeopardise educational careers (Jackson, 1987, 1989). Carlen *et al.* (1992) found that 50 per cent of their sample of absentees were or had been in residential care.

The overall concern of the research reported here is to explore the correlation that has been found between bullying and criminality (Eron *et al.*, 1987; Huesmann, *et al.*, 1984; Lane 1989; Olweus 1980, 1991) and to investigate the sources of deviant behaviour among young offenders. Longitudinal studies have identified certain factors that exist in childhood and are linked to negative adult outcomes. However, this study is concerned with a deeper analysis of how these links are actually formed. Central to this is an investigation into the part played by school in the formative experiences of young people, some of which include various aspects of exclusion. Thus the experience of exclusion is firmly embedded in the overall experience of the pupils. This helps us to question some of the common assumptions.

In relation to exclusion, Imich (1994) found that a small number of schools in one particular LEA accounted for a majority of exclusions, indicating that school factors may be a more significant predictor of pupil exclusion than the actual behaviour of the pupils. Galloway also found that 'the cause of exclusion, if not the disruption itself, lies to some extent in the attitudes, policies, and practices of the school' (Galloway, 1985, p. 60). This has implied a shift in attitude from automatically blaming the pupil to trying to understand the overall circumstance.

Since the mid-1970s, for instance, many researchers have preferred to use the term 'absenteeism' as opposed to 'truancy' (Carroll, 1977; Eaton and Houghton, 1974; Galloway, 1976; Reid, 1985, 1989), thus shifting the emphasis away from the characteristics of individuals to look at wider factors in the home, school, neighbourhood and society (Carroll, 1977). The term 'absenteeism' is psychologically more neutral and suggests a concern to explore the underlying causes of the phenomenon through the actual experiences and complex attitudes of children. This involves an exploration of the significant factors that make an impact on the tension between personal feelings and official policies.

There is a debate as to whether or not truancy, like exclusion, should be defined as a deviant act. According to Stoll and O'Keefe (1989) absentees are not deviants but 'rational thinkers' who have rejected the curriculum and made a conscious decision to absent themselves from school: 'It must be associated literally with physical absence, though as a form of alienation or rejection it overlaps with phenomena such as bad behaviour or switching off in class, which do not entail actual and physical absence' (Stoll and O'Keefe, 1989, p. 13).

From a different perspective others argue that the 'problem' of truancy is the result of the historical development of compulsory schooling as a way of controlling certain sections of the population. Gleeson (1992) defines truancy as a form of social exclusion that has its origins in the history and politics of compulsory education and maintains that the explanation of truancy as a form of individual pathology is over-simplistic. These researchers define truancy as a 'social phenomenon' rather than a behavioural category: 'Both truancy and the laws in which it is constituted are rooted in the class and political interests of an increasingly divided society' (Carlen et al., 1992, p. 180).

It is argued that, rather than a type of individual deviance, truancy is socially constructed, a result of the ways in which policies have been developed from political programmes and the ways in which they have been embedded in institutions: 'There has been a shift from varying patterns of attendance being a taken-for-granted aspect of varying ways of organising social life, to the production of the problem of irregular attendance' (Paterson, 1989, p. 179).

From their analysis of qualitative interviews, Carlen et al. (1992) concluded that, underlying the explicit reasons given for truancy, the young people and their families had a pervasive awareness of powerlessness and economic deprivation which they believed could not be remedied by attending school regularly. Much can be learned from talking to those who are involved, the young people themselves:

> If we examine the reasons for school absenteeism and indis-cipline, if we search beneath the surface of labels of truant, phobic, disruptive or maladjusted and ask why young people behave in this way we may begin to comprehend what could be done to improve the system.
>
> (Carlen *et al.*, 1992, p. 15)

The whole range of issues that affects children in school deserves further exploration; their motivation, their attitudes towards the curriculum and their responses to teachers and to each other. In particular, there is a need to know more about the way in which children learn disaffection with school and how they come to feel psychologically as well as physically excluded from school life (see Cullingford, 1993; Cullingford and Brown, 1995; Measor and Woods, 1984).

METHOD

In this study qualitative methods were employed as they offer the required degree of sensitivity and flexibility essential to the investigation of social processes and the generation of attitudes (Hammersley, 1990; Sampson and Lamb, 1992). Lengthy, semi-structured interviews were conducted with twenty-five young offenders between the ages of 16 and 21 in order to gain the empirical data. The research was undertaken at one male and one female young offender institution and the number of males to females interviewed (twenty to five) reflects the dispropor-tionate number of males to females in the prison population as a whole. Contact was made in the form of a letter, sent to each of the young people, requesting their permission and reassuring them of total confidentiality and anonymity. Each respondent was interviewed individually in a private room within the institution, away from prison officers and other members of staff.

The data were then analysed in order to establish how the interviewees view, categorise and experience the world and to identify sources of knowledge. In the semi-structured interviews certain set themes were explored. In order to avoid contamina-tion of the data, however, it was crucial that questions were open ended and not directed by the interviewer. To avoid any

assumptions, hints or guessing of the 'right' responses, the participants were not aware of exactly what it was the interviewer was
seeking. The young people assumed they were being asked for
general reflections on their experiences of school, unaware of the
specific focus of the research, lest they thought they were being
typecast into a particular role.

This technique allowed young people to develop their ideas
and to define attitudes, concepts and experiences that were important to each of them. Throughout the conversations the
interviewer explored childhood memories and retrospective
accounts of young offenders' whole experience of school that
included their feelings and attitudes towards the curriculum,
bullying, truancy, friendships, relationships with teachers, and life
outside school including family relationships.

No pre-formulated definitions were imposed. A central premise
of the research was that concepts can only be defined through
actual experience. For definitions to be accurate, the perceptions
of those involved should be given prominence. Concepts were
allowed to emerge from the empirical data after careful and
complex analysis. For example, the terms 'truancy' or 'exclusion'
were invoked by the respondents themselves, rather than by the
interviewer.

The approach to theory was therefore inductive. A hypothetico-
deductive model would be inappropriate to the type of research
concerning effects, responses and attitudes. The true nature of
the phenomena being studied may go undiscovered if it is
constrained by assumptions built into the hypotheses. (Glaser and
Strauss, 1967; Hammersley, 1990; Robson, 1993; Strauss, 1986).
It must be stressed that gender differences in the experiences
being reported were not found. Indeed, the findings are very
consistent, not in particular or ephemeral terms of factual and
personal details, but in terms of underlying tone, attitude and
circumstance.

RESULTS

All the young offenders in the sample had experienced 'exclusion' of some kind. This may have been formally imposed by the
school, self imposed through truanting, or both. Fighting and
aggression were prominent among the reasons given for being
formally excluded. It appears, however, that these episodes were

the culmination of a lack of communication leading to frustration and ultimately a breakdown in relationships.

The *de facto* exclusion from school may be preceded by a feeling of psychological exclusion whereby the individual feels that he or she no longer has a stake in either the formal or social aspects of school life. This experience leaves young people with a deep sense of not belonging and thus they may seek acceptance in alternative systems:

> They chucked me out of school and I nicked this car ... coppers ... they caught me like, took me down to the police station.
>
> (Male, 16)

> I got suspended, I went home for a week, and that's when I started thieving, robbing.
>
> (Male, 18)

> I really started gettin' into trouble ... 'cos like I got expelled from school, didn't have no money, I was bored.
>
> (Male, 19)

> that's when I started gettin' into trouble ... 'cos you're off school, you've got nothin' to do, you got no money for fags, so you just go round and if you see somethin' in a car, you think, well, there's money there I could just get it, and that's what I did.
>
> (Male, 16)

In addition to those physically excluded from school many children suffer from a sense of social exclusion. This form of exclusion is manifested in more subtle psychological forms and is often the result of being bullied or 'picked on' by others. From the point of view of children the experience of bullying involves unintentional as well as deliberate acts and thus emphasis on intentionality is misleading as it excludes the feelings of children who fall victim to unintentional hurtful acts (Cullingford, 1993; Cullingford and Morrison, 1995). It is the sense of hurt incurred by the victim, however inadvert, that counts. Children feel hurt and isolated, often as a result of behaviour in which the deliberate intention to cause distress is absent. Such actions can be psychologically devastating, leaving children feeling severely victimised.

The problem of bullying is not a matter of clearly identifiable incidents and isolated individuals. It is pervasive in less obvious forms which are difficult to detect and define. From the point of view of those who are 'picked on', it is not only children but teachers who are involved in more subtle forms of bullying behaviour that can be embarrassing and hurtful and ultimately cause feelings of alienation and social isolation.

They embarrass you 'cos they know probably you ain't very good at reading and that. They'll just pick you out of the whole class and say, 'Stand up and read that paragraph to the class' and you say, 'No I'm not doin' it' and they'll say, 'Right, if you're not doin' it you're goin' to the exclusion room', so I just grabbed my bag and just walked out, and everyone was takin' the piss and that.

(Male, 16)

Some teachers used to make me go into other classrooms and spell words on the board that I couldn't, that they knew I couldn't spell, to show me up and I didn't like that either.

(Male, 17)

These young people perceived teachers as unapproachable and irrational, the respect they are expected to show to their teachers not always being reciprocated:

There was a couple of all right ones, but the rest of them had a bad attitude. ... Just talking to you like you're a little kid and that.

(Male, 20)

They should like talk to you as if you're a normal person, instead of treating you like a big kid.

(Male, 20)

The Headmistress ... you couldn't talk to her, y'know, just normal, she'd just start shoutin' at you and that.

(Male, 20)

Whatever their intentions, the teachers isolated these particular young people who felt they were unfairly 'picked on' or rejected. This rejection was more severely felt when they were experiencing some other form of rejection, perhaps from peers or even at home:

Well, it was mainly to do with family problems, y'know what I mean, me mum and dad breakin' up. And, well, even before that I started runnin' away, didn't like it at all.

(Male, 20)

Gradually they felt alienated from both the formal and informal aspects of school life, and eventually from school as a whole:

They put me in classes where there was a teacher who could control me, y'know a big enough teacher, y'know I couldn't hit. They put me in classes like that, so I just went from there.

(Male, 19)

I weren't allowed to take me exams when I was here ... 'cos of me behaviour ... no teachers would have me.

(Female, 20)

I ain't had no education for about three year now, since I was thirteen, fourteen. I got kicked out of school ... that was it, you're on the streets.

(Male, 16)

Teachers who do not have the resources, time, or necessary skills to cope with children who present a challenge may feel forced to exclude them from the rest of the class. This exclusion occurs on a psychological as well as a physical level. It is here that the distinction between truancy and exclusion becomes blurred. Truanting by disruptive or 'difficult' children may be met with relief as it removes the 'problem' without the necessity of resorting to the formal mechanisms of exclusion (see, additionally, Stirling in this volume). A pattern developed whereby the individual, experiencing frustration at being ignored by the teacher or isolated from the rest of the class, chose to withdraw himself or herself voluntarily rather than confront the anticipated rejection:

What you couldn't even understand, he makes you do it, and if you don't do it you get detention after school. So that's why I used to just go to the exclusion room every time we had a language lesson, 'cos I knew for a fact that if I went to the class he'd end up sending me there anyway.

(Male, 16)

All's I can remember was them shouting at me all the time, sending me out of the classroom, that's all I can remember ... I didn't really like classes at all.

(Male, 18)

There is, then, a tension between formal exclusion as a type of punishment or sanction imposed from outside and the kinds of psychological processes that lead one to impose exclusion and isolation on oneself through truancy. The association between truancy, ostensibly the responsibility of the pupil, and exclusion, the responsibility of the authorities of a school, is so close as to be difficult to separate. This type of psychological exclusion remains an unexplored area. The resulting feeling of alienation may manifest itself in more extreme forms of attention seeking behaviour. The sense of frustration and deep resentment that results from experiencing social isolation may be the cause of further disruptive behaviour which may culminate in a total rejection of the system itself. This is not, however, expressed as a rejection of the intrinsic value of school and education, rather as a rejection of their place in the system as it exists.

If the school itself is seen in terms of a system into which children must fit, teachers are not only part of that system but also can act as a barrier to children feeling an accepted part of it. Some teachers are perceived to discriminate between pupils:

, I used to think they had their favourites ... and I used to sit there and they sort of blanked me out and talked to the others all the time ... so I used to sit there most of the time on me own, nobody to talk to. So I used to sit on me own, and then I used to think, oh God, I'm not coming tomorrow. 'Cos I knew if I stayed at home me mum and dad would talk to me, but they [at school] wouldn't.

(Female, 21)

Tension may be caused by the fact that the child is simply unable to meet the demands of schoolwork because they have difficulties with learning or keeping up with the rest of the class:

Some of the work at school I found really hard and I couldn't do it ... and that put me off as well. ... It used to make me angry inside, 'cos I couldn't do it and all the others used to be there writing and I couldn't. Teacher had to help me all the time. I used to feel stupid. ... It can be quite frustrating though, can't it, if you can't do it and others are there writing away.

(Female, 21)

I didn't like school much, but it were all right. I can't read very good, y'know what I mean, so that's why I've skipped it out, ... I still can't read very good, ... I didn't like paperwork, don't like paperwork, do y'know what I mean.

(Female, 21)

The feeling of being stigmatised as 'different' is felt by many. Individuals may be defined as different and placed outside their peer group for a variety of reasons, such as physical characteristics or for more personal reasons such as something in their family background. These differences are used to identify and label others and they are powerful weapons which children use against each other. Teachers are also involved in generating labels and defining particular pupils as 'different'. Once a pupil has been defined in this way he or she may be ostracised by peers and in turn become the victim of hurtful teasing and taunting:

I'm not good at maths, English and things ... they called me about me work, or me writing, 'You can't spell, you're thick', and things like that.

(Male, 20)

The process of differentiation can begin by excluding a pupil from the classroom. This experience is extremely hurtful to those who experience it. Having been 'singled out' or segregated the pupil stands in contrast to other 'normal' pupils. Pupils who attend special classes are often labelled by their peers, and in turn label themselves, as 'stupid' or 'thick', reflecting feelings of inadequacy and low self-esteem. Many of these young people recalled incidents in which teachers had denigrated their efforts or showed them up in front of the rest of the class:

If yours didn't turn out right she used to patronise you, you didn't try hard enough ... 'cos even though you were trying, she ought to say, well, at least you tried. Makes you feel better for starters, even if you have to throw it in bin.

(Female, 20)

Measor and Woods (1984) demonstrated that pupils have a particular notion of what is 'normal' and that individuals who deviate from this are prone to intense ridicule. They found two groups with which children did not wish to be identified; the 'too conformist' and the 'too deviant' types. Those regarded as 'too thick' were prone to insults, teasing and aggression and were frequently labelled by insulting nicknames. Pupils who needed remedial reading were known as spastics or 'spassies' (Measor and Woods, 1984, p. 133). From our own analysis it is clear that teachers can play a significant role in creating deviant identities that in turn provoke rejection and hostility from peers.

The difficulty of making clear demarcations between the official and the personal is highlighted by the fact that children who display difficulties with work are stigmatised and excluded not only by teachers but also by other children as well. If children are perceived as different from the others they may have to endure taunting and teasing as a result. From these experiences a sense of social, as well as intellectual, inadequacy is incurred:

> I got a lot of stick for being in that class. . . . Not just teachers, friends as well . . . just 'cos I couldn't read. . . . If you had to have spellings at end of week – you get ten spellings on a Monday and on a Friday you have to read 'em out – I couldn't remember one of 'em.
>
> (Male, 17)

> You get skitted and everythin' . . . well, you're thick, aren't you? 'Cos all them are in the top classes and that, and you're just a dunce, 'cos you're down there in the unit, that's why I didn't like school.
>
> (Male, 21)

This teasing and taunting can turn to retaliation and aggression:

> They used to call me this name . . . and I used to get really mad when they used to say it and they just used to wind me up and wind me up all the time, and I'd start crying and they'd carry on and carry on, y'know, till they'd really get you mad and you'd do something.
>
> (Female, 21)

I'd lose me temper easily, so if someone says somethin', I'd just start gettin' angry anyway. So I was havin' a lot of fights over that. ... It depends how they said ... things. ... I could ignore somethin' when someone's really gettin' at me, but I'd snap at a little thing.

(Male, 20)

Some children impose exclusion on themselves through truanting or 'switching off' and refusing to participate in class-room activities. This type of mental absenteeism is a form of 'hidden' truancy that must be very common:

I just used to read books instead of listenin' to what they'd do, and ... don't know, just never got on.

(Male, 20)

Virtually everyday I was goin' to school, its just that I wasn't doin' nothin' once I got there.

(Male, 20)

Pupils like these who felt a particular resentment and who ended up being formally excluded are merely carrying this behaviour to extremes. This is the more private form of playing truant; it is the mental rejection of school. It is through the ambivalence, the tension between the private and the public that pupils appear to have lost their ability to cope. Children's culture consists of an informal social structure of friendship, hierarchy and status which contrasts with the official, academic and organisational structures of the school. Children will be unable to enjoy school to the full if they cannot cope in both of these structures simultaneously. There is pressure from teachers and their alternatives, the peer group:

Well, the lads who I used to be with, they used to ... never be interested in work ... they wouldn't let you. They'd try 'n' stop you, they'd start messin' about, throwing things at you, paper at you, through the room, all that kind of stuff, and then that just distracts you then, and you can't do nothing.

(Male, 18)

I didn't like lessons ... too much disruption went off in class, so I just used to join in with 'em ... mainly lads ... when they used to flick rubbers, so we just started doin' it.

(Female, 20)

Although the interviewees spoke of their own bullying and aggressive behaviour, they clearly felt unfairly 'picked on' or victimised by particular teachers. Having been labelled as a 'problem' they were aware of the difficulties of changing teachers' perceptions of them as a deviant influence:

> I don't think they really liked me for what I was, a trouble-maker.
>
> (Male, 18)

> I was in trouble with the police in school as well.... And I think the teachers, the school, didn't really want me there either, 'cos of what I'd been charged for, especially for the possession of cannabis. They might of thought I was bringin' drugs to school, which I wasn't. Um, think they wanted me out as well.
>
> (Male, 19)

Possibly as a response to segregation and rejection there is a sense in which children clash with both the formal and social systems, resulting in anger, and frustration:

> Just the atmosphere and that around. The teachers were horrible. Just don't like getting told what to do.
>
> (Male, 20)

> I hated school, I don't know why.... I suppose it's when you're young and that, it's just school, you've gotta go.
>
> (Male, 20)

When communication has finally deteriorated, the sense of frustration and anger can be so powerful that it manifests itself in physical violence:

> I remember punching one in the stomach ... 'cos I walked in the class and I had me coat on and he just started dragging me out of the class, by the hood of me coat, so I turned round and punched him. I got suspended.
>
> (Male, 20)

> Didn't get on with them, was always fightin' and that, all the time, ... it was me and me sister really. Me sister would start arguin' with one, when I'd be another class – y'know two years younger than her – then one of her mates would come and

tell me she's fightin' with the teachers, and I'd just start fightin' with them as well then.

(Male, 20)

People will react against the system that has stigmatised and rejected them. They may even adopt strategies to bring about a final physical exclusion from the school system, recognising that there is an implied agreement that this should be so. After all, there are few protests to being excluded:

I didn't do nothin' much to get expelled, I seen people get away with worse, but I think they just wanted me out of the school anyway, and they knew I wasn't trying. I think they knew it's what I wanted.

(Male, 19)

I just told myself, I'm not goin' through with this at all. I was startin' to do things to try and get myself expelled ... not work, answer back, skive off.

(Male, 19)

Again the issue of complicity is highlighted. In some respects the child's decision to exclude him or herself may bring relief to teachers who are struggling to cope. It is easier for teachers if difficult pupils detect that they are not welcome, although formally teachers would deny it. In this sense, then, the formal exclusion may be seen as a reward for both teacher and student:

I was glad 'cos I was happy, 'cos I had time off school.

(Female, 21)

The children do not reject school totally but they feel that the system as a whole, as it exists, cannot respond to their needs. Rather than blaming teachers, they show an awareness of the pressures and demands they have to cope with in large class-rooms. Those who have felt unable to cope with the intellectual pressures of the curriculum explain their desire for more time and attention.

They should have teachers to so many pupils, just like three teachers to ten pupils, where they can walk round and help you continuously. ... He can just come up to you and give you the help you need.

(Male, 21)

They feel let down by the system and are aware that their difficulties could have been eased if teachers had more time to provide more individual attention:

Smaller groups, smaller classes would help.

(Male, 20)

More quieter, less people in classroom, 'cos then if you've got problems you can go straight to the teacher, can't you? Instead of having to wait for an hour.

(Female, 19)

There is a sense of inner failure as well as difficulties in meeting standards. There is isolation, a sense of personal exclusion, from all sides. The relationship between the formal work of school – the curriculum and standards – and the alternative world of teasing, competition and criticism from peers is a close one.

It is evident that a correlation exists between subjects and teaching styles and between teaching styles and attitudes to pupils:

It wasn't the learnin' what I didn't like doin', it was just the way they done it. So, if they'd had somethin' more interestin' I could've been OK 'cos I used to learn, 'cos I used to read books anyway. ... If it was maths there'd be a test but they'd say turn to one page, I'd go to another page and learn somethin' totally different. So ... don't know, just the way they do the teachin.

(Male, 20)

Practical subjects were preferred because they were more relaxed and less structured, offering an escape from the pressures of intellectual demands:

I used to hate maths and English. I used to go home in them. I used to like art, biology, sciences, woodwork ... I've always liked doin' things like that, practical, rather than doin' sums.

(Male, 19)

There were particular lessons in which pupils felt less threatened which was reflected in their relationships with the teachers of these subjects:

If I didn't like the subject, I most probably didn't like the teacher either, 'cos I just didn't wanna know about the subject, like German or French or somethin'.

(Male, 16)

In art and that you could talk a bit and do pictures and that . . . more laid back teachers who weren't so, y'know, mouthy. And then the lessons, I think I would work a bit more 'cos I felt more at ease there.

(Male, 19)

I remember the woodwork teacher. He was all right, 'cos he was dead easy goin'. We used to have a laugh and that, crack jokes, and I got on with him alright.

(Male, 19)

Clearly, pupils preferred some parts of the school, in which they felt at home, to others from which they felt alienated. It appeared that were are particular places, classrooms, or teachers and their teaching styles from which pupils did not wish to play truant and from which they did not feel psychologically excluded. These were often places where working with others rather than in isolation was the norm and where the set task was not so clearly defined as something which they would fail:

Well, I learned to read and write and that and I can draw. That's the only thing I was really interested in was drawin' and sports and stuff, . . . I just left everything else, I just wasn't really concentrating on anythin' else.

(Female, 21)

School just wasn't me, man. I just didn't wanna do it, I didn't like it. I just liked games and PE, know what I mean? I were in the netball team.

(Female, 21)

The previously unexplored area of psychological 'exclusion' is again illustrated by the tension between the sense of being unable to carry out a task and the refusal to do so:

I just stopped doin' work. 'Cos I was doin' well at school, gettin' all top marks and all that, and then I just, I just weren't interested after that.

(Male, 20)

I just couldn't hack it. ... All the teachers used to say, 'If you tried you could be a really good pupil' but I didn't try ... I think I was average. I was, yeah, a bit below average, I think yeah.

(Male, 19)

I could do all the work and that ... but I just didn't bother with it.

(Male, 20)

The relationship between the terms 'I can't' and 'I won't' is psychologically very close. A sense of inability or incapacity, or a dislike of doing something, very easily turns into a refusal. This can be achieved merely by a question from a teacher, by a demand that turns indifference into defensiveness. The more we gain insights into the inner lives of children the more certain definitions seem unhelpful. There are, after all, places and subjects in school that present an acceptable world in which pupils feel included and in which they have a part to play. There are tasks such as 'paperwork' which are alienating from a personal point of view and set tasks such as the Standard Attainment Targets against which failure is carefully measured.

CONCLUSION

Although truancy is a concept which implies personal choice it has a very close relationship to exclusion. Throughout the analysis it became impossible to separate and study the two concepts in isolation. From the pupil's perception, exclusion not only exists in its formal or physical aspects but also includes the personal sense of social isolation that leads the pupil to impose exclusion on him or herself through truanting. In addition, it becomes evident that truancy does not necessarily involve physical absence from school but can be manifested in behaviour such as refusing to work and participate, or simply 'switching off' in class.

Through subtle forms of bullying behaviour that labels, differentiates and excludes, teachers can act as a barrier to particular children feeling that they are an accepted part of the system. It is a difficult task trying to satisfy the individual needs of large numbers of pupils and, as a result of heavy pressures and demands inside the classroom, teachers are relieved if numbers are reduced through 'illness' or other absences. Thus, they may welcome absentees, particularly those who present an added burden on their limited resources because they display difficulties with work or behaviour. Only when teachers have reached their very limit and can no longer cope will they impose exclusion as a formal sanction and actually force the pupil out.

Usually, long before this, excluded pupils have experienced feelings of alienation and isolation as a result of more subtle psychological processes that can occur within the school and classroom, of which the teacher may be unaware. The feeling of exclusion starts in certain lessons and grows until the individuals no longer feel that they have a part to play in the social and academic life of the school. In anticipation of the final sanction they may choose voluntarily to withdraw themselves and reject their part in school altogether.

The results also suggest that a relationship exists between exclusion, in its various forms, and the development of delinquency. This is not to make the simple analogy of implying that all excluded pupils necessarily become criminals. However, all the young offenders in the study had experienced some form of exclusion. Once excluded from the school the frustration and boredom of having nothing to do, combined with pressure from peers, often led to 'getting into trouble' and the development of petty crime.

Chapter 11

Tales from the exclusion zone
The views of teachers and pupils

Susan de Pear and Philip Garner

INTRODUCTION

Since the establishment of the National Exclusions Reporting System (NERS, 1990) the topic of pupil exclusion has been of increasing concern to educationists and others who work with children and young people. The current interest has a long pedigree and, while it is not our intention to provide a historical review, it is worth acknowledging the work of Galloway *et al.* (1982) and Grunsell (1980). These authors help to consolidate a view that the current scenario, in which exclusion from school is primarily a birthright of the disadvantaged, represents a picture of educational conditions that have changed little over time.

Moreover, the evidence they present suggests that who gets excluded, and at what rate, is remarkably immune to educational politics in the widest sense. Government initiatives to deal with allegedly 'difficult' pupils in schools, and their regional (Local Education Authority) equivalents, have been notable mainly for their inability to provide long-term solutions. On the other hand, writers such as Rutter *et al.*, (1979) and Reynolds and Sullivan (1981) have shown that investigations into the organisation of schools and studies of the responses of small groups of 'at-risk' pupils (both of which have become popular devices to initiate developments in effective behaviour management) have a similar, but far more successful, historical tradition. These examples lead to the suggestion, explicitly outlined in this chapter, that it is the micro-politics of schools which exert a more significant influence on pupils' responses to schooling. Ultimately, it is argued, the interpersonal relationships that are developed within the school

(Hargreaves, 1967) have a crucial part to play in matters relating to exclusions.

The recent background to the question of exclusions has been widely reported (Imich, 1994; Lloyd-Smith, 1993; Stirling, 1993) and the current legal framework is enshrined in the Education Act 1993. The arguments presented by both legislators and educational commentators focus upon causal factors. Significantly these are ascertained using official (DfE or LEA) and 'unofficial' (obtained by individual researchers or research organisations) data which represent the views of teachers, administrators and parents rather than that of the pupils themselves.

In May 1994 the Department for Education issued a set of six consultation papers grouped under the heading 'Pupils with Problems'. Amongst these was Circular 10/94, entitled *Exclusions from School* (DfE, 1994b). This focused upon the changes in the existing law relating to exclusions covered by the Education Act 1993, and gave schools guidance on the effective use of exclusion procedures.

Parallel to the continuing debate concerning standards of discipline in schools, to which the circulars relating to 'pupils with problems' have contributed, has been a growing interest in the rights of individual pupils. Child-centred educationists have been influential in this relatively new development and there is currently a significant growth in the literature in this field. Moreover, some practices adopted by schools, following the advice of the Elton Report (DES 1989), have encouraged more significant participation by pupils whose behaviour is regarded as inappropriate. This group has been amongst the most marginalised and disenfranchised group of pupils in schools (Schostak, 1983).

The Code of Practice relating to special educational needs (DfE, 1994d) has sought to build on these developments. The Code states that steps should be taken to 'take into account the ascertainable wishes of the child concerned' (p. 3). It goes on to reinforce the principles of both the Children Act 1989 and the UN Convention on the Rights of the Child (1991) by indicating a belief that children can provide 'important and relevant information' and that they 'have a right to be heard'. Moreover, there is an explicitly stated belief that pupils should be involved in decision making. Significantly, however, Circular 10/94 (DfE, 1994b) in dealing with exclusions, makes little or no overt mention of the role of 'pupils with problems' in the decision-making processes of the school.

The OFSTED inspection schedule introduced in 1993 highlights the importance of 'discipline' and 'behaviour management' as indicators of effective schools. Elsewhere there is an accepted belief that the level of 'problem behaviour' by pupils in a school is a factor which can be used to judge the climate or ethos of the institution (Cooper, 1993). Exclusions are an important consideration in this respect, in that they provide hard evidence of how a school is coping with its most difficult pupils.

This chapter considers elements of all three issues outlined above in the context of what excluded pupils themselves have to say about their schooling. The argument is that exclusions from school, listening to pupils and school effectiveness are inextricably linked. We will imply that the current emphasis upon exclusions themselves is dealing with consequences rather than causes. The debate concerning exclusions fails to acknowledge the mutual dependence of each of the factors mentioned within what has been conceptualised as an ecosystem (Bronfenbrenner, 1979). Bronfenbrenner's argument is that a resolution of one problematic issue cannot take place when an imbalance exists between parts of the system. In this case, developing an effective school is inhibited by the lack of involvement in decision making by those pupils who are viewed as 'problems' and who are eventually excluded because of their behaviour.

Determining the views of pupils who have been excluded appears to be a sensible way of establishing a dialogue, especially if such views are considered alongside those of teachers. This approach has been significantly absent in much of the literature concerning exclusions and the resultant information gap has been frequently noted. Schostak (1983), for example, has remarked that 'in general, research has not tended to focus on the experiences of the young'. More recently an increasing emphasis on eliciting pupil-views has been discernable (Garner, 1994; Lloyd-Smith and Davies, 1995), illustrating the value of this strategy. The present chapter attempts to extend this way of thinking by providing an example of ways in which pupils' experiences may be used to promote institutional development.

GATHERING THE EVIDENCE

The information obtained in this chapter has been gathered from a series of conversations with six pupils who had been excluded from mainstream schools and who also had special educational needs. Of the six, two were girls, and all six young people were white. This was indicative of the location of the research sites – in non-urban Surrey and Kent. The interviews took place in special schools, where the pupils had been placed following exclusion. The interviews were taped and then transcribed. They were based on a format which was adapted from Schutz's FIRO-B (Behaviour) schedule (Schutz, 1978) by one of the writers (de Pear, 1994).

FIRO-B is a schedule based upon a three-dimensional theory of interpersonal behaviour. It enables comments to be elicited from the pupils which are indicative of their self-concepts. The schedule allows for a distinction to be made between wanted and expressed needs in three areas. It considers: first, the pupils' need for *inclusion* – the desire to feel significant and worthwhile; second the pupils' need for *control*, – the need to feel competent and responsible; and finally, the pupils' need for *affection* – the feeling that they themselves are loveable and liked by others.

Each of these criteria provided a means of analysis. The elicited responses of the pupils, and an indicative case study, form the substance of this chapter.

The views of seven teachers from the excluded pupil's main-stream school were also gathered as a means of establishing an insight into the effectiveness of current aims and practices in rela-tion to the management of behaviour. A series of 'prompt' questions, contained in a semi-structured interview schedule was used to elicit these views (de Pear, 1994) The current chapter does not report these views directly but uses them to build a picture of the organisational 'health' of schools. Such an analysis of schools, used in conjunction with the pupils' views, provides a means of highlighting important discontinuities in both policy and provision.

Little justification has to be given for the use of these quali-tative approaches. The use of data gathered directly from school children for research purposes has gradually increased in the last fifteen years (Armstrong *et al.*, 1993) and it now has a respected, if fairly recent, pedigree. In part this has been a result of the growing acceptance of qualitative approaches in social science research in general. In education, the impact of teacher-directed action research has enabled research activity to get closer to classrooms and, especially, to the reality of the children who participate in them (Bell, 1994). It is equally true, however, that the views of those pupils in schools who are the cause of 'behaviour problems' are seldom considered (Schostak, 1983). This is in spite of a number of influential contributions to this area of inquiry (Everhart, 1983; Willis, 1977; Woods 1979). The views of pupils who have actually been excluded appear to be even more infrequently investigated.

TALES FROM THE EXCLUSION ZONE

In part, the data obtained from this small group of pupils suggested that, whilst they were sometimes not able to take responsibility or make decisions regarding their emotional or educational lives, they paradoxically felt a need to feel competent and responsible. The conversation transcripts, for example, show the significance to these pupils of activities such as childminding, catering and bar work. On the other hand, the data tell us of incidents in school where feelings of incompetence caused these vulnerable young people to lose control.

In more detail, the study indicated that firstly, and without exception, the pupils' *wanted inclusion* scores are higher than their *expressed inclusion* scores. As *inclusion* refers to one's general social orientation the high *wanted* scores mean that the pupils have a strong need to belong and to be accepted. The lower *expressed* scores mean that the pupils are generally uncomfortable around people and will tend to move away from them. This evidence highlights a conflict of emotions for pupils with special educational needs. Thus, it may be hypothesised that the pupils, having been labelled and marginalised by their learning difficulties, may have a strong wish to feel significant in academic terms but their inherent fear of failure keeps them distanced from other learners. The resulting tension causes them either to withdraw from educational encounters or, as in the case of most exclusions, to act out their frustrations (see also Cullingford and Morrison, and John in this volume).

When considering the pupils' *wanted* and *expressed* need for *control* the results, with a single exception, show the same pattern.

The pupils' high *wanted* control scores suggest abdication of responsibility and lack of leadership behaviour. The lower *expressed* scores indicate that the pupils avoid making decisions and avoid taking on responsibility. The picture, then, is that these pupils, all of whom have special educational needs, are not able to take responsibility or make decisions concerning their emotional or educational lives.

At the same time they do have a need to feel competent and responsible. Indeed, the responses of the pupils in this study suggest that it may be too simplistic to assume that they do not wish to participate in the education process. A view is expressed, therefore, that the pupils were given little opportunity to succeed, exemplified by the comments, 'You get shoved to the back of the class' and 'Teachers don't help you when you put your hand up'. Moreover, as the comments of teachers in this study suggest, the preoccupation with control issues by some teachers ensures that they perceive the classroom as a contest-arena, between themselves and those pupils who do not want to work.

The third section of the interview schedule refers to the pupils' need for *affection*, that is to say, deeper relationships. About half of the excluded pupils appeared to be *overpersonal*, which suggested a fear of rejection and a strong need for affection. The majority showed a lower *wanted* score which might indicate (according to FIRO-B) that they are very selective about the people with whom deep relationships are formed. Although the higher *expressed* need for affection scores would normally suggest persons who would readily become emotionally involved with others, in this case it would be a mistake to draw such conclusions as most of these high scores were due to repeated mention of one favourite friend, relative or teacher. Most of the pupils in the study had been let down emotionally and in consequence found it very difficult to trust anyone else.

In their interview responses, the pupils in this study highlight a number of misconceptions generally held about excluded pupils. They point to a general commitment to mainstream education, to an ability to appreciate certain professional qualities in teachers and to the need for an atmosphere of mutual respect. The indications are that these young people are far removed from the alienated, aggressive and anti-social individuals that they have traditionally been thought to be. Moreover, their comments can be used in a dynamic way, helping to illustrate the shortcomings of schools in particular and society as a whole. This may, of course, be one reason why we do not wish to listen to them.

A CASE STUDY: PUPIL 'L'

Many of the contributory factors to the exclusion of a pupil from school can be illustrated by individual case studies. 'L' is in Year 11 and has been excluded from two schools, having been in trouble for most of his time in secondary school. He blamed his last exclusion on the influence of his group, who disrupted lessons and never did as they were told. He was not the leader, just 'one of them', and although they all damaged a lift he was the only one excluded, confirming his perception of being unfairly targeted by half of the teachers:

> Yeah, anything I'd done, they'd be on my back; shouting at me, screaming, throwing me out of class. But the thing was, it was only me that it happened to.

Working in class depended on the teachers – whether they liked and trusted him or not. He admits to having a conscience following disruptive incidents and when asked if it was generally peer pressure that made him act in such a way, answered:

> Yes, especially when there are five of them going on at me, 'You boffin, getting on with your work'. So I used to think, 'Right, I'm not going to do no more'.

He does not mention special needs specifically but does say:

> I feel stupid when a teacher says something and I can't think of an answer to give – so I shut up. . . . I don't like it when they're all laughing at me.

He seemed, at the interview, to be a sensible and sensitive boy who had hope for the future and had decided on a career as a chef. He realised a little late that, owing to his exclusions and behaviour, he had been 'falling behind' with his education:

> At first it's just a laugh but when you think back, you think, 'I should've been there, done it.'

'L' is similar to most of the others interviewed in that he, too, comes from a broken home. At the time of the trouble at school he lived with his father. He is now residing with his mother and much younger step-siblings whom he resents:

> If anything goes wrong in the house it's down to me, . . . it's my fault.

However, he admits that things are working out a lot better with his mother, although he is worried because he has not seen his father since he was excluded. If left alone:

> I can sit down, on my own, and think about him. Like, I don't know where he is . . . whether he's still alive . . . but if I'm with other people I don't really care.

He needs to talk about his problems with a trusted person but says he has not yet found that person. He has at least found relative happiness at his new school because:

> Everyone knows everyone; no-one hates anyone here; everyone likes each other – which is the best part . . . it's really good.

According to his high *wanted* and *expressed* need for *inclusion* scores 'L' is clearly *oversocial* and, like the other excluded pupils, would seek others incessantly as he hates to be ignored. With an underlying feeling that no-one was interested in him, his response would be to *make* people pay attention to him. His very high *wanted control* and lower *expressed* score suggest he is an *abdicrat* and so, as can be seen in his case summary, he feels incapable of responsibility and tries to avoid situations where he feels stupid. His high *wanted* and *expressed* need for *affection* scores indicate that he is *overpersonal*, being motivated by a fear of rejection and a strong need for affection.

WORKERS' TALES

The views of seven teachers from one school provide an illuminating, if somewhat depressing, counterpoint to the views of the excluded pupils. In analysing the responses of the teachers a systems perspective was used, adapting Seddon's (1992) model of 'organisational integrity'. This offers insights into what influences the behaviours of the individual participants (teachers) and into how the procedures and protocols of a school help to sustain such behaviours over a period of time. The logic of this approach is that relationships, as they are not simply linear, have to be interpreted and analysed in a non-linear way. Exclusions, for example, are often believed to be about 'cause' and 'effect'. This naivety obscures the truth and frustrates remedial action.

One school portrayed by the teachers in the example selected, presents as one in which the dominant belief-systems prevent any incorporation of the views of those pupils most likely to be excluded. Thus, the school is conceptualised as one in which leadership is administration-focused rather than strategy-focused. There is a bureaucratic hierarchy in which a teacher's implicit role is to serve a line manager rather than the pupils. Supporting this is an administrative culture which addresses problems by writing policies and invoking procedures rather than by attempting to understand a problem as a first order task.

There is considerable emphasis placed upon outputs, the school's reputation is seen as important in this respect, and the desire to control problem behaviour (rather than establish its root cause) is a natural concomitant to this. Feedback from senior managers to the workers, especially in the form of praise, is frequently lacking, while there appears to be little collective involvement in, or ownership of, the difficulties faced by pupils who have special educational needs. Finally, there is an implicit belief that a lack of control or discipline is the most important cause of behaviour problems.

CONCLUSION

The views of excluded pupils in this study suggest an amplification of the danger, expressed by Lloyd-Smith (1984), of providing 'family-based pathological explanations' for behaviour. Such medicalisation often diverts attention from the real cause of the problem and leads, additionally, to an amplification of the original 'problem'. Of course, many schools have become accustomed to a high degree of self-scrutiny as a means of improvement and we would not wish to assume that the negative picture of school-systems as painted by both pupils and teachers is universal.

Nevertheless, from the illustrations given in this chapter, there is an uncomfortable correlation between the position the excluded pupils found themselves to be in and that of the teachers. We have stated that the views of individual pupils who are viewed as 'behaviour problems' in school are frequently disregarded.

But this is hardly unexpected, given that some schools are viewed by the teachers who work there as rule-governed establishments. The interpretations of both teacher-workers and pupil-workers should be given equal currency. And if schools want to inhibit the rate of exclusions they must develop procedures and an organisational culture which regards incorporation of both into decision making as routine and justifiable.

Chapter 12

Damaged goods?
An interpretation of excluded pupils' perceptions of schooling

Pippa John

INTRODUCTION

My experiences during my own school years and time as a teacher have resulted in my interest in researching excluded pupils' perceptions of their schooling. My professional interest in the subject of exclusion began in 1990 when I started working in a centre for young people who had been permanently excluded from school. In conversation with these young people it became apparent that the parallels between my own school experiences and theirs were striking. At school I was unjustly blamed for girls four years older than me taking up smoking, I did almost anything 'for a laugh', I worked hard for the teachers with whom I had a good relationship, and had little respect for those who could not control the class.

This leads me to wonder what is really going on in some schools. Twenty years after my own exclusion from school young people still felt the same way as I did then. Despite all the educational research and the changes in initial teacher training there are still some teachers who do not realise or accept that teaching is about making relationships and that it is their responsibility to ensure that they are good ones. My concerns have deepened since the ramifications of the Education Reform Act 1988 have become apparent to me in that I believe that it will become increasingly difficult for teachers to work with young people experiencing emotional and behavioural difficulties in mainstream schools.

Exclusion from school may be seen to solve 'the problem' for the school but what are the consequences for the excluded pupils? The effect upon the self-concept of the young person excluded and the implications that this has for his or her future merit investigation. Apart from damage to self-esteem, exclusion from school can have other effects on young people and it appears that very little has been done to elicit their perceptions of this.

Teachers are undoubtedly in a difficult position, trying to meet the needs of both the individual disruptive or difficult pupil and others attending school. Schools differ tremendously in their capacity to tolerate and deal effectively with pupils experiencing emotional and behavioural difficulties. This depends on their philosophy and determination to help such young people. The skills and experience of the teacher determine whether the young person can be catered for (Lowenstein, 1990).

When talking with parents Galloway found that: 'It was clear . . . in the interviews that by no means all the children presented problems at home as well as school' (Galloway, 1982, p. 208). This begs the question of what part, therefore, do schools and teachers play in the exclusion process?

McLean (1987) studied six schools with low exclusion and minimal disruption rates and found that they shared a child centred ideology with whole school, flexible discipline systems and support structures. There was a positive, proactive style of pupil management and much involvement of senior staff with 'problem' pupils. Galloway (1982) concluded that schools with a well developed form-teacher pastoral-care system tended to have lower rates of disruptive behaviour while McManus (1987) found that such schools probably had fewer exclusions.

There are, then, variables within a school which can significantly contribute to the exclusion or non-exclusion of pupils. McLean concludes that: 'Because there is no widely accepted evidence for one major cause or several minor causes of disruption, the choice of solutions is ideological. The choice depends on, and to a certain extent reflects, the values of the school' (McLean, 1987, p. 304).

Lowenstein (1990) argues that exclusion from school is damaging to young people in that it leads to either a feeling of rejection or an unhealthy feeling of power that they can make it happen (see also Cullingford and Morrison, and de Pear and Garner in this volume). He believes that there is little evidence to show that exclusion has any positive effect upon the subsequent behaviour of the pupil and states that:

It is vital for those who are involved in dealing with young-sters who may ultimately be expelled or excluded to be aware of what can be done in the first instance to prevent such deci-sions being made and under what circumstances they might be necessary.

(Lowenstein, 1990, p. 35)

While working in a centre for young people who had been excluded from school, I carried out an investigation into their perceptions of the centre and their schools (John, 1991). In this study I sought to find out what they thought were good and bad things about the centre compared to their mainstream school. The major negative point raised was that the centre was small and students had very little choice of friendship group – just because they have all been excluded from school it does not mean that they have anything else in common. This made me aware of the fundamental importance of the role of the school in a social context for its pupils, which is something which has subsequently been emphasised over the years in my conversa-tions with young people. Students also missed playing team games and further resented the restricted academic curriculum (we had no science and language laboratories or on-site sporting facilities).

These points were the immediate negative experiences of a small group of young people who had been excluded from school. From my own experience there may be further nega-tive consequences for excluded pupils in the future. These may be related to employment prospects, college applications and status in society in general. While being in the centre was seen as a positive experience in many respects by all pupils, there are definite disadvantages. This has been one of the moti-vations for my research in finding out more about what could have been done to keep such young people in mainstream education.

Through conversations with my students there can be little doubt that mainstream schools have failed to meet their needs, yet that is where most of these young people would prefer to be educated. Many people see young people experiencing emotional and behavioural difficulties as 'bad' and 'naughty'. This is a doubly handicapping special educational need. Learning difficul-ties arouse compassion; emotional and behavioural difficulties

arouse anger and frustration. Young people with learning difficulties get help with their difficulties; those with emotional and
behavioural difficulties get punished for theirs.

METHODOLOGY

I used the ethnographic method of data collection because this
method intends to gather data which describe both the behaviour and perceptions of the 'actors' who are being studied. I
believe that the notion of the self-concept of the pupil is of paramount importance when looking at their behaviour within the
schooling system; that an individual's experience and, therefore,
perception is subjectively real to him or her. If we, from the
objective perspective of an outsider, deny their reality we can
only move further away from our own understanding of their
behaviour (Plummer, 1983).

I believe that pupils' perspectives – especially those of pupils
excluded from school – are marginalised and that either they are
denied a voice altogether or the perspective of the teachers is
held up as 'the truth'. Galloway *et al.* found that:

> The significance of an event can vary from individual to indi-
> vidual depending on his part in it. The fact that pupils and
> teachers may describe the same event in different ways does
> not mean that either description is false.
>
> (Galloway *et al.*, 1982, p. 48)

In this research I wanted to hear the pupil's perspective and
was not concerned with looking at the school's official versions
of what happened. The official records of the schools will undoubtedly contain a different version of events. Humphries (1981)
studied the perspectives of elderly people reflecting on school
experiences in the early part of the century. He argues that education was intended to elevate working-class children to middle-class
morality and that the only way to study the resistance of these
impositions was through oral history because the official records
so often distort the evidence.

My study was phenomenological in orientation and ethnographic in context. Critics of the interpretative approach claim
that it is methodologically unsound. Their primary argument is
that it is not scientific and that, in general, it is impossible to
make the necessary predictions in scientific terms owing to the

small number of cases being studied. Positivist researchers argue that their methods are more rigorous, scientific and pure. The ontological and epistemological assumptions of positivist research paradigms cause researchers to set up investigations which exclude the subjective and are based on the notion that there is such a thing as objective reality which can be measured and proven. I would argue that such procedural purity is untenable in research in the social scientific area and that we, as researchers, bring to it our own beliefs, attitudes and values which must be acknowledged. Positivist research tools such as questionnaires can only gather data looked for by the researcher because of the prescriptive nature of questions and the fact that the outcome may be biased by the way that the question is phrased. I believe that interpretative research is not therefore more subjective than positivist research, it is merely that its subjectivity is more overtly stated. I have chosen to work within a phenomenological framework because I want to know the students' perceptions, not affirm or deny my own.

Such an approach to data gathering has a long tradition. During the nineteenth century researchers took a great interest in personal documents, oral histories and life stories. The tradition in Chicago sociology at the University of Chicago 1920–55 took this approach still further. This tradition was concerned with researching marginalised individuals and groups and urged researchers to pursue through field observation and life-history work the detailed, the particular and the experiential. Chicago sociology emphasised how critical it was to understand the perspective of the 'actors'. Values and attitudes were studied alongside the objective, the need to look at how people make sense of and understand their own world was stressed as crucial (Plummer, 1983).

This seems to me to underpin my fundamental beliefs in my research. In order to understand the ways in which excluded students perceive and make sense of their experiences I must ask them and therefore gain knowledge from the individual's account of his or her own behaviour, its causes and effects. Young people have a right to be heard, their views are both relevant and enlightening.

In my research I carried out unstructured interviews which have been used as data collection techniques in many different research projects, both on their own and with observational material and personal documents. They have been used in the collection of life histories, oral accounts and to clarify and expand personal documents such as diaries (Burgess, 1984).

I asked students to look back on their mainstream schooling and tell me their stories, feelings and views on a past experience. Interviews are a useful way to gain access to past events, life history and details of situations which the researcher did not witness (Burgess, 1984). Unstructured interviews give scope for the interviewer to probe deeply in the conversation and to introduce new material into the discussion. Cottle remarks: 'Without allowing people to speak freely we will never know what their real intentions are, and what the true meaning of their worlds might be' (Cottle, 1978, p. 12).

In order to help the reader to picture these students when reading the accounts of the interviews I describe them in terms of their home situation and a brief educational history.

Colin

Colin is sixteen and lives in the inner city in a housing association property with his parents. He has attended one comprehensive school and had five periods of exclusion lasting two to fourteen days over a four-month time-span. He then attended an off-site education unit until his placement at the centre in year 11.

Colin lacks confidence, having poor literacy and numeracy skills which he masks by putting on a front of physical and verbal bravado. In private he will acknowledge his learning difficulties and is a caring person who is supportive of both staff and his peers. He is liked by other pupils in the centre.

Charlene

Charlene is sixteen and is an African–Caribbean pupil who lives in a housing association property in the inner city. She lives with her mother, a lone parent who works part-time and is in receipt of Family Income Supplement. She has attended two comprehensive schools, having left the first one voluntarily after several periods of exclusion. Charlene lasted a very short time in her second school before being permanently excluded. She was out of school for two months before attending an off-site education unit for one term prior to coming to the centre.

Charlene has some learning difficulties which I believe are part of the cause of her low self-esteem which she masks by being 'stroppy' and very demanding. She does not communicate very readily, is monosyllabic and a loner in the centre. She is an independent young woman whose trendy image is very important to her. Charlene finds it hard to take on some responsibility for her difficulties at times and finds it easier to blame other people. She has a strong sense of her own culture but I feel that her feeling of self worth has been damaged by living in a racist society (Mac an Ghaill, 1988; Troyna and Williams, 1987).

Luke

Luke is sixteen and lives in the inner city with his 'guardian'. He has presented difficulties from a very early age and was excluded from primary education for months at a time. He was statemented as having special educational needs while in primary school. His secondary education has been in a special school where he has had several periods of exclusion, the final one being permanent and precipitating his placement at the centre. His home life has been very unstable from infancy with periods in the care of the local authority and various relatives.

Luke has low self-esteem yet appears very sure of himself. His literacy and numeracy skills are poor and he often refuses point blank to attempt anything written. He is a friendly young man yet can be extremely violent, which leads to his peers being very wary of him.

Margaret

Margaret is sixteen and lives in a council house outside the city with her mother and brother. She has attended one comprehensive school and had a period of six months out of school after being excluded permanently. Her next educational placement was at an off-site unit until she came to the centre in year 11. Margaret has had a turbulent childhood, having coped with the death of one parent and the severe illness of another as well as periods of homelessness.

Despite all this Margaret is a friendly and mature young woman, who has good communication skills and is appreciative of the help that she has received. She has low self-esteem when it comes to her academic abilities yet is quite easily motivated and has enjoyed some measure of success in this area. Her attendance has been fairly erratic but I believe this has, in part, been due to the long distance which she has to travel in order to get to the centre.

Carl

Carl is sixteen and lives with his siblings and his mother who is a lone parent in receipt of income support. They live on a large council housing estate in what is predominantly a white, working-class area of the city. His difficulties in school are documented from year 7 in a comprehensive school where he had several periods of exclusion. He was statemented as having special educational needs before his permanent exclusion and was then sent to a residential special school. He has been out of school for long periods of time having been excluded for four months from his special school before returning to be permanently excluded shortly afterwards. He then had to wait for five months before we were able to offer him a place at the centre.

Carl has very little confidence in his academic ability and often refuses point blank to attempt any tasks requiring literacy skills. Through my experience of working with him I would say that he has very low self-esteem and, to a certain extent, he has compensated for this by becoming extremely adept at stealing cars. In other ways, Carl is a mature and caring young man who listens to others and is able to take responsibility for his actions. Despite his occasional violent outbursts Carl is well respected and liked by peers and staff.

Martin

Martin has just turned sixteen and lives in the inner city with his parents. He has attended one comprehensive school and has had several periods of exclusion leading to a permanent exclusion in year 10.

He is the least mature of all our students and is very dis-organised and attention seeking. Martin has a very short concentration span, even when apparently well motivated to complete the task. He is constantly wandering around disrupt-ing the other students, who find him difficult to be with and are very dismissive of him, yet he is a very caring and friendly young man.

THE ROLE OF SELF-CONCEPT IN PUPIL BEHAVIOUR

My research suggests that excluded pupils have low self-esteem even though many of them present a front of self-confidence or even arrogance. In the late 1960s and early 1970s much research was done into the nature of self-concept and the effects of low self-esteem upon individuals and their schooling (Barker Lunn, 1970; Burns, 1977; Pederson, 1966; Thomas, 1973). Maines and Robinson (1988, p. 4.) define a person's self-concept as: 'his perception of his unique personal characteristics such as appearance, ability, temperament, physique, attitudes and beliefs. These determine his view of his position in society and his value to and his relationships with other people.' It has been suggested that self-concept has three aspects: self-image, ideal self and self-esteem (Lawrence, 1973; Maines and Robinson, 1988).

Self-image is the idea that we have of our social, intellectual and physical self which we obtain and modify according to not only how we are accepted and valued by 'significant others' such as parents, teachers and peers but also the events we experience. Often these experiences are of an extreme or persistent negative nature, occurring in childhood, such as physical, emotional and sexual abuse (Bass and Davis, 1988; Mearns and Thorne, 1988).

Ideal self is our image of what we would ideally like to be and is based upon our knowledge of qualities which we know are valued from our interactions with 'significant others'.

Self-esteem is the degree of respect that a person has for himself or herself and affects us all in our ways of interacting with others and in our behaviours. The greater the difference between our self-image and our ideal self, the lower our self-esteem is. Pupils with low self-esteem will find it difficult to attempt new ways of behaving. They will cling to old patterns of behaviour, regardless of how much trouble they get into, in order to behave in a way which is consistent with their poor self-image (Maines and Robinson, 1988).

This then becomes a self-fulfilling prophecy, with adults responding to the negative behaviour rather than what underlies or causes the behaviour. Given that behaviour is mistakenly seen as an intrinsic part of the person rather than a symptom of underlying distress, the young person will begin to internalise the negative messages that everyone around is giving and continue to believe that he or she of no value (Mearns and Thorne, 1988). The themes identified in my interviews with these young people illustrate this (John, 1993).

THEMES IN PUPIL–TEACHER RELATIONSHIPS

Respect

The issue of lack of respect by staff was a common grievance expressed by the students in all the interviews. Indeed, it is widely expressed by the majority of young people with whom I work whether in the centre or in mainstream schools.

COLIN	The teachers gotta show us respect before we show them respect.
MARTIN	Innit?
CHARLENE	Yeah.
COLIN	It's true . . . They didn't respect me at all so I didn't respect them. No-one respects me, I don't respect them. I respected Mr Midford a lot 'cos he respected me a lot . . . He had to do his job – that used to mean me getting into trouble but he was a nice man.

Being treated with respect is a key issue in self concept work. If we are to value ourselves we need to be made to feel valued by 'significant others'. Lack of respect by teachers reinforces the low self esteem of the students and often has the effect of making them feel that they are being treated as young children.

P.J	What about the other teachers that you liked, did you respect them?'
COLIN	Mmmm.'
P.J.	Why?'
COLIN	'Cos they respected me they didn't treat me like a kid, right? Didn't treat me like a two year old. You know you don't treat me like a kid. I've had a lot of teachers treat me like a kid, right? If you're gonna treat me like a kid an' not respect me, right, I'll just muck about. If you want me to act like a kid then I will.

The feeling of not being respected was mainly generated by the way that teachers spoke to the pupils.

CARL   I didn't like the attitude from the members of staff.

COLIN   It's the tone of voice.

CHARLENE   'Come over here and pick up that book NOW! Go on'. Just 'cos they're a teacher.

COLIN   Yeah, you can tell by the tone of voice, innit? Like for instance, if Pippa asks Carl to pick up that book it'd be, 'Oh Carl, can you please hand me that book', but if it were Lewis now, he'd say, 'Get me that book!'

Fairness

Fairness was an issue for these students in that they felt that they were not listened to.

COLIN   They didn't sit down and say, 'Why did you knock off school?', something like that. At the end of the day he gave me a note, saying, 'Right, get out. I don't want to see you again'. That was it.

This issue was also highlighted with positive comments by students.

P.J.   What was it about the German teacher and your welfare officer that was different?

MARGARET They liked me. I liked them because they respected me and that was just really nice. Like Ann, she would listen to what I 'ad to say and understand my side an' understand the teacher's side as well.

COLIN   My head of year, right? He used to go into a classroom an' he'd say, 'How are you doing, Colin?', an' we'd sit down an' have a chat, you know.

The students also felt that they had been picked on at times.

COLIN   He goes, 'Colin, pick that up!' I goes, 'No 'cos I didn't put it on the floor. Why should I pick it up?' There's everyone round me, right? But he got to pick me, yeah?'

CHARLENE   You're allowed to wear rings but not so many rings, only one or two. I wasn't the only one who had loads of rings.

The following example illustrates how a pupil perceived an incident as very unfair and the power as all on the teacher's side. When it came to a confrontation with a member of staff it appeared that it was always the pupils that were deemed to be in the wrong.

MARGARET They always take the teacher's point of view. It was just about most of the time. Everyone didn't want to help me, they didn't care. They want to hear what they want to hear, that was it really. . . . I didn't like it at all, I mean I didn't think it was fair. It's not very nice when you're in school an' you don't get any support an' they won't listen to you an' it goes on an' they still won't listen to you, like no-one's listening to you. It's a really horrible feeling.

Such incidents serve only to reinforce the students' feeling of not being valued. If they have low self-esteem these perceived negative messages will become internalised, lowering their feeling of self worth. Young people with low self-esteem internalise the negative messages that they receive and seem to generalise these. This becomes apparent in that the students felt that staff did not like or care about them, although it is hard to believe that 'every single teacher' felt this way.

COLIN They've always got someone they like the most and they've always got someone they hate the most, right? In Linkside, right, every single teacher hated me.

One student felt that staff had not cared enough about her to help her to succeed in school.

MARGARET My head of year, . . . if I had done something, she was more interested in the other person . . . not trying to help me, trying to tell me where I've gone wrong or whatever, or 'Do you realise what you're doin'?', or things like that. It's all about them, them, them an' . . . not stopping me . . . trying to help me out a bit . . . Stupid.

Trust

Trust is an important aspect of any good relationship. Our self-image can be damaged considerably by negative experiences such

as abuse of any kind. Such abuse of children by adults is fundamentally an abuse of trust, hence trust becomes an issue of
primary importance to these young people. It appears from the
data that these students feel little mutual trust in their relationships with many teachers.

LUKE   So he breaks his word ... when it comes to the
            thing, it's a completely different story.
COLIN   Have you ever said to a student, 'take this to so-
            an'-so', another teacher in the school? Like a little
            messenger, to take to the other teacher?
P.J.   Sometimes I'd say it.
COLIN   Right, and that's what our teacher always used to do,
            right? But he never ever done on me an' I used to say,
            'What's wrong? Don't you trust me?', an' he used to
            say, 'No, Colin, I don't. I don't trust you, not one bit'.

Humiliation

For students with a fragile self-concept, public humiliation is an
intrinsic attack upon their self-esteem. Students reported many
incidences of having been shown up by teachers which added to
their resentment.

COLIN   He always tried to show us up, all the time.
CHARLENE   Teachers show you up in front of other people as
            well.

Colin, whose low self-esteem comes, in part, from having difficulties with learning, recounted another way in which he felt
shown up.

COLIN   If we was doing a discussion he knew I wouldn't
            read, right? An' then he used to show me up by
            saying 'Colin, will you read this out?', knowing that
            I can't read it an' I just used to look up an' say,
            'Sir, I can't read it'. You know, one of those things,
            can't do it. That did show me up. That showed me
            up something rotten. It would show anyone up, you
            know, them things. I used to go all red, you know,
            but it was horrible. He used to do it on purpose
            'cos he knew I couldn't do it.

Racism/gender

Some students highlighted the issue of racism in schools. One student in particular, being African–Caribbean, had experienced what she perceived to be a lot of racism in her own mainstream schooling. This was supported by other students. There is a feeling that groups of black pupils are threatening to staff and that they will often get moved on when chatting when groups of white pupils will not.

> CHARLENE   They're just feisty, man, innit? I know they're racist just by the way they look at me. They pick on black kids like me and then say it's our fault. They say they're not racist but they are.

The two young women whom I interviewed both alleged that there were times when they felt that they had been treated differently because of their gender. Charlene said that staff gave her harsher punishments than the boys for physical assaults on other students.

> P.J.   Do you think there's been times when you've been treated ... in a certain way or differently, 'cause you're a girl?
>
> MARGARET   Mrs Ford said, 'Oh, you come into school and you don't wear your make up an' you get all moody', and she goes, 'You're better off coming to school and start wearing your make-up again'. An' I thought that was really stupid, really.

Margaret also drew attention to the language used by some staff.

> MARGARET   He called me a tart once, that was way out of order.

Physical contact

There was also discussion about times when staff had physical contact with students which provoked them into reacting violently themselves. Such behaviour is difficult to cope with in mainstream schools as it puts other pupils and staff at risk physically. I believe that these situations need to be looked upon differently; indeed I believe that we should ask ourselves when physical contact with young people *is* appropriate. There are, undoubtedly, several

young people in our schools who cannot bear physical contact.
I would assert that it is likely that such pupils have been subjected
to inappropriate physical contact in their past and that, when it
happens in school, their reaction to it stems from all the feelings
of powerlessness and fear stored up from previous experiences
which is vented as anger. This may go some way to explain what
staff often see as an over-reaction by students.

MARTIN   I walked out, he grabbed me an' he started draggin'
me back into the room by my neck, so I just turned
round an' went smack!

MARGARET So I walked off and this teacher called me and I
looked behind and I just carried on walking and
she came up behind me and grabbed me. So I just
turned around an' hit her. But she did grab my hair
and that was it, really, . . . I got suspended for that.

LUKE   An' they don't listen, an' they're close near you an'
they gets hit an' then they go, 'Oh, we tried to
control 'im', but you're warnin' 'em to go away.
You're tellin' 'em if they go near you an' start
handlin' you they're gonna get hit. . . . This teacher,
she threw [something unintelligible] in my face so
I put it back in her face an' she drag me up, 'oldin'
my 'and an' I just told 'er to let go before I punch
'er in the face an' Mr Church comes in an' says,
'Look, let him go!', 'cos Mr Church knows.

THEMES INVOLVING THE PUPIL'S ROLE

Having a laugh

'Having a laugh' is an important strategy for young people when
dealing with boredom at school. It can also be used by pupils to
make teachers feel uncomfortable or excluded. Woods (1979) sees
laughter as a form of resistance and says that both disruption
and truancy can often be enjoyable activities especially compared
to the dullness of daily life. He states that:

Some pupils, already alienated from school by virtue of
their background, social class and culture and similarly structurally located in school as their parents are in work, also
cope, largely through humour and laughter. For them, in fact,

it transforms the situation into one that they consider is of advantage to them.

(Woods, 1979, p. 222)

MARGARET   I suppose it was just for a laugh, sort of thing. I would laugh at school a lot.

COLIN   An' we want to have fun, you know. If it takes throwing frogs around the classroom, that's what it takes.

My research data not only reinforce the importance of having a laugh but also suggest that these pupils have taken on the role of the person who ensures that everyone else can have one. This role in their peer group was also seen as a contributory factor in getting into trouble. Longworth-Dames (1977) asserts that, by secondary-school age, pupils will have a definite reputation to maintain and that labelling means that they are also unable to lose face:

Peer acceptance is often a stronger determinant of behaviour than adult acceptance, especially where the latter precludes the former. Excluded children could be behaving in a very socially precise way to maintain their image in their sub culture.

(Longworth-Dames, 1977, p. 171)

This certainly seems to be the case for these students.

MARTIN   Class entertainer, innit? They gee you up an' you do it for them, innit?

COLIN   They used to say, 'Colin, throw a rubber at the teacher's 'ead', an' I'd do it. I'd just do it for the crack.

MARGARET   Some of 'em would encourage me ... 'Oh go on, go on, go on, go on,' an' they used to be the goody goodies in the class and I used to be the one taking notice of them, doin' what they're sayin' and gettin' into trouble.

Reputation

The students also highlighted the importance of 'reputation' and its effect upon their behaviour and that of the teacher (see, also, Marshall in this volume). This reinforces my assertion that the problem of low self-esteem can be exacerbated by teachers labelling students as disruptive, causing them to become more challenging.

CHARLENE The teachers just know that I'm bad, everything
          that I do I was gonna get in trouble for – they just
          make it worse, really.
COLIN   As soon as you get a bad reputation, that's it.
CHARLENE Then you just get in more trouble again innit?

This feeling was echoed by Margaret in her interview.

MARGARET As soon as I got into the first bit of trouble, everything
          went from there, . . . I can't remember what it was – I
          think it was something, just something stupid like
          skiving off school – and ever since then, from that first
          day, they've been watching out for me.

Most students that I interviewed individually felt that they had
been labelled as 'trouble' because they had siblings who had
attended the school and had been difficult to handle.

MARGARET Because once when I got into trouble they were
          like, 'Oh, you're Peter's sister', just like that.
COLIN   I knew that they didn't trust me anyway 'cos my
          sister wasn't exactly Miss Popular you know.'

Cicourel and Kitsuse (1968) argue that the labelling of young
people by peers and teachers can lead to a delinquent career.
Wright (1987) uses the following quote from an African–
Caribbean student which illustrates my point:

  I suppose it makes me behave bad, they pick you out, on your
  colour. They tend to say, oh well, he's black, so it's to be
  expected, they're bound to do that, so when they give you
  that kind of attitude, you think, oh well, blow them, if that's
  what they think, why not act like it.

                                        (Wright, 1987, p. 183)

Robinson and Maines (1988) explain this by putting forward the
notion that if a person's ideal self is completely unobtainable he or
she may then substitute one which is more easily achieved. It may
be argued that a young person who is consistently feeling that he
or she is 'not good enough' will be pushed into becoming a member
of a 'delinquent' group because within that group he or she will
be seen as 'OK' and his or her self- esteem will rise within that
situation. As teachers there can be little doubt that we may see
ourselves as 'significant others' in a young person's life and that, as

such, we can and do influence a pupil's self-esteem (Pedersen, 1966; Zahran, 1967). Burns (1982) stated that:

> Teachers can reinforce the poor opinion a child already has of himself when he begins school, but they can also, in fact, help to reverse this opinion and to create in the child a more positive view of himself and his abilities.
>
> (Burns, 1982, p. vi)

Aptitude

In the individual interviews I asked the students whether they felt that the work that they had been set was within their capability. Many young people with low self-esteem will often refuse to attempt work which they feel is beyond them or they may say that it is 'crap' or 'boring'. Both of these strategies are employed in order to reduce the risk of failure and to protect their self-concept.

MARGARET   I found it hard ... an' I didn't get any help with it. Like sometimes I'd get an easy piece of work an' I'd think, 'Yeah, this is all right'. I used to like that. As long as it was straightforward an' I could do it then I would do it.

COLIN   Some of the work they used to set me was ridiculous, you know. I couldn't even flippin' read it 'cos of how long the words were an' all that. An' I was just saying, 'How do you expect me to do this?', an' they'd say, 'Well, you should be good enough to do it', an' I'd say, 'Well, listen ... I'm not, so I want to do something else', an' they'd say, 'No, do it!'. An' that was what it was like, you know.

Some of the students that I have worked with over the past three years have survived quite well in mainstream education with the help of learning and behavioural support units. Quite a number of these young people have ended up being excluded from school when this level of support has been withdrawn. This has been the experience of one of the students that I interviewed.

COLIN   The first and second years I was in remedial for bad behaviour and in the third year they said, 'Right, go into mainstream, go to all the proper classes'. But I wasn't used to having all these kids around, you know, all my mates. It was just my luck that all the bad kids were put into the one class an' that was all of us. They just stuck me back in, they didn't ask me nothin', they didn't ask me shit. They just said, 'You're going'. From the day I went into mainstream things just went wrong.

Sanctions

There was discussion about the nature of sanctions employed in the students' schools, particularly with reference to the threat of exclusion – the ultimate sanction – and its efficacy

P.J.   In the end did you want to be thrown out of school or not?'

MARGARET   I was worried by ... what my mum might think but I knew damn well that if I was to get into trouble I'd be out.

P.J.   It sounds like you feel kind of a lot of pressure really from the school by the end of ...

MARGARET   Yeah.

P.J.   What effect did that have on you?

MARGARET   It made me a lot worse. I think that's what did make me worse actually.

P.J.   If you look back now and try to put yourself in their position what would you do with ... a student like yourself? What would you do to try and help?

MARGARET   I don't think ... I'd punish them but they used to punish me by suspendin' me but I don't think that's a punishment. I would ... like my mum says, 'God, she's got five weeks off of school. That ain't punishment. That's great, innit? That ain't punishment at all'. I think punishment is going out collectin' the litter or somethin'. ... Stayin' behind at school for two weeks every day ... stayin' behind. But they didn't never used to punish me like that you know. I think I, if I was them, I'd punish them and talk to 'em, try and think, guide or something, ... I dunno, just I don't think suspending is a punishment actually. If I had really wanted to have time off of school for the summer, I suppose all I had to do was get into trouble and be suspended.

Notion of self

The notion of self-concept is central to the humanist perspective of psychology. At the centre of this model is: 'the individual's perception of himself (his self image) and his unique perception of others and the world around him' (Davie, 1989, p. 53).

From within this paradigm, effective learning and positive behaviour may be seen as a result of the ways in which teachers and pupils interact (Reid *et al.*, 1988). From my data I would argue that the young people I interviewed have low self-esteem. This is reflected in their feelings of not being liked or cared about, in their perceiving very little trust or respect; in fact, it is apparent through everything that they have said. It is, perhaps, summarised by the following conversation.

MARGARET Back then I wouldn't 'ave thought by now I'd be, doin' me GCSEs. I don't think me mum would either. I don't think anyone would.

COLIN Teachers really didn't expect me to do work. I could just go in there an' not say a word, right? An' they'd write 'excellent' 'cos that's a real vast improvement to what I was in the last lesson, you know.

P.J. Do you think they should have expected more of you?

COLIN I wouldn't have expected more out of me myself at that time.

I would argue that the concept of low self-esteem goes some way to explain what the difficulties have been for these young people who have been excluded from school.

IMPROVING PUPIL–TEACHER RELATIONSHIPS

I asked the students what might have helped them to stay in mainstream schooling. The suggestion was made that *good* teachers would make a difference. When I asked what characteristics made a good teacher the students said:

COLIN Sense of humour.

CARL Someone you can tell 'em something an' they ain't gonna go round, sit in the staffroom an' tell all the rest, innit?

COLIN Personality.

MARTIN Good at controlling their anger.

Margaret highlighted 'labelling' and felt that being treated as a 'normal' pupil would have made all the difference to her:

MARGARET   I think if the teachers wouldn't have looked at me as Peter's sister . . . they could've . . . accepting me as just a normal student doin' her work. . . . What I done wrong first of all, they wouldn't of judged me on that.

The students talked about what had made it easier for them in the centre:

MARGARET   I get a lot of respect off you and John . . . and trust . . . and we talk to each other as if we were friends. You help me, you don't go, 'Oh, Mrs so and so'; it's 'Pip'. It's a shame that people can't start off in a school like the centre. Maybe if it was bigger, like a normal big comprehensive. School could be like that. Just get on with your work. . . . They can teach you without upsetting anyone.

I believe that those students who took their GCSEs at the centre were motivated by doing so and that it raised their self-esteem to be continually convinced that they were capable of this. In conversation with Colin, I asked him what made him attend the centre on days when he was tired and when he had not done so anywhere else.

COLIN   Even though I've been out all night partying an' drinkin' till five .. six in the morning, that's because I want my GCSEs, you know.

Their final suggestion for what might have helped a student to stay in mainstream schooling was to have a part placement in an off-site unit to support them.

CHARLENE   With my brother now, when . . . I don't know why he got thrown out or whatever . . . but he used to go to Longhill two or three times a week an' come to Sunnydale still. They should've done that.

P.J.   Right. So, if you could've come somewhere like this a day or two a week . . . you could've stayed in school, yeah?

CHARLENE   Yeah.

This is something which we tried successfully in our centre.

CONCLUSION

Having undertaken this research and reflected upon it, drawing on my wider experience, I feel that I could make several recommendations that would improve the situation for these young people. However, my analysis also tells me that the prioritisation necessary to meet their needs is unlikely to happen because the policy context, both educational and economic, is driving us in the opposite direction. Nevertheless, I should like to identify a number of strategies that would improve the situation were there to be a culture that would support them.

Young people experiencing emotional and behavioural difficulties need a great deal of support to maintain their places in mainstream schooling. This, in turn, requires both financial and human resources in order for it to be a positive and successful experience (see also Parsons in this volume). Ultimately this also depends upon the ethos of the school and the commitment of its teachers. Funding and training are a core requirement in order to bring about the changes necessary to ensure that these young people can succeed in our system.

The integration of pupils with special needs into mainstream schools, advocated by the Warnock Committee and embedded in the Education Act 1981, gives teachers the responsibility for meeting a vast range of needs within their classroom. This requires a large amount of work, including producing differentiated work for young people with a wide range of abilities and supporting their learning. In-class support becomes the order of the day, rather than the withdrawal of young people requiring this level of learning or behavioural support. Many teachers do not have the confidence or expertise necessary to work in this way and such a fundamental change in ways of working requires proper resourcing in order to be successful.

The introduction of the National Curriculum and associated assessment has led to teachers being under tremendous pressure with an increasingly heavy workload (Muschamp et al., 1992). This, in turn, means that staff are already overstretched in time and resources and have very little time or energy to deal constructively with pupils with challenging behaviour (see also Searle in this volume). The plethora of government legislation has undermined the professionalism of teachers and served to lower their self-esteem and if we do not respect and support our teachers how can we expect them continually to respect and support our pupils?

In my research, the pupils had plenty of positive suggestions to make when they were asked and I wonder whether it might be a good idea to evaluate our practice in this way more often. It can be a threatening thing to do but does enhance the teacher/pupil relationship and makes students feel far more valued. As teachers we must take on the responsibility of making and maintaining good relationships with our pupils. As argued previously, self-esteem is of fundamental importance and teachers and 'significant others' should be aware of this and take into account how low self-esteem can affect behaviour. Every gesture and word can have a profound effect upon another person and negative messages will be internalised by those with a poor self-image.

Schools are agents of socialisation, reflecting the white, middle-class values of our society and intrinsically valuing those who are born into such homes. Schools should be making a more sustained and overt effort truly to value cultural diversity which seems to be of vital importance when looking at success and failure in our schooling system.

If more people were familiar with this way of thinking it would help them to interpret what is happening for these young people. This may, in turn, enable them to look upon some pupils differently and to understand them better. I hope that this model will be taken seriously by staff and that it may inform practice through both formal and informal In Service Education and Training (INSET) work.

Policies such as those concerning integration appear to be made not necessarily to meet the needs of the pupils but to meet the needs of the pupils as perceived by other people. This is not the same thing. Such pupils do succeed and achieve in small units on-site in schools where their socialising can take place in the main body of the school. Mainstream schools can offer these pupils the opportunity to take part in team games and use the facilities that smaller off-site units do not have. Is it not possible to put the two good things together in an attempt to meet the needs of these young people? I believe that they should have a safe, secure environment within a mainstream school where their academic education can take place, yet still have the benefits afforded by a larger establishment.

These young people, above all, have a real need to be treated with respect, to have trusting relationships and to be in a situation where adults have a true commitment to valuing the pupils' culture, raising their self-esteem and their achievement. As teachers, we are failing these pupils if we do not give them the positive regard that we all, as human beings, need. Excluding them from our schools is merely perpetuating the vicious circle of failure in their lives, engendering the feeling within them of being worthless and sending them out into life without the necessary skills to cope. By excluding these young people I believe that we are colluding in the construction of their 'deviancy' and creating future generations of pupils whom schools cannot educate.

Part III

Preventive strategies and policies

Chapter 13

The Staff Sharing Scheme
A school-based management system for working with challenging child behaviour

Dinah Gill and Jeremy Monsen

INTRODUCTION

This chapter describes the development of an action-based project designed to assist teachers to become more effective in managing the challenging behaviour of children and young people. The Staff Sharing Scheme was originally developed in New Zealand during a period when additional Government funding to schools was limited. Schools were expected to re-examine their use and management of existing resources. The Staff Sharing Scheme involves an educational psychologist training a group of staff to operate a problem-solving framework and then to support its operation through consultation. Underpinning the consultative basis of the Scheme is a problem-analysis/-solving framework which staff use to clarify problem situations, plan and evaluate interventions. To support this model, staff also receive training in specific process and content skills. Once training is completed the Staff Sharing Group meets regularly to suggest, devise and evaluate interventions. The Scheme also focuses on increasing the educational psychologist's effectiveness by providing a model which allows for more meaningful input to teachers and pupils. The Scheme was brought to England in 1991 and following further developments is currently being used in several English schools.

In summary, the Staff Sharing Scheme aims:

1 To establish within a school a resource network of staff who meet regularly to assist each other in solving problems, using a structured problem-analysis/-solving framework.
2 To train staff in behaviour observation, analysis and management as processes for measuring and modifying problem situations and behaviour.

3 To increase staff competence in communication with pupils, colleagues, and parents/carers.
4 To encourage staff to be more objective in their perceptions of problem situations, thus reducing stress.
5 To provide staff with the opportunity for practical school-based training.
6 To encourage greater school responsibility for managing difficulties and thus reducing the need for extensive outside input.

BACKGROUND AND RATIONALE TO THE SCHEME'S DEVELOPMENT

The Staff Sharing Scheme was first implemented in New Zealand by Gill in 1982 (Gill, 1986). Since then it has developed in scope and format as a result of improvements made following its use in schools across New Zealand and in England. Despite cultural differences many of the issues which first led to the Scheme's development in New Zealand were evident in England. In England in 1991 there was a real demand for schools to manage more effectively the limited resources they had at their disposal. It has proved possible to adapt the scheme successfully to conditions in East London and in Kent where it has been tried so far.

In New Zealand in 1982 when the Scheme was launched in a pilot school, the term 'resources' included teachers, parents, pupils, school dental nurse, secretary, teacher's aide and the caretaker. In this, school staff members were being used in additional ways to support children within the school. For instance, it was recognised that the dental nurse was in a good position for one-to-one discussions with children. She also served as a neutral figure at times when children were engaged in conflict, becoming a valuable member of the Staff Sharing Scheme. A similar involvement occurred with the school secretary and caretaker in the East London school where the programme was first run in England.

The title 'sharing' was applied because of its non-threatening, non-hierarchical connotation and in our experience the ability of most people to share with others when encouraged to do so.

The Scheme originated from the need to find more effective ways for psychologists to work with schools who presented large numbers of referrals. The traditional approach of individual assessment and a follow-up psychological report was neither an efficient nor effective use of time. These steps did not necessarily enhance teachers' ability to learn from the referral process or develop skills for solving future problems. The view then was that to provide more meaningful input to schools the psychologist needed to shift from focusing solely on the individual child to include work with groups of children and teachers. The framework of psychological support to schools required a shift to a more consultative and preventive orientation.

It was recognised that, owing to various issues affecting the community (for example, unemployment, working parents, abuse, ineffective parenting, truancy, cultural differences), many pupils were presenting schools with a complex range of problems. These problems required a greater degree of management than the single classroom teacher was often able to provide. It was thought possible that when resources within the school and wider community were 'pooled' there would be a greater chance of having some positive effect.

A major aim of the Scheme was a need to assist staff to take more responsibility for developing their own problem-solving networks. Part of this process involved challenging some of the staff's existing belief systems. Schools believed that a referral to the link psychologist would result in some 'magical cure' or at least the psychologist would take responsibility for the 'problem pupil'. Many staff appeared to be searching for something 'wrong' within the pupil that could be identified, diagnosed, labelled and 'fixed' through the involvement of the psychologist. This internal attribution model of describing pupil problems does not recognise the many complex factors affecting children's behaviour (Christenson *et al.*, 1983). Such a view is a disservice, both to the pupil, in assuming that the problem resides solely within him or her, and to teachers, in not giving them enough credit for being able to work effectively with diverse groups of children and young people when given appropriate support. Thinking along the internal attribution model may deter teachers from making systematic attempts to implement interventions prior to involving the psychologist or other support staff.

Many staff prior to the Scheme's implementation reported that they did not know how to implement interventions, and in any case, 'that was the job of the psychologist'. They had doubts about their own abilities to solve problems and regarded problems as 'things' to be feared. Especially difficult was the 'unsolved problem' that reflected teachers' own feelings of incompetence. Hence defensiveness and an attachment to the internal attribution model is hardly surprising. Part of this self-doubt about solving problems comes from what McPherson (reported in Christenson *et al.*, 1983) describes as a perceived lack of dignity. McPherson sees dignity as being one of the core constructs which teachers use in guiding their behaviour in a range of situations. We notice this in the way a teacher walks, acts and speaks. We can be suddenly aware of its absence in ourselves and others. While dignity can be influenced by others, ultimately it is a condition that is within the control of the individual.

Lortie (1975) found that the achievement of teacher dignity comes about when the teacher is able to produce affection and respect from pupils, get work out of them and is effective in gaining their compliance. The Staff Sharing Scheme assists teachers to enhance their dignity by modifying some of their beliefs about problem situations and their roles. Westera (1985), in evaluating the Staff Sharing Scheme in New Zealand, found that training in the problem-analysis/-solving model and in learning specific content skills resulted in teachers reporting less stress and more confidence in their ability in managing children's behaviour.

A CONSULTATION MODEL AS THE BASIS FOR THE STAFF SHARING SCHEME

Before the development of the Staff Sharing Scheme most schools with which Gill was working had been used to a psychologist responding to a referral, 'seeing' a child (usually in the medical room) and then writing a report. The report usually recommended what would be in the child's best interests. Often the recommendations in the report were stated in what Argyris (1993) calls 'applicable knowledge' terms. This assumes that staff have the necessary skills and understandings to carry out the suggestions made (for example, 'Richard requires a differentiated curriculum, social skills and self-esteem training'). In Argyris's view the reports would lack 'actionable knowledge' and therefore most of the suggested interventions would not be implemented effectively. (For example, how does one differentiate and how does one run a social skills/self-esteem group?)

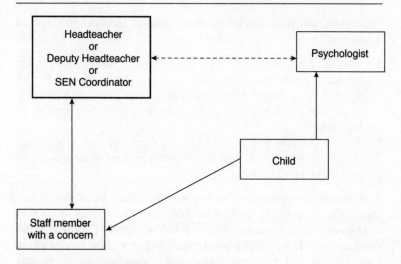

Figure 13.1   Traditional model of working

Most school requests for help were prompted by the assumption that to get extra assistance for a child or for something to happen 'we had to go through the psychologist'. Often the implication was that problems can be solved by simply providing extra adult support. It is a paradox that pupils with the greatest difficulty are often assigned the least skilled workers and that this is then perceived as an adequate solution to the problem.

The psychologist may not have discussed the 'problem' with either parents, teachers or the pupil in any depth. In many cases the report confirmed in 'esoteric' language the referrer's 'lay' impressions. In other cases cognitive data were presented but inadequately explained, which only helped to mystify the teaching–learning process. The referrer was often left with a gulf between the report and the action that would make a meaningful difference in a child's development. The psychologist's report and efforts were often of little long-term practical input. This we call the traditional model of working and is shown in Figure 13.1.

Gill found that when she checked out her concerns about the traditional model of working, schools too were dissatisfied but did not know how else to work. The two main points of concern specified by schools in New Zealand and later in England were that:

1   Psychologists were not in the school enough and their reliance upon the 'test and tell' method often left the schools with information confirming what they already knew about the pupil but with little assistance with intervention or follow-up.
2   After a referral had been made, teachers were often no more skilled or able to manage problems than they were before the psychologist's involvement.

Although an assessment and report may have been made, and there was a tangible sign that something had been done, no change had actually taken place. Bardon stated: 'people ask for services they do not really want, often because they do not know how else to get services. They make assumptions about the responsibilities of psychologists (and others) that are not always warranted' (Bardon, 1980, p. 22).

In Bardon's view:

> the educational psychologist must find ways to try to increase the impact of services offered. From such large pupil–psychologist ratios in New Zealand (1–8000) comes the necessity to offer a wider range of services, consultation with educators and parents, in-service education and co-ordination of the service of others must become necessary ways of working for educational psychologists.
>
> (Bardon, 1980, p. 23)

In Gill's mind there were compelling reasons why the way psychologists worked with schools needed to undergo a change. A consultation process underpinned with a problem-analysis/-solving framework, supported by skills training, appeared the most appropriate innovation.

Gill's early work reflected what is fairly typical in staff development approaches, namely one or two training sessions in which information is shared. Participants often report a 'feel-good' factor after attending such sessions. However, generalisation of understandings or skills back to the classroom is rare unless this is planned and supported by some on-going process. Gill therefore provided participants with a conceptual framework and the practical skills to make the Staff Sharing

Scheme work. Without this conceptual underpinning we found that staff did not have the necessary skills to work in a consultative way. Staff Sharing Meetings without these skills merely reflected the giving of advice with no understanding or motivation on the part of the teachers or, at worst, reversion to the traditional model of thinking.

ELEMENTS NECESSARY FOR EFFECTIVELY IMPLEMENTING A CONSULTATIVE MODEL

The elements necessary for working a consultation model are emphasised by Gordon *et al.* (1985) and more recently by Argyris (1993) and Wagner (1995). They note several assumptions which underlie a consultation model and which are essential to its success. The first is the assumption that consultation involves shared power and collaborative decision-making. The consultant is viewed as a resource to the consultee with power shared equally between the two. The final decision regarding the selection of interventions lies with the teachers in order for them to have 'ownership' of those interventions. A second underlying assumption is that, for most referrals, the indirect involvement of the psychologist with a pupil is more efficient than their direct support. However, indirect support (consultation) should not be viewed as being incompatible with direct work but rather as on a continuum with it. There will be certain issues where the direct involvement of the psychologist is warranted to help to clarify the dimensions of the problem situation. However, the information so gained is then fed back to the consultee to be processed along with other information within the problem-analysis/-solving model.

As a consultation process the Staff Sharing Scheme assumes the adoption of an ecological perspective when viewing pupils' behaviour. The many factors that affect children's learning and behaviour are taken into account when defining the problem areas, selecting a priority problem on which to focus and in intervention planning.

The Scheme emphasises indirect rather than direct support to pupils. They are helped indirectly through assistance provided to their classroom teacher, thereby helping greater numbers of pupils with existing resources. It also utilises psychologists' skills in more efficient ways. It ensures that resources are directed at providing intervention assistance to those people with the most invested in solving the problem. These are usually the classroom teacher, Special Needs Coordinator and parents/carers.

The Scheme affirms the principle of prevention and ensures that problem situations do not escalate and that future problems are more effectively managed by increasing the skill and knowledge of teachers. The problem-analysis/-solving model and skill development sessions are crucial to the Scheme's functioning as they help to support the consultative way of working.

Curtis and Meyers (1985) note that there are important skills which are essential when working a consultation model. They describe four skill areas:

1   interpersonal skills: such as, communication skills, rapport building, listening skills, effective questioning and negotiating techniques;
2   problem-analysis/-solving skills: that is, knowing how to identify, clarify, analyse and generate hypotheses and to evaluate the often confused problems with which people are involved;
3   content expertise: such as, specific knowledge of child development covering not only cognitive but also social-emotional and physical development, and a range of intervention approaches;
4   an understanding of systems theory: that is, understanding the process of change, understanding systems variables in classrooms and schools which reflect on the presenting problem.

The skill development sessions include learning in each of these areas.

THE CONSULTATION STEPS USED IN DEVELOPING THE STAFF SHARING SCHEME

In developing the Scheme we used the following consultation steps which are described with illustrations from both New Zealand and English schools.

Phase 1: Assessing existing school processes for managing challenging child behaviour

Testing the need for a change in model of service delivery

This involved advocating, with concrete examples, the advantages of a consultative way of working and the difficulties we were having with the traditional model. We endeavoured to test out openly our attributions and assumptions in a way that encouraged school staff to inquire and challenge us. The result was a clearer understanding of the issues involved (Argyris, 1993).

Entering into the school system and preliminary contract with the school

In our experience most of the schools we approached were prepared to try a new way of working and then review its effectiveness. The key factors for the psychologist at this stage were to have the rationale and framework of the model clear before meeting with the headteacher and school staff, and to check out and clarify any assumptions or attributions being made.

Data gathering and assessment of existing processes and resources

This involved undertaking a needs analysis of the school's existing processes for managing challenging behaviour. This was carried out through questionnaires administered to all staff who worked within the school, selected spot interviews with staff and senior management members, classroom observations and a review of school documentation (for example, policy documents on behaviour). All staff were involved in this process, including caretakers, secretaries and dinner staff.

The main questions we used are presented below followed by a discussion of the themes extracted from New Zealand and English schools.

1 Is there a need for a different way of working in the school?

2 Is there a wish for a different working model?

Most schools indicated a need for a different working relationship with the educational psychologist (and other outside support staff) but most did not know of other models or how they worked.

3 What are the number of referrals/requests being made by the school to the psychologist?

The numbers of referrals being made by schools to the psychologist ranged between ten and twenty per term. In many cases the requests arrived in batches which made it impossible for the psychologist to respond to them all on an individual basis. The schools continually stressed that formal requests were only the 'tip of the iceberg' and they would like more children 'seen' by the psychologist.

4 What are the types of referrals being made to the Psychological Service?

The types of referrals being made to the psychologist were mainly requests for help with behaviour management issues. This was supported by annual statistics data which indicated that the largest percentage of referrals were for behaviour issues in boys aged between 7 and 11 years.

5 What are the diverse range of problems with which teachers are being confronted?

The range of problems with which school staff had identified was very wide. Reference was made to not only behavioural but also intellectual, social-emotional and psycho-sexual problems. Some staff also referred to their own issues in relating to colleagues, the increasing workload, curriculum changes and lack of management and resources.

6 What are the management strategies that are being used?

The management strategies mentioned by staff covered a wide range. For example, one school's data included (described in teacher terms): behaviour management techniques (praise, rewards), peer assistance, ignoring, talking to the child/giving individual attention, talking to mother/caregiver, set limited work, growling, moaning, peer pressure, avoiding confrontations, detentions, withdrawal of privileges, regular work checks, threatening, send to headteacher or other senior staff, given classroom responsibilities.

It was apparent that within all the schools surveyed, prior to implementing the Staff Sharing Scheme, teachers said that they were using a wide range of strategies. Some staff reported success while others appeared not to be so successful. Classroom observations undertaken in several schools indicated that although certain staff said they used a wide range of strategies, in practice very few approaches were actually observed. It was inferred that staff had some understanding of basic behaviour management principles but perhaps lacked the knowledge to apply effectively their understandings. Staff also acted in ways which indicated that they did not have an objective framework for thinking about their own behaviour, the environment and the young people in their care.

Teachers were presenting themselves as resourceful skilled people, but perhaps lacked consistency of application, and required a refinement of their existing skills and some new learning to develop a more effective approach. A further point which emerged from the data and discussions was that in many instances teachers were utilising their skills alone and were isolated from any other assistance from within the school.

7 Who within the school is providing assistance with problems?

Teachers identified the following people as those from whom they either sought assistance or from whom they received it: headteacher, deputy headteacher, senior teacher.

8 What type of assistance is being made available?

In relation to help available (for example, advice, demonstration, observation, relief, share child, design work programme for child and other), the majority of teachers indicated that in the main they received advice and on occasions the child was removed for a time. There were very few instances across the schools where demonstrations occurred, or where a colleague was able to make a classroom observation to assist a teacher or where individual help to design programmes for children was available.

9 What stressors are prominent for teachers?

Staff listed a wide range of stressors. Some of those mentioned are included below, again as they appeared in the questionnaires and interview notes:

- Continual interruptions during the discussion part of a lesson.
- Children who will not own up when they have been caught out.
- Equipment/books that are borrowed and not returned and have to be chased.
- Noise – especially on wet and windy days.
- Noise – from a variable space classroom.
- Sports teams during lunch hours or after school.
- Pressure from the hierarchy.
- Constantly disruptive children.
- Trying to cater for children who range from special class to above average and 'still have time for my husband and personal interests'.
- Constant reminding to make the children work.
- Rudeness.
- Workload.
- Relationships with colleagues and parents/carers (dominating, non-supportive, undermining).

From our point of view it was important to establish, through the questionnaire and interviews, how staff perceived and felt stress, because one of the aims of the Scheme is to reduce staff perception of stress.

10 What else would staff find helpful in managing problem situations?

Most teachers left this question blank and during the spot interviews most staff reported that this question was the hardest to answer. Of those who did offer some suggestions the following responses were fairly typical: more adult assistance with behavioural management, especially the use of rewards and class contracts, more skill in being able to 'diagnose problems', more time to 'counsel' children, as well as how to solve problems more effectively.

11 What are the school procedures for managing challenging behaviour?

School procedures for managing challenging behaviour varied greatly. In one school there was a total absence of any formal procedures. Individual staff were expected to deal with 'their problem kids' alone or with limited support. In this school, problems were perceived as being within the child and 'if teachers couldn't cope it was because they were useless' (headteacher comment). In another school, an attempt had been made to develop a staged process. For example,

- Stage 1: teacher to manage pupil by self.
- Stage 2: discuss with Special Needs Coordinator.
- Stage 3: discuss at syndicate meeting.
- Stage 4; send child to headteacher.
- Stage 5; headteacher to take over; contract/reward system implemented – if improvement observed, certificate given at school assembly, if no improvement, invite parent(s) to school.

While this procedure had some merit it also demonstrates some shortcomings. The problem is again seen as largely residing within the pupil; the problem is passed up the ladder, finally coming to the attention of the headteacher. This process shifts the responsibility for action further away from the teacher. There is no attempt at joint problem-solving, therefore little change of real learning and a change in action. It is likely that the teacher will be no more skilled to deal with future difficulties. In terms of self-acceptance and credibility, staff within the school system will be motivated to continue to protect themselves by using various 'defensive routines' and the result will be that the problem situation will remain largely unchanged.

12 Who has overall responsibility in the school for ensuring the appropriate management of challenging child behaviour?

The person with overall responsibility for ensuring appropriate pupil behaviour was perceived by most staff as being the deputy headteacher and/or the headteacher. Very few staff identified that everyone has a vested interest, including pupils and parents.

13 How effective are the espoused/actual management strategies being used in the school?

During interviews, most of the headteachers and senior staff viewed the management strategies which existed in their schools as having limited effectiveness and agreed there was a need for new and creative ideas.

14 How many staff have recently attended in-service training courses on behaviour/classroom management?

In most schools visited few staff had experienced recent in-service training courses. Those who had received some training tended to report that it was mainly on curriculum-related issues.

Diagnosis, feedback and re-contracting

Soft systems and problem-based methodologies assisted us in sorting the information obtained and in presenting this back to the whole school staff (Frederickson, 1990, 1993; Robinson, 1993). The emphasis here was on trying to clarify and present the differences between the staff's espoused theories of action ('as a staff we help each other with problems') and the actual theories of action being used to deal with problem situations in their school (in fact most staff reported feeling isolated and dealt with problems on their own for fear of being seen as incompetent). We were hoping to assist staff in taking a 'snap-shot' of what was currently happening rather than what was said to be happening. For example, in many of the schools we visited, it was reported by senior management that staff 'worked in teams

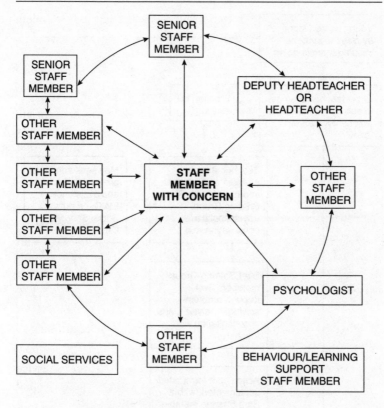

Figure 13.2 Consultative model of working

and shared problems'. Yet when this assumption was tested out very often the headteacher managed staff as individuals and staff reported feeling de-skilled and isolated (Argyris and Schön, 1974).

Following discussions and feedback of the assessment data, school staff are presented with a model of operating a problem management system within their school. The following components are central in negotiating a school's commitment to and acceptance of working with the psychologist in a more collaborative way:

1 Presenting an operational model of the Staff Sharing Scheme (see Figure 13.3).

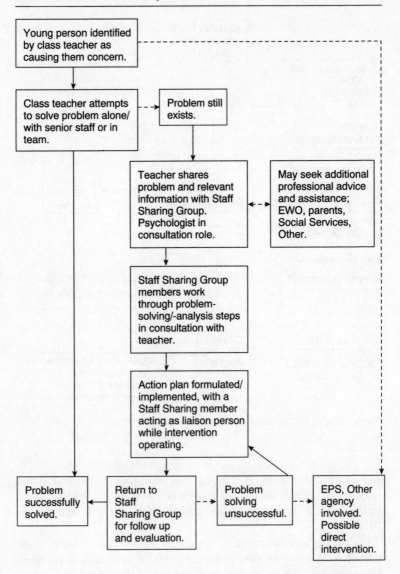

Figure 13.3   An operational model of the Staff Sharing Scheme

2   Discussing the traditional versus consultative models of work (see Figures 13.1 and 13.2).
3   Presenting the aims of the Scheme, the rationale for the problem-analysis/solving model and skills development sessions, which underpin the workings of the Scheme.
4   Outlining the content of the training sessions and the logistics of running the Scheme.
5   Outlining how the Scheme runs following training.
(Guide notes on the above are presented in the Training Manual.)

Phase 2: Skills development sessions

Action steps

The Skill Development Training Manual provides a structured account of all ten sessions. The objectives of each session are outlined along with a guided sequence for the instructor, plus supporting hand-outs and transparencies. Each session lasts approximately two hours. Further details of the content are provided in Table 13.1.

We developed the skill development sessions to enable staff to formulate behaviour management interventions following careful observation and analysis of problem situations. Training gives permission to staff to consult with others in a supportive team atmosphere rather than merely providing or receiving advice. It also ensures that staff have equivalent understanding of problem analysis, consultation and management skills, and do not feel threatened or isolated. The approach adopted also encourages staff to see their link psychologist and other support people in an equal-power role. In our experience this results in the Staff Sharing Group being more focused and productive.

Underpinning by a problem-analysis/-solving model

The Scheme is underpinned by a problem-analysis/-solving model which guides staff in structuring problems using a common framework and language. In our work with teachers we found that when they approached problem situations, they tended not to make sufficient use of the information available. They based their

Table 13.1   Relationship between the problem analysis model and the skill training sessions. This framework is used for the functioning of Phase 3 of the Staff Sharing Scheme.

Problem analysis checklist	*Corresponding skill development session*
Step 1: Defining the problem situation (a) Clarify your problem situation: • Avoid assumptions or interpretations. • Check validity of all items of information collected. • Describe behaviours objectively. • Systematically collect objective data. • Include your own personal feelings and goals. • Generate tentative hypotheses which will help guide and focus your sampling of areas of the problem situation.	*Session 1* 1 Problem-analysis-/-solving framework. 2 Behaviour analysis and behaviour management. 3 Objectivity v. subjectivity – *how to define behaviour clearly.* 4 Behavioural measurement – *how to measure behaviour.*
(b) *Sample* from the following to help build up your understanding of the problem situation: • Communicate with the child concerned. • Observe situation(s) where problem is occurring (e.g. behaviour observations). • Collect and examine work samples. • Consult records (academic and behaviour).	*Session 2* 5 Behaviour measurement: • Time sampling. • Event recording. • Duration recording. • Graphing.
• Examine environmental/classroom organisational factors (e.g. seating, grouping, instructions, difficulty level of work, adult–child and child–child relationships). • Seek comments from other staff on their views (e.g. what they have tried). • Interview parents/carers to gain their perspectives on the problem situation.	*Session 3* 6 Behaviour analysis – hypothesis generating and testing: • Baseline, trend, level. • Demonstration of behaviour change. • Graphing procedures.
(c) Seek relationships between specific pieces of information collected: • Categorise and compare items of information.	*Session 4* 7 Antecedents, behaviours, consequents. 8 Reframing behaviour – *goal setting.*
(d) Write a short description of the priority problem (or problems) bringing together all relevant items in a clear statement looking at possible causal hypotheses and ways forward. (If you have difficulty with this, consult with one or more of the following: headteacher, deputy headteacher, senior teacher, syndicate leader, other staff within your school, social services, psychological service or other agencies.)	*Session 5* 9 Antecedents and consequents – *the specifics of.* 10 Behaviour management: • Increasing behaviour. • Reducing behaviour. 11 Implementing management programmes.
Step 2: Consider approaches to problem (a) Generate possible approaches and list: • Include approaches used with similar problems previously encountered. • Include 'commonsense' or 'natural consequence' approaches.	*Session 6* 12 Behaviour management – maintenance and generalisation: • Continued individual assistance provided to each staff member for the implementation of the management programme.

Table 13.1 continued

Problem analysis checklist	Corresponding skill development session
• Include possible environmental changes. • Consult with others and include their ideas (e.g. child, parents/carers, support agencies). • Consult the literature for ideas.	Sessions 7 and 8 Problem management and communication skills.
(b) Evaluate the approaches by predicting the possible outcomes of each alternative: • Seek advice regarding possible outcomes if necessary. • Discuss alternatives with those most concerned to gain their perspective (e.g. child, parents/carers).	Sessions 9 and 10 Communication strategies and conflict resolution in the classroom.

(c) Select the best approach (and a second 'back-up' approach). Criteria for selection may include:
  • Maximum involvement/commitment of child (children) concerned.
  • 'Realistic' involvement of staff, parents/carers in terms of time and effort required to implement the approach.

Step 3: Make a plan for action
  • Specify who will carry out what action and when this will occur.
  • Record this in sequence. (This may take the form of an Individual Education Plan.)

Step 4: Implement plan
(a) Ensure Plan is implemented adequately:
  • Give clear instructions and check out individuals' commitment to action.
  • Institute checks to ensure action is carried out.

Step 5: Evaluate
(a) Pinpoint fault(s) in problem analysis/solving if not fully successful:
  • Identify information omitted from the initial problem definition.
  • Identify incorrect information or unrelated information in problem definition.
  • Identify faults in action plan.
  • Identify inadequacy of implementation plan.
(b) Evaluate the current status of the problem situation and report this back to those concerned:
  • Consider further actions that may be needed (e.g. reviews of progress).
  • Consider maintenance procedures to ensure that the problem does not recur.
  • Obtain the views of the child, parents/carers, other staff.

interpretations of the information they had on untested assumptions, tended to be distracted by irrelevant lines of investigation, often failed to link pieces of information, and usually did not recognise their own feelings and agendas which were involved in the problem situation.

The Scheme has adapted both the problem-analysis model developed by Robinson (1987, 1993) and ideas from the work of Argyris (1993) and Schön (1983, 1987, 1991) and Argyris and Schön (1974). Through the training sessions staff internalise the problem-analysis/-solving model and learn to use a common language when analysing and addressing problems. We argue that once staff are able to define clearly the presenting problem, to identify and sample its dimensions and to generate hypotheses to help to explain why certain things are happening, they will be in a better position to select appropriate interventions which will have real influence. Table 13.1 shows the relationship between the problem-analysis/-solving model and the skill training sessions.

Phase 3: The staff sharing scheme in operation

Evaluation of actions taken and the setting up of the Staff Sharing Scheme

The Staff Sharing Scheme establishes within a school, after a period of training, a problem-solving network which meets regularly to deal systematically with school-based issues. The psychologist is one member of this team and all his or her work with the school arises from decisions made at the Staff Sharing Meeting. The Scheme is based upon the following underlying principles:

1   No one person within a school has sole responsibility for the well-being and learning of a child.
2   Problem ownership is a responsibility of staff, pupils and parents/carers.
3   Staff in schools have personal resources which are not always collectively utilised for the benefit of other staff members and/or pupils.
4   Staff in schools are welcoming of continuing education in the form of school-based training as a means of increasing their effectiveness in the management of children.
5   School staff are motivated to find ways of reducing job stress.

Dealing with inter-professional jealousies and defensive routines

In our experience, both in New Zealand and in England, the staff we worked with were welcoming of receiving collaborative assistance. During evaluation sessions staff reported liking the idea that they did not have to 'go it alone' with any particular problem, and that the responsibility was being shared with their colleagues. This resulted in a reported perception that something practical and real would be/could be done to help in what were often initially seen as 'hopeless situations'.

What we found during the training sessions was that individual teachers changed the way they perceived their pupils, themselves and their colleagues. In many cases this change represented an alteration in core guiding principles, thus increasing the likelihood of a consistent change in actual behaviour. Collaborative problem-solving meant that teachers needed to learn and apply the skills of observing, gathering data, generating hypotheses and solutions, so that they could then explain their understandings to their colleagues in a way that was helpful. Staff learned that in order to receive assistance, they needed to provide specific data upon which colleagues could make assessments. The traditional model which encourages teachers to complain about pupils, see problems as solely residing in individuals, and to make many untested assumptions and attributions, would not work within the structure of the Staff Sharing Meetings. The group expectation, following training, was that more specific objective information was required before assistance could be planned. Teachers were led to realise that they were the ones with the knowledge about their pupils and their situations. Outside agents such as the educational psychologist are often strangers to pupils, yet there has always been an expectation that the psychologist has some 'magical insight' to intervene more successfully than could the classroom teacher.

What was important during the Staff Sharing process was to remind teachers that in most cases they had the solutions and knew what to do, but required reassurance, guidance, and some extra skills. In our experience, although staff in the early stages of training found some of the ideas challenging and complex (for example, problem analysis, checking out understandings directly, being objective and rational), resistance was short-lived as most people could see the logic of working and supporting each other.

When resistance was encountered it was dealt with directly by requiring specific examples and testing out any assumptions being made. We both attempted to model open ways of dealing with conflict and involving the group. We both saw and still see conflict as being productive if managed openly (that is testing out assumptions, being clear about rationales for doing particular things) and here the work of Argyris and Schön (1974) and Robinson (1993) influenced us greatly. Because of its premise about equal status the Staff Sharing Scheme does not work in authoritarian systems or when senior management members are not committed to the principles of the Scheme.

Ironically, it tended to be psychologist colleagues who resisted working in the Staff Sharing way. For some it was perceived as a threatening way of working because it would mean greater exposure of self and ability, often to a whole school as opposed to one teacher, a parent and a child.

The Scheme worked for us and other psychologists, because we were used to being in and working with schools. We were clear about what our role as applied psychologists working in educational settings actually meant and what we could and could not offer. We avoided the temptation to 'be all things to all people' and to take on what were clearly other people's responsibilities. Our position was and is that we could assist people to acquire further skills to be able to undertake their role more effectively, but it was still their role. For us to work as members of a problem-focused team was a logical procedure.

CONCLUSION

The Staff Sharing Scheme was first developed by Gill as a way of working more effectively with her set of schools. It has since been used by educational psychologists in a wide range of facilities including mainstream schools, special schools and social services institutions. The content of the Scheme has been greatly enriched by the contributions of all those involved in its development from 1982 and we have benefited from the joint working relationships involved in its operation. The Scheme has developed from school to school and from New Zealand to England and this is still an on-going process.

We have found that the number of referrals requiring our direct input drops significantly following the introduction of the Staff

Sharing Scheme. We also noticed that teachers became more skilful in managing problem situations. The Scheme is still being run in some Auckland schools fourteen years after being introduced. Clearly the Staff Sharing meetings have changed and developed as staff have come and gone, yet schools report that the framework is still helping them to manage problems more effectively. In looking at the reasons why the Scheme has lasted in some schools for so long it appears that one key factor is the continuity and commitment of senior management members, especially the headteacher. This is an important consideration for those who are thinking of setting up the Scheme. Training is costly, in terms of time, so high staff turnover is counterproductive.

More and more literature continues to appear on systems interventions for educational psychologists, organisational development with schools and school-based consultation (Wagner, 1995). There is also the powerful influence of government legislation which outlines explicit models of practice and working for educational psychologists, such as the Code of Practice on the Identification and Assessment of Special Educational Needs (DfE, 1994d). In light of these developments we are led to review our beliefs about the role and function of an educational psychologist working with schools and to reconsider the basis of this Scheme.

In the mid-1990s it appears that many schools are presented with increasing numbers of challenging young people and little likelihood of further resourcing. Schools often say, 'What can we do?. This Scheme reflects one way of working with schools differently and creatively and may well address this question. Hopefully, it also emphasises the positive professional relationship which can form between outside agencies, schools and young people.

Chapter 14

Resisting the trend to exclude

Catherine Benson

INTRODUCTION

The free market strategies of competition, choice and consumerism fostered by the education reforms have served to decrease tolerance levels towards pupils with problems. Meanwhile, newly forged links between pupil numbers and school funding and pressure to publish national assessments and attendance levels in league tables continue to force schools to give priority to academic results and able pupils whilst difficult or disturbed pupils become unwanted.

Exclusion has become one means of back-door selectivism in this free market where the reputation and 'attractiveness' of the school are an important part in its survival. Despite the so-called 'fining' of schools who exclude pupils by ensuring that finances for that pupil do not stay with the excluding school but follow the child, successful schools which can attract large numbers of pupils can easily 'fill the gap', often, they claim, with better behaved or more academic children who were unable to enter the school the 'first-time round'. Such an atmosphere does not promote any real incentive to reintegrate excluded – or those who have become known as 'high risk' – pupils.

There is also the new danger that in the short term, unofficial 'sink' schools will develop, schooling the 'surplus'. In the long term, faced with the same resource problems as other schools but with the additional problem of a 'bad' reputation, such schools may be forced either to close or officially to recognise themselves as a form of 'special' school. These schools would essentially cater for the less able or less academic, making the gulf between such schools and the 'successful' academically orientated schools substantially wider.

It would seem, then, that to exist, schools must 'play the game', excluding 'unsaleable goods' (Blyth and Milner 1996; Lloyd Bennet, 1993) whilst concentrating efforts and resources on the academically orientated, the regular attenders and those viewed as 'model pupils'. It would also seem that with increasing amounts of young people excluded nationally each year and suggestions that official figures are only the tip of the iceberg, schools are doing just this.

Research conducted in one County Council, however, reveals that such a trend has not captured all remaining players and that resistance to exclusion by headteachers in some schools is strong and firm. The diversity of reactions to free market philosophy and the new utility of exclusion as a means of selection has been frequently overlooked in both official and academic literature. As such, an analysis and explanation of resistance to these powerful national discourses remains neglected. Although the present research has been conducted in only one locality, it provides an important foundation for understanding and indeed turning such a trend whilst providing an insight into the impact which future official reforms may have.

THE RESEARCH

This chapter is based on the findings from an eight-month research project whose chief purpose was to examine the processes involved with, and the influences on, exclusion from mainstream schooling. Its aim was also to analyse the processes of reintegration into the mainstream schooling system.

Thirty-eight secondary schools were contacted through means of a postal questionnaire, resulting in a 79 per cent response rate. The qualitative data were backed up with a representative sample of ten headteachers who were approached to be involved in a series of more in-depth interviews and case studies with the researcher.

Resistance to exclusion, however, cannot and does not simply stem from headteachers, who must have the backing of their teachers, or at least the majority of teachers, in order to be able to endeavour with resistance against a trend which many teachers would see as in their own interests.

Indeed, there has been a catalogue of studies conducted into the role of the teacher in the disciplining process and their importance as the 'front liners' in any behavioural problems in the classroom, an important point which cannot be undervalued. Even experienced and highly respected headteachers have to work extremely hard to negotiate the support of their own staff when it comes to pupils who are, or are perceived to be, problems (see also Searle in this volume).

The headteacher, however, does retain the power of the 'gatekeeper' over processes of exclusion. Headteachers decide whether to exclude, what to exclude for, how long the exclusion should last, and whether the child should be returned, if at all, to the school. For this reason, an analysis of the headteacher's views about the role of education and its future is thought to be essential; not because the headteacher's power is exclusive over processes of exclusion, indeed the teacher's role is equally important, but because it is one which has frequently been neglected. As the Department of Education and Science (DES) asserted, the headteacher's role in promoting good behaviour in school 'cannot be evaluated as directly as the effectiveness of the individual teachers in classroom management' (DES, 1989, sec. 4:38).

Reynolds (1985b) touched upon the point of the headteacher's power when he stated that what makes some schools 'good' is their headteacher. To date, he remarks, there has been no research focusing on the quality of leadership generated by the headteacher. He continues: 'this is a marked contrast to the situation in America where the "effective school principal" has been an obsessional interest for at least a decade.' He concludes: 'the fact that we have no distinct British evidence is a major embarrassment' (Reynolds, 1985b).

Case studies of the secondary schools have been examined here in order to distinguish three different typologies of school which account for the diverse trends in exclusion in the Authority and which are no doubt alive in other areas. According to Schutz and Luckmann (1974), the way we understand the behaviour of others is dependent on a process of typification, by means of which the observer makes use of the concepts resembling 'ideal types' to make sense of what people do. These concepts are derived from our experience of everyday life and it is through these, claim Schutz and Luckmann, that we classify and organise our everyday world.

In themselves they represent pure forms of their typology, although in schools there may well be a mixture and overlap of the different types. Thus the particular case studies examined here are 'ideal types', chosen to illustrate the clearest extremes of responses. One always faces the problem of generalisation in pursuing an in-depth study of single cases, opening the danger of creating stereotypes. Nevertheless, such types are important to help to understand and distinguish similar trends in other areas. Through these typologies the research aims to highlight two important points. First, the free market approach to education which encourages a selective emphasis to schooling does not yet have an outright majority. Hence we must not fall into a complete impossiblism, something which is easily done given the existing situation. Second the essentialness and quality of any positive initiatives to avoid exclusion must be recognised and highlighted, in the hope that this will guard against such schools being given only two options to survive either by becoming an existing 'sink school' or joining a segregated group of 'Special Needs' Schools. Such projects must be elevated to a state of importance and thus made more attractive to other schools.

CASE STUDIES

School A

Profile

1   The school's catchment area is predominantly upper working class, with a small percentage of ethnic minority children.
2   The school roll contained approximately 900 pupils (mixed sex).
3   Permanent exclusions averaged twelve per year over a two-year period.
4   The school had Local Authority status (although at the time of research the school was in the process of a move towards grant-maintained status).
5   Resources were described by the head as 'reasonable' with plans for several new computers to be given to the Information Technology department. There was a remedial class with one full-time teacher for 'slow learners'.

6   Parents were invited to come to the school at designated times through a traditional yearly parents' evening. Apart from this, they had little contact with the school.

School aims

We are committed to raising the standards of our school and to provide an education which will help the individual succeed in adult life. We help students to realise their potential and their responsibilities by rewarding effort and achievement and setting the highest possible expectations. Our school environment encourages students to develop their skills and talents in a disciplined and stimulating environment in order that they can succeed and excel in education. These commitments are offered to all of our students, regardless of gender, race or belief.

(*Statement of Aims*, School A)

The headteacher saw the role of education as giving those who wanted to 'get on' in life an opportunity to succeed. Those who did not were seen as an unfortunate by-product of compulsory schooling and he held little patience for those who rejected schooling in some way, remarking that they were often lazy or delinquent. Outside pressures stemming from family or friends and the often subtle processes within school which can disproportionately disadvantage some pupils though racism, sexism or bullying were given little weight. The headteacher argued that pupils have to learn not to bring their outside problems into the school and explained that if they did find themselves experiencing bullying inside the school, 'they have established and proper procedures to follow'. These procedures seemed straightforward to the headteacher although they seemed poorly constructed and advertised to the pupils, which would perhaps explain why he asserted that 'we've rarely had any need for such recourse'.

'Everyone has the chance to succeed here,' he stated. 'The rest is simply up to them.' He also felt that there were certain 'types' more prone to 'disruptive' behaviour. He was, however, unable or unwilling to say what they were and he strongly believed that the reasons for such behaviour stemmed from individual pathology and bad parenting, which he stated were not problems with which his school should be concerned.

In this school, exclusion in all its forms was an essential part of the school disciplinary process. The aims of exclusion were not only to highlight that such behaviour would not be tolerated but also to remove the risk of any disruption and potentially negative influences on the other children. The headteacher explained that his staff and the other students needed to be protected from a disruptive and unpalatable few who, he confidently asserted, could be readily recognised by his staff when the initial problems arise. 'I do not interfere in the normal disciplining of pupils handed out by my staff', he remarked, 'and when a member of staff feels that exclusion is called for, I assume that if the situation has deteriorated this much, then I must support my staff.' This is the least he thought parents would expect, although the limited contact he had with parents would suggest that he assumed more than he was willing to admit.

The long-term negative consequences of such a move were denied. Rather, exclusion was sometimes seen to be a positive step to discipline the child, as he argued: 'Our society has always removed those who cannot abide by the laws firstly for a punishment, secondly to make sure they haven't the opportunity to repeat the behaviour and lastly in the hope that they will reform.'

Reintegration was also not thought to be possible until the pupils could satisfy the school that they had modified their behaviour. This was something that the headteacher felt was not taken seriously in other 'alternative' forms of schooling where discipline was often not a high priority. It was therefore difficult to imagine a situation where the headteacher would be satisfied that the problem behaviour had been modified, if indeed such a situation did exist. Indeed he angrily remarked that: 'The LEA can put all the pressure they want on me to take excluded children, it doesn't matter because my school will not become a dumping ground. We have standards to keep and I will not let them be brought down.'

He sympathised with those who had learning difficulties but did not recognise that there might be a link with what he frequently referred to as 'disruptive' behaviour. He concluded: 'The remedial class we run is not really ideal. These sorts of pupil would be better catered for outside mainstream schooling.' This was despite the fact that current discourses on special needs are consistently in favour of integration into mainstream schooling. In this headteacher's view there were many 'types' of pupil who would be better catered for outside mainstream schooling or at least, as he remarked, 'outside his school'.

The headteacher admitted that any indication of what he called 'problem' behaviour at pre-secondary level encouraged what could only be described as subtle persuasion on his part to identify the potential of other, better equipped schools. He held no doubts about dissuading a small minority from opting for his school, especially as the school was consistently over-subscribed enabling him to essentially pick and choose pupils for the school. He was confident that the standards set by his school were the best in the local area and humorously remarked that the competition should 'look out'.

School B

Profile

1   The school's catchment area in mainly middle class with a very small proportion of ethnic minority children.
2   The school roll included 1,400 pupils (mixed sex).
3   Permanent exclusions were about four per year over a two-year period.
4   The school has Local Education Authority status (although at the time of research the school was exploring the possibility of becoming grant maintained).
5   Resources were described by the headteacher as 'unusually' excellent, with 'no complaints from staff'. The school has an 'on-site' unit for disruptive, disaffected pupils with one full-time member of staff.
6   Parents were encouraged to come to the school at any time with queries although there seemed to be little motivation from staff and little evidence that this actually happened except during the traditional yearly parents evenings.

School aims

The school aims to provide an education which is broad, balanced and relevant to all individuals, regardless of gender, ethnic origin or capability. Non-academic achievements will be valued in the same light as academic successes in order to stress the multi-disciplinary nature of education. Pupils will receive all the support they need in which to achieve their full potential in order that they may lead satisfying and stable lives and develop a sense of responsibility towards others. It is hoped that by creating such an environment our pupils will develop as useful members of society, playing a constructive role in a democratic society.

(*Statement of Aims*, School B)

The headteacher saw the role of education as a right for all children and stressed that academic achievements were not the sole concern for the school. Under-achievers were frequently encouraged and supported, as were 'disruptive' and 'disaffected' pupils, in a somewhat luxurious and reasonably well equipped 'on-site' unit. 'I feel that education is important to these children [those in the unit] as they often have negative self-attitudes and family problems,' argued the headteacher. 'For these children we aim to provide a little extra support in the hope that they can eventually return to full-time education in the mainstream.'

However, he explained that there were limits to the school's tolerance for those who would not cooperate with the unit. Thus he stated, 'there must come a time when a school cannot be seen to condone behaviour and the child must be excluded temporarily or permanently as an example to others.' The negative consequences of exclusion, that the exclusion might disadvantage the child and the family further, were acknowledged by the headteacher but he felt that others should then be stepping in to make sure that this did not happen. He mentioned a frustration amongst his staff and himself concerning lack of outside support and concluded that, by actively supporting the unit, he and his staff were doing all they could to help the children's problems.

Unfortunately the unit was due to close because the space was needed for expanding pupil numbers and the full-time member of staff was needed for the mainstream curriculum teaching. This increased the danger that the school's exclusion rates might soar over the next few years. The headteacher voiced small concern and saw no other way around the closure. The pressures being put on him by the need to 'compete to survive' had made him rethink resources and direct them towards more attractive facilities. He was extremely conscious of the competition from other schools in the area and he asserted: 'We're in the same game as everyone else – raising standards, redirecting funding and recruiting in order to show that we have actually achieved success. It's an unfortunate but real strategy for survival.'

This was quite a turn around from the enthusiastic attitude which he had held with regard to the unit when it had been set up in the early 1980s, amid a climate of positive initiatives for special needs and 'disruptive' pupils. The only explanation offered was the rather flippant remark that 'things change', although it seems notably more so for children in need of support from the school.

He admitted that, until specialised internal support was given to the school, the school would no doubt be forced to utilise processes of exclusion, without the possibility of reintegration, especially from other schools which the headteacher thought were 'recipes for disaster', being transferred to a strange environment without proper support. Without such support and the closure of the unit the headteacher felt that he could not expect his staff to operate under even more pressured circumstances. As he explained:

> I don't like exclusion as a policy at all but you're being forced to consider it more now because a school's reputation is a marketable thing and if you can't market the school on a good reputation, then you aren't going to have the other children in school that you need to place yourself high in the league tables. It's a real problem.

However he added that some of his staff do put a lot of time into work with 'difficult' pupils and he encouraged this but he concluded that he felt 'there must come a time when, regrettably, we've done all we can and someone else must take over'.

School C

Profile

1 The school's catchment area is overwhelmingly working class with a large proportion of ethnic minority children.
2 The school roll was about 850 (mixed sex).
3 Permanent exclusions average out about one every two years, over a two-year period.
4 The school had Local Education Authority status.

5   Resources were described by the headteacher as 'poor'. Some classrooms were in need of repair, specialised resources such as computers were thinly spread and there was never any 'spare cash left over'. There was a special needs class for pupils who were having trouble with basic English or maths, run part-time by a member of staff who was aided by a parental volunteer. A school governor also worked voluntarily with some of the older young people who might otherwise have been on the verge of exclusion, in an initiative resembling an outreach project where the pupils would be in school for some time, and out with the governor the remainder.

6   Parents were encouraged to come to the school at any time to monitor their child's progress or to talk over any problems. The parents' group were an active body at the school, helping out where they could and collectively discussing any problems. They also helped to produce a 'link' newsletter every month, allowing outsiders, teachers, parents and pupils to be aware of what was going on in the school and to recognise any achievements of pupils.

School aims

Education is there to ensure that students acquire academic, practical and recreative skills desirable not only for employment, but for living life to the full. Our school provides students with the skills, concepts, attitudes and knowledge necessary for them to meet, with confidence, the different demands made on them as and when they change roles during their lifetimes. The differences of gender, race, and capability are recognised and if necessary supported, but treated at the same time as equal. Academic excellence is proudly valued by the school and given every possible opportunity to develop, but at the same time the adage 'nothing succeeds like success' is and has always been as important. We therefore seek to provide young adults, as far as is possible, with happiness, a knowledge of self, self confidence, maturity, responsibility, independence and knowledge.

(*Statement of Aims*, School C)

The headteacher saw the role of education as a child's right and did not think that the school necessarily had a right, then, to re-select their school population 'through the back door' using exclusion and in so doing effectively deny some children a right to education. As the headteacher argued: 'Children are all different and it is a school's job to recognise and act on these differences, so that a policy of equal opportunity is realistically implemented.' Anything else he thought was rhetoric and would disproportionately disadvantage some pupils, setting them up for exclusion. 'Exclusion', he argued, 'is simply a way of ridding yourself of the "problem" in the hope that someone else will pick up the pieces. In today's climate this usually means the parents, and young people rarely wish to rely on them.'

'In today's world', he continued, 'young people don't have it easy growing up. Most of their problems stem from a troubled family life and the negative way they see their futures and for some, education seems of little use.' He felt that the school needed to be flexible and to show young people that school can help them, through such means as the off-site programme, which is available for those who readily admit that they have some problem with school. Here they are offered a stable relationship with an adult who can also act as an intermediary between pupils, parents and school. They also get a chance to learn survival skills such as examining opportunities offered on college courses, learning interview techniques, learning how to fill in application forms, learning about tax and insurance, and finding their way around job centres. They meet positive role models and are encouraged to stay in school for their basic education qualifications. As he explained, 'It helps to integrate things done outside with things done in the classroom, so they see a reason for learning it. It encourages them to see that an education is not purely schooling for the sake of it.'

There is no 'contract' as such with parents but, according to the headteacher, the parents on the whole are very helpful. 'For those whose children are on the programme we explain the reality of the situation.' He pointed out that 'A lot of parents think that if this school's not working for their child then they'll just find another. The government's ethos of "Parentocracy" encourages such a view, but it's just not the case for the parents of excluded children'. He exemplified the point by stating that it is more like trying to find a job in today's market with a prison record. The outcome seemed to be that even the most uncooperative families understood that the burden might fall completely on them if the school were forced to exclude. They also understood that their cooperation is vital in avoiding this and that the support will be two-way, more like a partnership, which, he noted, is indeed, one of the government's current catch phrases. The school also encourages a large amount of parental involvement in extra curriculum and fund-raising activities. This provides parents with the opportunity to participate in school events, promoting a greater understanding and communication between teacher, pupil and parent. This is further encouraged by a strong and active governing body derived from the local community. The head-teacher asserted that the school is, from all appearances, poorly resourced but is utilising community resources and strengths to help to fill the void left by official funding.

There is always a potential that off-site programmes, such the one here, may look attractive to those who are on the fringes of rejecting school, and thus that the scheme might encourage them to be further alienated from mainstream schooling. The head-teacher felt confident, however, that the support the school drew from the community helped the staff to show pupils that rejecting school is never in their own interests: 'Our whole ethos is geared to making a positive environment for all pupils and the staff are very much committed to recognising individual abilities and problems.'

The school frequently has meetings about any problems which crop up and some of these will be behavioural problems. No stigma is attached to failure to control or relate to a particular child, rather the staff are encouraged to talk about experiences with everybody so that the whole team can be a support. Here the fact that teachers 'share their clients' (Grunsell, 1980, p. 78) is used as a positive collective resource which removes the need for a staffroom grapevine. It has the added attraction that the use of stereotypes and labels can be guarded against, owing to scrutiny by other members of staff, and it also helps to dismiss the belief that children with 'problems' are problems in all lessons. Any improvements in behaviour can then be understood and techniques of handling different situations and different individuals can be utilised. Catchall phrases such as 'disruptive' and 'disaffected' which refuse to recognise the individual are also avoided. The staff are thus encouraged not to see the behaviour of the pupils as meaningless, mindless or irrational because these sorts of belief can often overlook potential problems.

If relations between pupil and teacher do break down, however, an informal meeting with the two parties will be set up. The headteacher said that he tried to be as impartial as possible so that both parties could feel that they have been heard and have been treated fairly; a procedure which is important for both the teacher and pupil involved.

The LEA frequently asked the school to take on excluded pupils from other schools but the headteacher did feel that there had to come a point where he was forced to put a halt on it. He explained that these were young people who have already experienced one form of rejection and the parents were sometimes slow to cooperate with the school as much as he would have liked. For these reasons alone, it is particularly difficult to find some common ground with excluded pupils from other schools.

The obvious danger with accepting a steady flow of excluded pupils, whilst not 'guarding' an exclusively academic reputation, is that of becoming a 'sink school'. The school was already struggling with falling numbers and a growing professional reputation of being a 'special' school. The headteacher was extremely aware of this danger, particularly of the insulting labels branded on his school which, in his view, 'completely defeat the whole purpose of comprehensive education, allowing an elite and underclass of schools to develop'. He concluded:

> Schools must be made to hold on to the children they have regardless of ability, background or race. There will always be some who need extra help, some who need more punishment and some who just totally reject the system, but to recognise every young person as an individual in their own right we must recognise these differences and not categorise them into good and bad but try to reach some common ground with them and their community.

CONCLUSION

It would seem that all three headteachers recognise that the government's competitive approach is putting pressure onto schools to be selective, albeit through the 'back door', under a guise of equal opportunities and education as a 'right'. This kind of approach has been welcomed by a minority of headteachers who are committed to the belief that education should only be available to those who both show a commitment to education and can achieve, primarily through academic achievement, within the system.

It also appeals, though not altogether comfortably, to the majority of headteachers who feel that education should be a right for all children but are concerned that their school succeeds and are open to persuasion that pupils who cannot cope in their school, or who have rejected school, are better off out of mainstream schooling for their own good and for that of the school. These schools are hesitantly beginning to accept the value that exclusion may have to their survival.

Its appeal, however, falls short for a decreasing minority of heads who are ironically committed to a policy of equal opportunity, but one which they point out can never be equal, unless we recognise that pupils start off from unequal bases. They recognise that some pupils and teachers will need support and that, rather than continually emphasising the lack of resources available for schools, they should find more imaginative ways around such problems by drawing on what little resources they have through their local community. They believe that education is a child's right and that it is dangerous to ignore the consequences of allowing a child to give up this right. They therefore condemn exclusion as a form of civic or social exclusion which can have specific negative consequences for the young person and his or her family.

The research goes some way to analysing the headteacher's role in relation to these dominant discourses in education. It shows that each of the different standpoints held by the headteachers stems from different beliefs about the role that education and schools should play in children's lives and has had a direct effect on exclusion rates; more so it seems than catchment area, ethnic mix of the school population, size, or even resources that the school has at its disposal. These different beliefs existed long before the government's education reforms, emerging from the old grammar and technical-school split.

Such standpoints or ideologies filter down through the hierarchies of teaching staff and, although there may not be total consensus, such views will have important and direct effects on school exclusion rates through school policies, teaching styles, support structures and disciplinary processes, effectively reducing any resistance to a state of constant struggle and isolation.

It is debatable to what extent recent changes in the curriculum, resources and ethos of schools have produced negative effects on pupil behaviour. Increases in exclusions over recent years, however, have clearly been directly affected by the government's free-market reforms which have effectively redefined the official role of education and with it the role of exclusion.

The reforms have helped to emphasise and actively encourage support for one type of belief: that of education in mainstream schools for the 'ideal' pupil, the academically able and well-disciplined child from a stable, often white, middle-class background. Any 'second-class goods', including slow learners, the academical underachievers, children with unstable homes, children looked after by local authorities and more frequently black children who are perceived to have or be a problem for mainstream schools, are just not wanted. Mainstream schools are no longer resourced or geared up to be able to educate any pupil who falls or is perceived to fall into these categories. As such, they are thought to be better off outside them, often permanently. Hence exclusion is justified on the grounds that it protects the good of the majority, or more realistically a growing minority, whilst the rest through a rejection from school are disadvantaged in their future lives.

The pressures to conform to such ideology are great, especially where funding is directly linked to standards. No doubt some headteachers have left the profession because of these pressures, given the restricted choice of conforming or the possibility of an increasingly recognised second-class status as a special school, or the fact of being overwhelmed with excluded pupils by LEAs. These constricted options can only serve to decrease the quality of education for existing pupils.

It is therefore important to recognise that positive initiatives, such as those exemplified by school C, can be equally influential through school policies, teaching styles, and so on, and that they represent a collective resistance to the acceptance of a free-market philosophy and the growing tide of exclusions. These initiatives should be praised and promoted financially. After all, such schemes have proved to be successful with all kinds of pupils, working with minimal resources, unlike the excessively expensive and separate special units. These are the initiatives from which much can be gained and little lost.

The Children Act 1989 emphasises the importance of the court's duty to assess the capability of parents to meet the child's needs. Perhaps it is time that the same emphasis be placed on the importance of a school's responsibility to meet their pupils' needs, not for a select few but, rather, for a whole range of needs. Equally importantly is a recognition of the government's responsibility to all pupils within its education system, and with this the necessity of a release of funds which will enable schools to try to fulfil their obligations. These are the long-term reforms needed if we are to safeguard all children's rights for the future.

Chapter 15

Primary school exclusions
The need for integrated solutions

Carol Hayden

PRIMARY SCHOOL EXCLUSIONS: A QUALITATIVELY DIFFERENT ISSUE?

With the exception of Parsons *et al.* (1994) and Parsons in this volume most exclusions research, if it mentions primary school children at all, does not analyse whether exclusion in this phase of schooling is of any more significance than later on in a child's school career. There has, however, been an expression of concern for some time from teachers who report that a minority of children are presenting with more difficult behaviour and at an earlier age (Coxon, 1988; Lawrence and Steed, 1986; TES, 1991). This concern was reflected, for example, in the *Elton Report on Discipline in Schools* (DES, 1989). Bennathan (1992) has written of educational psychologists and education welfare officers not being competent to deal with the growing incidence of what is often referred to as 'challenging behaviour'. Other professionals, such as Rutter, are of the opinion that there is a real increase in child psychiatric disorder and his research is providing evidence of this (Rutter and Smith, 1995). Rutter (1991) has previously considered a whole range of possible contributory factors in explaining this increase, such as greater relative poverty, unemployment and family breakdown, all of which affect more children in the 1990s than in earlier decades.

This chapter suggests that there are a number of issues in relation to the exclusion of primary-age children from school which make action to address exclusion at this phase arguably more urgent than in the secondary phase of schooling. For some young children school is a haven. It may be the one place where there is some consistency and predictability. For children living with their families, it is likely to be the only place where a child is monitored daily by an external agency. Primary-age children are more vulnerable than their secondary school counterparts by virtue of their relative immaturity and greater dependence on adults. Parents may not always be available and willing to take care of their children during the school day. Young children who are not properly supervised are at risk of harm in a whole range of ways, not least from accidents in the home or elsewhere but also through the possibility of becoming involved with older children out of school whose disaffection may be more marked.

Cohen and Hughes (1994) show that having a young school-age child at home is likely to cause difficulties for parents in a number of ways. It is likely to be restricting and stressful for some parents who are at home and faced with competing demands from pre-school children and other activities. Parents who are in work or further education and training may not be able to afford or, indeed, find appropriate childcare arrangements. These difficulties may damage the parent/child relationship; parents may feel they should be punishing their child for being sent home from school, rather than trying to help to compensate for the education he or she is missing. The exclusion of one child in a family may have an effect on other siblings who may see the exclusion as some kind of holiday and/or be resentful of the extra time the excluded child gets with a parent.

Primary school is the time when most children learn the basic skills of reading, writing and social interaction. Disrupted schooling and the social isolation that can sometimes go with it at this early stage may be difficult to compensate for in later schooling. Secondary-age children are more likely to have an established peer group independently of whether they attend school. It is already known that difficult and often aggressive behaviour is a main reason for exclusion of young children (Parsons et al., 1994). It is therefore particularly important that these children are given help and support to develop more positive interactions with their peers. Low self-esteem is often associated with negative behaviour towards others and an exclusion is likely to damage self-esteem even further by marking the child as clearly different from his or her peers (see also John in this volume).

Primary school exclusions may also be viewed as an indication of the constraints upon services which try to support families in difficulty and to work with schools to address behaviour problems with children. Emotional and behavioural difficulties may be seen as the poor relation in the scramble for special educational needs resources (Peagram, 1991). Such children may not be viewed as deserving as children with physical disabilities or identified learning difficulties.

The supposition that primary-age exclusion may be a qualitatively different issue from the secondary-age group is supported by Bennathan (1992) who argues that evidence available to organisations represented by 'Young Minds' has tended to show that most schools do everything they can to avoid permanently excluding a child:

> Some of the children excluded from school are seriously disturbed. This would tend to be true of younger children. ... Seriously disturbed children tend to make themselves known very early on in their school lives ... the picture that emerges, reading the files of young boys excluded from school, is not of unsympathetic teachers rushing to exclude any but the children who will do them credit. On the contrary, many of them have had immense amounts of attention, even affection, from mainstream teachers and continued tolerance from fellow pupils and their parents in the face of prolonged aggression, offensiveness and disruption of lessons.
>
> (Bennathan, 1992, p. 4)

The particular concerns about young children out of school, outlined above, influenced the decision to focus upon children excluded from school in the primary sector in the University of Portsmouth research. There are three stages of the research: a national questionnaire survey; case studies of contrasting LEAs and individual exclusion cases within them; and the identification of possible strategies to address school exclusion at this stage.

RESEARCH EVIDENCE

The national questionnaire provides evidence of the number and characteristics of excluded primary-age pupils as well as the reasons for exclusion from a wide range of LEAs across England and Wales during the 1992–3 academic year and during the autumn term 1993 (forty-six LEAs responded, 39 per cent of the total). Some key findings will be outlined here but more detailed analysis can be found elsewhere (Hayden, 1994a; Hayden, forth-coming). It is estimated that in the 1992–3 academic year over 10,000 primary age children had a recorded exclusion of which approximately 1,200 were permanent. These exclusions repre-sented 14 per cent of all exclusions in that academic year. Thus, although primary exclusions are relatively rare, compared to those in the secondary phase, they still represent thousands of children. However, in the permanent exclusion category most local authorities have only a handful of young children who are extremely hard to cater for in any of their facilities.

The great majority of excluded primary pupils were boys (90 per cent) and there were more exclusions in the older primary-school age groups. Ethnicity was often not recorded. Only fifteen LEAs supplied this information, which showed that white and Asian pupils were under-represented in exclusions, whilst African–Caribbean/mixed race/other categories were over-represented by up to three times their proportion in the local population. Social class may be an additional factor to consider in relation to African–Caribbean exclusions, in that there is an over-representation of this group in semi-skilled and unskilled occupations. Only half the local authorities could supply an analysis of reasons for exclusion and these centred around dis-obedience, verbal abuse and physical aggression.

The case studies which are used to illustrate the range of needs and possible responses to primary school exclusion are taken from two contrasting LEAs; a County Council (LEA 1) and an inner London Borough (LEA 2). In these two LEAs, a sampling frame of 218 individuals was created from which the more in-depth case studies were conducted. The great majority of these children were excluded for a fixed-term period only, in the time period under investigation (166 pupils, 76 per cent). About a quarter of the children were excluded. Of these, twenty-one pupils (10 per cent) were permanently excluded, thirty-one pupils (14 per cent) were indefinitely excluded. The information on file in the education offices on these 218 individuals shows that 81 per cent of families in LEA 1 and 90 per cent of the families in LEA 2 were already known to a range of agencies outside school, such as social services departments, child and family guidance clinics and the various education support agencies. Even these high proportions are likely to underestimate the level of outside agency support to these families, because not all support will be known and recorded on education files and because there was no information about individuals who had no special-needs file or education welfare support. Children known to the social services departments were the largest grouping in each LEA (37 per cent in LEA 1, 39 per cent in LEA 2). Special educational need was another feature in many cases; 38 per cent of children in LEA 1 had a statement of special educational need at the time of their exclusion and 18 per cent in LEA 2. In addition, 18 per cent of the excluded children in each LEA were undergoing assessment. As with the national data, the majority of children were boys and exclusions were more usual in the junior rather than infant-school phase of primary school education. In LEA 2, where race was recorded, there was a three-fold over-representation of African–Caribbean children.

Thirty-eight in-depth case studies were conducted across these two LEAs in which both home and school accounts of what happened, and why, were sought. These case studies were analysed, illustrating the needs of the children in the following way: evidence of special educational need; evidence of difficulties in the home background; evidence of both special educational need and difficulties in the home background; naughty and/or disaffected children. Individual case studies are used to illustrate some of the typical components to each of these categories. This is followed by a discussion of some of the initiatives which are attempting to address this range of needs. However, it must be emphasised that in many ways these categories are, at best, only a rough guide. Some of the children who have been categorised as predominantly 'naughty' rather than as in great social and educational need also have indications of some degree of difficulty in one or both of these areas.

Almost all of the children had some level of special educational need which had warranted in-class support, advice from an educational psychologist, requests for formal assessment or were already statemented, usually for emotional and behavioural difficulties. In only four cases was there *no* evidence of extra support for special educational needs; in three of these cases the children and families could be described as from more affluent backgrounds in which the family lived in their own home and the family had an income from paid employment. Yet it was rare for special educational need to be the predominant factor explaining an exclusion. The argument that exclusion could have been avoided if support for special educational needs had been properly planned is illustrated in the following case example.

Lenny lived with his mother and younger sister and was statemented for emotional and behavioural difficulties. He and his family have a range of long-standing problems which contributed and related to his educational difficulties. However, a key issue was a lack of planning for his reintegration from a special unit into a mainstream primary school at the start of Year 3. He had been excluded in his first year of schooling but had got on 'brilliantly' at his special unit, according to his mother. There had been no animosity between the mainstream school and his mother:

> It's not fair on the teacher in a big class to have a child who wanders about, hides under the table, disrupts other children, locks himself in the toilet. He's got no boundaries ... he hates to be sitting down all the time.

He was out of school for four months before obtaining a place at a special school where he settled well with the help of the NSPCC acting as a spokesperson and advocate for the family. At interview he became particularly enthusiastic when asked about his new school:

> I like swimming ... cooking ... (class teacher) she's nice ... she takes us out ... every term we have three lots of stars, we get money for the stars and we go to the shops to spend it. ... If we're good we get stars ... last time I had five stars. [What sort of thing did you get stars for?] ... finishing books ... being excellent ... doing as you are told ... ignoring people if they are rude and naughty.

Lenny's mother helped at the school, in a different class from her son, and had gained some insight and confidence in her handling of him. She said: 'To be quite honest, he hasn't got a behaviour problem now in the home. You can see the difference in him since he's been in this school [i.e. special school].'

Other cases where special educational need could be seen as an important factor in explaining an exclusion more typically centred around the issue of getting recognition that the child had a special educational need rather than being viewed as simply 'naughty'. Also the formal assessment and statementing process had often been held up in families where children had been in and out of local authority care, and/or where there had been numerous moves of location by and between parents. In more affluent families the parents were sufficiently concerned to pay for a private assessment of their child.

Tensions and difficulties in the family background of excluded children were present in almost all cases. Only four of the thirty-eight children lived with both original birth parents. These findings are consistent with those of Parsons *et al.* (1994). Related difficulties in this study included violent family relationships and various forms of abuse, as well as bereavements in the family. Some of the black and mixed-race families also mentioned racial harassment. This had led to rehousing by the local authority in one case. There was also evidence of a range of difficulties in the minority (four) of more affluent families. Three of these families focused more on their individual child than family or school circumstances in their search for an explanation of the child's behaviour. In one such case the parents had taken their son to a private psychiatrist, in two of the other cases the parents had an assessment carried out by a private psychologist. In the fourth case the parent was a psychotherapist herself and believed that she was the appropriate person to help her son.

Major difficulties in the home background were evident in more than half of the case study families. A typical example was Adam, a seven-year-old boy, who was accommodated by the social services department during the period of fieldwork. A social services team manager supplied the family and case history as no social worker had been allocated to Adam due to staff shortages. The picture supplied of this child's life was one of multiple stresses, disruption and trauma. Concerns about this family from the social services department were there before his birth in relation to older siblings, and he presented problems at nursery. He had witnessed violence from his father to his mother and had been threatened himself – on one occasion his father smashed the door down and threatened the family with a hammer. He had been physically abused by his older brother, who had often been left to look after him. He was described by the headteacher of his mainstream school as desperately unhappy and aggressive, wetting and harming himself:

> Adam is an intelligent, pleasant boy who is desperately unhappy ... concentration is very poor ... low self-esteem ... wanders around the classroom ... rips up and throws things

around ... but he has a good teacher, he has settled, he likes structure. Although we are only looking after him, sometimes he is observed rocking and making animal noises.

Adam received some additional in-class support from within the school's budget and has been observed by the educational psychologist. He had had one fixed-term exclusion from his current school.

An example of the overlapping nature of home/school problems, which featured in most of the families involved with social services, was illustrated by Sean and Peter's situation. These brothers, aged 8 and 11 years respectively, were permanently excluded within weeks of each other from the same mainstream primary school. Both had statements for emotional and behavioural difficulties and it had been suggested that Peter needed a therapeutic residential placement. These boys had lived at thirty-four different addresses, and had been rejected by two sets of foster parents and prospective adoptive parents. Their relationship with each other was described as so violent that the children's home could not have other younger children resident whilst they were there. Peter was the most damaged and had been receiving three forty-minute periods of psychotherapy a week which involved the loss of about 30 per cent of his school week when travel time to the therapist was added. He was placed in a special unit after his permanent exclusion. This unit was unable to take Sean who spent six months out of school receiving home tuition. The headteacher of the school which excluded them confirmed the view that a main issue for these boys was whether or not they should be kept together or apart; for example, he reported that they used to be brought to school in two separate cars from their children's home. The school had tried different strategies with the boys, for example:

We all went to speak to a play therapist who suggested that we allow the kids space to play, seeing as they had such massive problems. The problem with this was that if they could play for part of the day they couldn't see why they shouldn't play for the whole day.

The children's social worker confirmed that the school had put in a lot of resources out of their budget for these children. With reference to Sean, he said:

The statement was almost a waste of time ... fifteen hours Special Needs Assistant did not even start to meet the requirements of Sean. It felt like a paper exercise ... he needed full-time special teaching support. The social services support service became involved and tried to devise programmes to support him, but that failed before it got anywhere. There is no provision to get a resource in when it is needed, that is the same day. [Help is] ... too blinking late when it comes.

When it is considered that many children who have special educational needs and/or live in poor or stressful home circumstances do not get excluded from school, one has to consider the extra dimensions of 'naughtiness' and 'disaffection'. In particular, 'disaffection' is known to increase sharply in the early years of secondary school and disaffection does, of course, occur in primary school (Barrett, 1989).

A good example from the case studies was Danny. He experienced some disruption in his home background and received in-class support for special educational need. Both his mother and teachers saw him as a popular and likeable boy who was well integrated into his peer group but his disruptive behaviour was not as severe as that of the great majority of children in the case studies. Also, both school and parent were in agreement that a fixed-term exclusion was an important disciplinary tool. The headteacher said of this exclusion:

That exclusion worked. We treated it really seriously, mum too. That's a good example of a good use of exclusion. Fixed-term exclusions can be useful. It depends upon the age of the child and parental support for it.

The child's mother echoed much the same at interview, in particular the view that the fixed-term exclusion seemed to have worked and that her son did not want another one.

REDRESSING THE BALANCE: RECOGNISING THE NEED FOR AN INTEGRATED SERVICE

As several parents and social workers commented during the course of the research, if a young child is permanently excluded from school one day there should be somewhere else for him or her to go the next day. Whilst the integration of all children into mainstream education is a laudable aim, it is fairly clear that this is not likely to be successful without adequate funding (AMA, 1995b). Many of the children in this research were 'integrated' in the sense of being physically present in a school but this did not mean they were socially integrated. Too many of their inter-actions with other children were negative and only contributed to their already low self-esteem. What is clearly needed is a continuum of provision which recognises that some children will need to spend time outside mainstream education and even in residential and therapeutic environments. The aim should still be to reintegrate these children if possible but in a carefully planned way. There are a range of initiatives which are likely to address the needs presented by the majority of temporarily excluded chil-dren but it is obvious that there are no simple answers for children who have reached the stage of a permanent exclusion. An inte-grated response from a range of agencies is necessary. Setting up the structures at local authority level should mean that a child should not have to get to the stage of a permanent exclusion before all the agencies start to respond.

The main statutory agencies, education, health and social services, all have a part to play, indeed in relation to statements of special educational need there is supposed to be a multi-disciplinary assessment (see Normington in this volume). What is needed is multi-agency funding and provision for the 'exceptional' children. The case studies in this research have demonstrated that many of the excluded primary-age children are in major social and educa-tional need. Some excluded children clearly need the expertise of the mental health services. However, primary school exclusion is also about the perceived range of disciplinary options in some schools with lunchtime and fixed-term exclusions replacing detention or corporal punishment.

Behaviour support services exist in many local authorities and there is also a plethora of projects funded through the Grants for Education Support and Training (DfE, 1995a) which are attempting to address related issues of truancy and disaffection. For example, one of the LEAs in the study has an 'Inclusion' project to look at ways of keeping pupils at risk of exclusion in school. These services and initiatives were greatly valued. The teachers interviewed in the London LEA, who had access to the behaviour support service, generally wanted more of the same. Skilled teaching assistants were also very much appreciated. However, these education-based initiatives were viewed as insufficient to deal with children who had obvious major additional social needs.

Although permanent exclusion at the primary school stage is extremely rare, the research reported here would suggest that an important threshold has been crossed in which the unthinkable (that is, permanent exclusion of a primary school child) happens. Because these children are exceptional it is clear that their needs cannot be met by the education system alone. This is already recognised by a range of support services throughout the country. Primary schools, even more than secondary schools, are under immense pressures due to what Webb (1994, p. 5) has referred to as a 'deluge of directives' brought about by the Education Reform Act 1988 and the implementation of the National Curriculum. Webb recommends urgent action in a number of areas, two of which relate to better staffing and school-based social workers.

Some local authorities and schools already have a number of support structures, where funding comes from more than one agency. For example, LEA 2 funded a psychiatric social work service to work in school. Some schools fund their own counsellor, often with the help from grants from charitable foundations and local businesses. Some social workers and key workers in children's homes spend time trying to support children in schools. Certain local authorities have education support services within the social services departments which work with children 'looked after' by the departments (see Firth and Horrocks in this volume). Bringing the additional support services to the child and family in the school setting has been adopted, including drop-ins and clinics. Outside the school setting, a range of statutory agencies work with children (for example, see Hayden, 1993, 1994b) and families on their behaviour towards each other, but stronger links need to be made between such initiatives and what schools are also trying to do (additionally see, for example, Stephenson in this volume and Orbach, 1995).

CONCLUSION

The research reported upon in this chapter indicates that while primary-age children excluded from school are a relatively rare occurrence, particularly the permanent category, they are an especially vulnerable minority. They usually have some level of special educational need as well as disrupted and stressful family backgrounds. Their behaviour illustrates distress more often than 'naughtiness'. Although there are support structures and particular initiatives in some schools and LEAs trying to address the issue of behaviour and exclusion, these are unevenly distributed and may often focus on secondary-age children. Furthermore, the funding for such services is far from certain in a time of reducing budgets. Potentially preventive work may be sacrificed in favour of core activities in a range of services. Some children need more specialised help than they are likely to get through special needs support assistants in schools. Although such children and their families may be getting support for issues which are considered to be outside school, the reality of a full day in school for the child can be overlooked. The school day is often a source of additional stress for children who are already having difficulties with their peers and with their school work. School may also be a location where some youngsters feel safe enough to 'act out' in their cry to be noticed and helped. However, the appropriate help is not usually available at the time when a child presents such difficulties and the immediacy of the situation in a school classroom may not be fully appreciated by support services used to waiting lists and appointments.

The long-standing nature of the difficulties experienced and presented by most excluded primary-age children are well documented in schools and education departments and, from the evidence available, in other agencies as well. Exclusion from school was certainly a possibility, long before it became a reality in our case studies, unless the appropriate support for the child was forthcoming. Like schools, many education support services and other agencies are under pressure to deliver specified outcomes, within particular financial constraints. In such circumstances it can be tempting to focus only on statutory duties and the measurable and likely successful outcomes. Trying to support children with fairly complex difficulties and needs in school is likely to require the expertise and support of several agencies and professions, yet the time needed to do such work may be difficult to justify in terms of budgets and outcomes. However, once such children are permanently excluded from school they often create additional pressure on services outside school in a range of ways. In some cases, a permanent exclusion for a child has been followed by a period of time in the care of the local authority. Such an exclusion often precipitates a formal assessment for special educational needs, if indeed this has not already been undertaken. By allowing the situation to deteriorate to a permanent exclusion we are adding to the difficulties of an already vulnerable group of children. It is perhaps an obvious but nevertheless important point to make that if we fail to support these children now they are likely to present a range of unresolved difficulties in the future which not only will call upon the resources of a range of agencies but also, as Bennathan (1992) warns, will affect all of us as a result of the problems they are likely to present to society.

Chapter 16

Exclusion from school
The role of outside agencies

Joan Normington

INTRODUCTION

Pupils likely to be excluded from school are often the concern of several support agencies such as the education welfare service, social services, the educational psychological service, peripatetic support services, off-site unit staff, and so on. As permanent exclusions seem to be widely regarded with disfavour, it is preferable to attempt to prevent them. Where they do occur, rapid resolutions are needed so that pupils miss as little schooling as possible. This suggests that the various agencies should collaborate.

The requirement for schools to develop policies for special educational needs (DfE, 1994f), the Code of Practice on the Identification and Assessment of Special Educational Needs (DfE, 1994d) and the changes in the law on exclusions in the Education Act 1993 (see Blyth and Milner in this volume) have all helped to re-focus attention on discipline and behaviour. The general agreement seems to be that permanent exclusions remain undesirable but the stringent procedures now laid down mean that LEAs and schools have to develop policies and procedures for dealing with severe behaviour difficulties and preventing exclusion where possible (DfE, 1994a). The implication is that the various support agencies, therefore, must become involved and work cooperatively (Galloway *et al.*, 1989; Lowe, 1989).

A recent study focused on the work of support agencies with excluded pupils and some of its findings form the basis of this chapter. A number of shortcomings regarding the quality of inter-agency cooperation and collaboration are identified. Many of these arise from the perceptions and expectations the agencies have of themselves and each other, coupled with under-resourcing and shortage of staff. Good practice is described, particularly the consideration of how case conferences can be effective starting points in planning and coordinating inter-agency work when reintegrating pupils into schools and/or preventing their exclusion.

The work of a Pupil Referral Unit is considered positively; its role in supporting pupils with behavioural problems and their schools is described. The links with the stages of assessment as outlined in the recent Code of Practice on the Identification and Assessment of Special Educational Needs (DfE, 1994d) are discussed with particular reference to exclusion and ensuring that any pupils withdrawn from school are reintegrated as quickly and successfully as possible.

RESEARCH METHODOLOGY

In the late 1980s and early 1990s I studied the work of the support agencies involved with pupils excluded from school. I interviewed all the professionals working with a small sample of excluded pupils attending an LEA off-site unit, now a Pupil Referral Unit. I also studied all the files kept by the various agencies about the pupils concerned. In effect this was a series of case studies through which I could examine how agencies work together. Anderson (1990) argued that case studies are an aid to understanding how processes operate. This was my aim as I had a concern with 'how things happen and why' (Anderson, 1990, p. 158).

I chose to interview rather than administer a questionnaire as I wished to explore the views of a small number of people with relevant experience and specialised knowledge of multidisciplinary work, described as 'elite interviews' (Anderson, 1990, p. 223). I used a semi-structured interview schedule which was more a topic guide (Hedges, 1985) to remind me about the areas that I wished to cover than a series of questions for the interviewees. At all stages I tested my interpretations of the emerging data by returning edited transcripts to the interviewees for comment. This technique, 'member checking' (Kyriacou, 1990, p. 30), helped me to ensure that the data were 'trustworthy' (Guba and Lincoln, 1987).

The aim of the study was to investigate the nature of the multidisciplinary work with particular reference as to how the agencies collaborate.

FINDINGS

Most of the excluded pupils were already involved with one or more of the following agencies: the educational psychological service, education welfare services, peripatetic behaviour support services, social services. However, such involvement appeared to be random. There had been few attempts to involve the support agencies systematically and in a coherent manner. It would seem sensible to refer pupils for help before goodwill is exhausted rather than waiting until teachers feel that they have done all they can and that exclusion is the only remaining option (see also Parsons in this volume). It is necessary for teachers to recognise that other professionals can help them to solve problems rather than removing them (Murgatroyd, 1980). However, the problems associated with multi-disciplinary work have been recognised for many years but are not easy to overcome (DHSS and Welsh Office, 1977; Fletcher-Campbell, 1990; SSI and OFSTED, 1995).

Perceptions that the various agencies have of each other can be barriers to successful co-operation (Kyriacou and Normington, 1994). Education welfare officers (EWOs) see themselves as links between home and school, concerned for the welfare of *individuals*. This can clash with teachers' concerns for the greater good of the *whole class* or school. However, both groups ultimately have the same aim, that pupils should succeed. Educational psychologists are perceived as being influential facilitators, primarily because of their statutory (and increasing) function in formal assessments of special educational needs. Their role in exclusions was often one of supplying tacit approval for the schools' actions. They were frequently consulted only after the event when there was no hope of their doing any preventive work. This was not welcomed by educational psychologists who believed that they should have been involved earlier while there was opportunity to effect changes in behaviour. This would avoid the problems associated with 'debris management' as identified by Parsons in this volume. They saw their most effective attributes as being objectivity, empathy, listening skills and the ability to set out plans in clear and achievable steps (see also Gill and Monsen in this volume).

Social Services were frequently involved with excluded pupils, not usually as a result of the exclusion *per se* but because many excluded pupils were already part of a social worker's case load (see, additionally, Stirling, 1992a, b). The biggest differences of opinion existed between teachers and Social Services staff. This is a long-standing issue (Kahan, 1977) but little progress has been made in resolving the differences (see also Parsons and Hayden in this volume).

INTER-AGENCY COLLABORATION

A necessary requirement for improved inter-agency cooperation is that all agencies have a clear understanding of their own aims and objectives as well as being fully aware of their agency's role. This obviously means that they should have a similarly clear understanding of the roles of other agencies. They are then better able to recognise their own strengths and weaknesses as well as those of others. It should follow that the workers/agencies do the particular task for which they are best suited (Clarke, 1986; Evans, 1977; Galloway *et al.*, 1982).

The conflict between Social Services and Education Departments exists at all levels of the organisations and has been aggravated recently by the tensions resulting from budgetary constraints (see Sinclair *et al.*, 1994). Another source of this conflict stems from differences in personality, training and perspective (for example, social workers' prime consideration is with individuals whilst teachers have a tendency to think of the group, class or school as a whole), as well as from issues arising from confidentiality (Davie, 1977; Fletcher-Campbell, 1990; Jackson, 1987; Reid, 1986). The Children Act 1989 makes cooperation mandatory (see Blyth and Milner in this volume) and it is now incumbent upon the services to ensure that they do work together for the good of children 'in need'. The mandate is there, it is now up to senior managers in both services to give the lead to their staffs (Tutt, 1992). However, teachers and social workers can do much to improve the situation on their own 'patches' if they are aware of their differences and strengths. There is a deal of evidence to suggest that effective multi-disciplinary work depends on good inter-personal relationships (Davis, 1985; Lane, 1990). A useful starting point is for the workers in the agencies to make sure that they know their immediate colleagues in other agencies.

Strengths of inter-agency working are that there are wide ranges of skills, perspectives and knowledge to bring to bear on problems. Weaknesses can arise from those same sources – without a willingness to accept that others' viewpoints are just as valid as one's own, cooperation is unlikely (Blyth and Milner, 1990). Communication problems are the biggest single hurdle, whether they stem from the use of jargon (Murgatroyd, 1980) or from the practical difficulties of actually contacting the right person at the right time. Consideration of common records to prevent duplication of effort both in actually maintaining records and in the work done with pupils and their families could be helpful (DHSS and Welsh Office, 1977, 1988; Fletcher-Campbell, 1990; Scottish Office, 1989).

Joint training, perhaps during initial professional training, and some elements of in-service training may be helpful in breaking down barriers between workers in schools and allied agencies. There is a need to promote cooperation not merely deplore its inadequacies. Perhaps we should seriously consider joint children's services rather than separate departments, each jealous of its autonomy and budget (see also Stephenson in this volume).

Pupils excluded from school have usually given their teachers cause for concern for some time. The schools should, therefore, have commenced Stages 1, 2 and/or 3 of the Code of Practice on the Identification and Assessment of Special Educational Needs (DfE, 1994d), hereafter called the Code. This procedure does not apply only to learning difficulties. There should already be written evidence of the action the school has taken to help (individual education plans) together with minutes taken at reviews involving parents and other professionals. This applies at Stages 1, 2 and 3. Swift action is required to ensure that excluded pupils do not miss more than a few days' schooling (see Parsons, and Mitchell in this volume). A case conference called in response to a given situation and attended by school representative(s), parents, support agencies currently working with the child or who may become involved, and anyone else with relevant knowledge is one way of beginning interventions. The aims of such meetings are to exchange information, take decisions, make recommendations, coordinate the efforts of the various agencies, allocate responsibility and form clear action plans – perhaps even a recommendation to move to Stage 4 of the Code: a multidisciplinary assessment.

These meetings are most effective when the participants know why they have been asked to attend, have prepared their information and are empowered to take decisions on behalf of their agency. They should result in clear statements outlining action plans and detailing specific tasks to named individuals. Monitoring and review arrangements should be agreed. Minutes should be circulated to all involved within a week. Although detailed planning should be left to smaller groups of workers, pupils and parents, conferences open up the planning process and are the means of delegating tasks to named individuals who will be accountable at subsequent reviews.

There is a danger that conferences can become more involved with past history than planning for the future. However, it is important that what has happened is made known so that repetition can be avoided and decisions made that are firmly grounded in accurate information. It also helps to ensure common understanding.

Effective chairing of case conferences is important. The chairperson should ensure that all opinions are aired and minuted, that the meeting arrives at a consensus if possible but does not neglect alternative views (Blyth and Milner, 1990; Scottish Office, 1989). Cline (1989) recommends training for conference participation and this was also advocated by many of the professionals interviewed. This could be one element of a joint training initiative.

There should be a clear agenda and code of practice for case conferences, setting out who to invite and why they are needed. It should be understood that case conferences can often be the beginning of preventive work with pupils in danger of exhausting the school's efforts and reaching exclusion – a Stage 3 meeting could be used to develop a workable individual education plan.

THE PUPIL REFERRAL UNIT AS FOCAL POINT

Despite current anxieties that Pupil Referral Units may be no more effective than the 'sin bins' of the 1970s (see also Stirling, and John in this volume), such an off-site unit can be a useful element at this point if its purpose is clearly defined (DES, 1989; Galloway et al., 1989; Lovey et al., 1993). If properly staffed and resourced, such a unit can assess pupil attainment and difficulties, review in-school factors which may have contributed to the problem, offer time-out from stressful situations, prevent further escalation of problems, offer remediation both academic and behavioural, and assist in planning for and supporting reintegration.

The PRU of which I am currently the headteacher has evolved from being the educational provision at a Social Services Observation and Assessment Centre. We initially offered some day places to young people who were trying to rehabilitate themselves in other community homes, foster homes or their own homes. In this way they were having to adapt to only one change at a time. We realised that admitting into the education unit all of the young people who were residents at the Centre was not necessarily a good idea. When the time came for them to return to their own schools, the pupils had not only missed work but often did not want to go; we were creating disaffection. We determined to admit only those with existing school problems such as chronic non-attendance, severe behaviour difficulties and some learning problems. This left some spare capacity which the LEA used, so that we could help to provide advice in connection with assessments of pupils with special educational needs. As the social services' care and accommodation philosophy changed – assessment becoming 'a process not a place' – our involvement with the LEA increased. Since September 1994 we have been registered as a PRU and work solely with pupils referred to us through the education system.

We have a Referral Panel which consists of senior teachers from secondary schools on a rolling rota: an educational psychologist, the head of the newly formed Service for Pupils with Emotional and Behavioural Difficulties, PRU staff, occasional representation from the peripatetic support service for pupils with emotional and behavioural difficulties and the Home and Hospital Teaching Service. The Panel meets weekly to discuss pupils referred by schools. The pupils' problems are usually behavioural but there are often associated learning difficulties. Pupils may be accepted for a maximum of six weeks for assessment, remediation and behaviour modification. Admission is usually effected within two to four weeks of referral being accepted. Waiting lists are not long as there is a regular 'turnover' of pupils. Reasons for rejecting a referral may be varied; for example, chronic non-attendance, problems that seem to be so entrenched that short-term intervention would seem to be inadequate, difficulties that are centred in home and social circumstances. However, all referrals are treated individually and there are no hard and fast rules.

The LEA's Exclusions Panel, of which I am a member, also refers some excluded pupils to the PRU. Pupils permanently excluded in years 7 to 10 are admitted *only* when another school has agreed to put them on roll. These pupils also attend the PRU for a maximum of six weeks and are then reintegrated into the 'new' mainstream school. This prevents the PRU being used as long-term provision or a 'sin bin'. Year 11 pupils join a transition programme at the PRU which prepares the pupils for the transition from school to work and is an alternative to an ordinary school curriculum.

Of necessity we have to reintegrate pupils into mainstream schools. Success depends on many factors; among them the pupil's own wishes and determination to go back, the willingness of receiving schools to be seen to adapt their practices to accommodate the pupil, the reliability of our support to the school, the general ethos and expectation at the PRU that ordinary school is the 'best' and, therefore, that is where the pupils should be, and the care taken in planning the return with everyone involved, especially the school (Galloway *et al.*, 1989; Normington, 1992a). It follows that we need a school prepared to work with us. It is easier if that school is identified at the outset rather than having to try to 'sell' difficult pupils to unwilling schools. It also saves time. If a pupil is not attending a school at all, then the sooner one is named, the sooner work for reintegration can begin. If the pupil is attending the PRU without a named school, there is no sense of urgency in finding one, delay seems to be inevitable and extended stays result.

We have used the academic year 1994–5 as a pilot year and have involved the agencies and the secondary schools in our planning and on-going evaluation. We have worked with colleagues from the education social work service, the educational psychology service, officers of the LEA, headteachers and senior staff from the high schools. We are following the Code (DfE, 1994d) and are involved at Stage 3 – 'teachers and the SEN co-ordinator are supported by specialists from outside the school' (DfE, 1994d, p. 3), with occasional overlap into Stage 4 – 'the LEA consider the need for a statutory assessment and, if appropriate, make a multi-disciplinary assessment' (DfE, 1994d, p. 3).

The major aim of the PRU is to prevent exclusion wherever possible although when pupils are excluded then we seek to reintegrate them into alternative schools. Success depends on our own credibility as a service. We aim to be flexible and responsive to the needs of individual pupils and schools.

The services we offer are:

1   The collection and collation of information to inform decision making about pupils' educational needs. This helps in identifying the precise nature of problems.
2   In-school support to attempt to maintain pupils in mainstream schools.
3   'Time-out' placements to give time for all concerned to be more objective.
4   Time-limited placements at the PRU to allow for remediation of specific learning problems or modifying particular behavioural difficulties.
5   Individually planned courses for all pupils linking closely with mainstream work and geared to raising the pupils' expectations by providing success and attainable challenge.

> A PRU is a place of learning. Careful attention will have to be paid to ensuring that the curriculum is appropriately selected and integrated, that work assignments are well planned, differentiated, challenging and attainable within the time that a child is in the unit.
>
> (DfE, 1994c, p. 13)

6   Subsequent reintegration using a variety of strategies ranging from part-time or gradual re-introduction to going back full-time with the support of the PRU's teaching and support staff: Support may involve in-class help; regular sessions with pupil and teachers to review progress, discuss targets and modify individual education plans; specific help with learning problems; arranging rewards for success; allowing time at the PRU for pupils to return to see staff or join in particular activities – it is flexible and responds to individuals.
7   Prompt, realistic support for schools and pupils. This is planned for individual situations but can be available 'on demand' in emergencies.

The emphasis in the PRU is on ensuring that time spent out of school is kept to a minimum and on facilitating successful reintegration. Schools are at all times encouraged to take responsibility for their pupils, the onus of arranging reviews and of monitoring progress remains theirs. Realistic target setting enables evaluation and helps to avoid unnecessary delay in ensuring that schools and pupils receive the help they need. If it is obvious that the individual education plans are not being effective this can provide evidence for further assessment, perhaps even Stage 4 multi-disciplinary assessment leading to a statement and the statutory provision of further support.

Planning for all pupils is multi-disciplinary and detailed. Before admission, an individual education plan is developed by staff at both the PRU and the named school. These plans are modified in practice during the pupil's time at the PRU. Before the pupil returns to school we hold a case conference, now called a reintegration meeting, involving the pupil, parents, PRU staff, school staff, education social worker, other agency representatives and an educational psychologist where possible. Progress is discussed, reintegration is planned in detail and the individual education plan modified for use in school. If the school has completed a referral to the educational psychologist at Stage 3, this is regarded as a Stage 3 individual education plan, and is then monitored and reviewed by the educational psychologist with a view to progressing to Stage 4 assessment procedures or reverting to Stage 2 as outlined in the Code (DfE, 1994d). This review normally indicates the end of our involvement with the pupil.

THE ROLE OF THE PRU WITH OLDER PUPILS

It is inadvisable to mix older pupils with no hope of return to ordinary schools with younger pupils working to that end. This is because an important factor influencing reintegration is the prevailing ethos in the PRU; if the expectation is that all pupils return to school then they are more likely to do so. If younger pupils see older ones remaining in the PRU for extended periods of time, they perceive that reintegration is not the only option. Hence our transition programme for Year 11 pupils who are permanently excluded from school.

The programme includes:

1 Distance-learning packages.
2 Frequent supervisory sessions at the PRU but in a separate part of the building.

3   Regular sessions of outdoor education to boost self-confidence and to help build good relationships with the PRU's staff, an essential requirement for effective work.
4   Work experience through the Trident Scheme (a national scheme for organising and sponsoring work experience) but monitored and supported by the PRU staff.
5   Careers guidance and the help of the Careers Service.
6   Links with schools to enable examination courses to be completed where applicable.
7   Links with tertiary colleges.
8   Community service.

During the academic year 1994–5 we worked with a group of Year 11 pupils, numbering five at the beginning of the year and increasing to fifteen by the end. They attended the PRU for two mornings each week to return work for marking, to receive further work and for specific teaching when necessary. The work was based on Units of Accreditation for the Northern Panel for Records of Achievement. The pupils received a fortnightly careers input from the specialist careers officer. Work experience was arranged for one, two or three days a week in blocks of two to three weeks. Assessment and information visits were made to the local technical college, Careers Fair, Job Centres and various training providers. Some pupils worked with a local special school, helping their older pupils at the Sports Centre. One pupil who had been entered for GCSE by his mainstream school was enabled to sit the examinations by the PRU staff arranging invigilators and escorts. Outdoor education sessions were organised and the pupils were taken canoeing, caving and rock climbing. All the pupils completed their final school year without further incident, four found permanent jobs (direct results of their work experience placements) and the others went on to training schemes.

This alternative to school is proving to be popular all round. Its future development is intended to enable us to offer a more comprehensive and concentrated educational programme covering the transition from school to the world of work.

CONCLUSION

Our reintegration work seems to be successful although it is as yet too early to evaluate the long-term effects. Of the thirty-nine pupils referred to us during the year only one has since been permanently excluded from his high school. He is about to be assessed as having special educational needs on behavioural grounds. We withdrew a Year 10 pupil to prevent his permanent exclusion and are negotiating a design and graphics college course for him for his final school year. The rest are still in their schools.

The response from the schools suggests that they appreciate the referral procedures and genuinely feel that they have a role to play in admissions to the PRU. The detailed planning and information exchange is essential in enabling pupils' return to school. There are signs that the schools are examining their internal procedures, particularly with regard to the Code and its use for pupils with behavioural difficulties. There has been a tendency in the past to assume that special educational needs referred only to learning problems but this is changing.

We have not had the anticipated flood of referrals; schools consider our involvement very carefully and only use what is a scarce resource for those pupils they feel will benefit the most, often those with the most complex difficulties. This is leading us into cooperation with more agencies including social services and the specialist support services.

It is also interesting to note that the number of permanent exclusions within the LEA has fallen. I do not claim that this is a direct result of the work of the PRU but it is a factor; the major one, however, being the attitude of our high schools towards disruptive and disaffected pupils. It is evidence of cooperation between all the schools and the agencies that exist to support them.

Despite the poor 'press' given to off-site units in the past (HMI, 1989; Mortimore et al., 1983; OFSTED, 1993a) I believe they can serve a very positive function provided that their educational rationale is clearly understood. Referral procedures, admission and discharge criteria should be agreed and defined with the support and help of the schools who will use the unit. Planning to meet individual needs should be precise with definite targets outlined and review and monitoring arrangements inbuilt. The opportunity for pupils to find success, both academically and socially, should be built upon in such a way that their return to ordinary schools can be eased.

The needs of disruptive and disaffected pupils are as special as those of children with more obvious handicaps. They should be assessed and provided for with the same assiduity if we are to prevent an increasing number of alienated adolescents growing up into unfulfilled adulthood.

(Normington, 1992b, p. 355)

Chapter 17

Cities in Schools
A new approach for excluded children and young people

Martin Stephenson

INTRODUCTION

This chapter contends that the current institutional and legislative framework coupled with professional divisions can often exacerbate the social exclusion of young people with multiple problems. The underlying reasons, the possible scale of the problems and the inadequacy of traditional approaches are reviewed in terms of inter-agency deficits. An alternative approach is then proposed.

It could be argued that the shape of health, social welfare and education services available to people who have extra needs mirrors the prevailing organisational structures and processes of the predominant form of production in a society. In the United Kingdom in the nineteenth century, the response to people with mental health needs or children without parents was to create, in effect, a factory system of care. Where people required support they were removed to an institution where economies of scale existed. Regimented practices echoed the production line processes of Victorian factories and mills.

In a post-industrial economy based upon high technology, small flexible teams and the integration of functions through comprehensive information systems, such models may be redundant. In both the private and public sectors large institutional organisations relying on bureaucratic cultures are experiencing a gradual revolution. Social welfare and educational institutions working with children and young people with multiple problems cannot avoid the impact of these changes.

The broad thrust of reforms since the mid 1970s in health, social services and educational provision has been to include groups of people in need within the mainstream of services but the pace of change for children and young people with multiple problems, who often display challenging behaviour, has lagged behind those children with, for instance, physical disabilities. There is a seductive simplicity in the removal and segregation approach to young people who challenge schools and local social services resources severely (see Booth in this volume). Unfortunately, this approach cannot be justified in terms of educational outcomes, effective use of scarce resources or longer-term benefits to local communities through reductions in offending, increased employment and participation in training.

Young people with multiple problems can, in effect, be excluded from mainstream services in a variety of ways. Permanent exclusion from school is a stark statement of our inability to cope with them. In practical terms young people excluded from school can arrive at a variety of institutions ranging from secure accommodation units, young offender institutions, residential special schools, community homes with education, off-site units or some form of day-care provision. It is of even more concern that significant numbers may go nowhere initially (SHA, 1992).

Underlying difficulties will have impelled them along various routes to these destinations but exclusion and time out of school may well in themselves accelerate this process. Their chaotic educational and care careers are often an indictment of the fragmented response of the relevant agencies and can be in part caused by organisational inadequacies (see also Firth and Horrocks, Parsons, and Cullingford and Morrison in this volume).

The separation between several agencies of services that meet the needs of children and families has been widened by changes in recent years. This division is deepened by the tendency of professionals to line up along agency boundaries. It can be a meaningless question to ask whether a child who has been excluded needs a teacher or a social worker when the causes of the problem may lie within a family but can be affected significantly by the school.

Each agency has bureaucratic systems processing these categories of young people into a disparate array of services. These systems all operate on an assessment–plan–review cycle. A child with special educational needs will be subject to this process under the Education Act 1993. If this child were to be prosecuted for an offence he or she would be assessed for a Pre-Sentence Report and, if a Criminal Supervision Order were the sentence, would have a detailed plan (including education) and regular reviews. If this same child had also been subject to abuse he or she might have undergone the assessment and planning required by a Child Protection Case Conference and subsequent registration. If a family breakdown were to occur then this child might need to be looked after by the local authority. Under the Children Act this would necessitate a detailed assessment and care plan (including education) with statutory reviews. The complex if not downright confusing interplay between these processes coupled with the underlying difficulties experienced by this child could easily result in behaviour likely to lead to exclusion from school, in which case the child would be subject to the exclusion procedures laid down in the Education Act 1993.

Activity under one process may trigger another process in an unpredictable manner. An exclusion, for instance, might precipitate a child into entering residential care which would activate the care planning process. Equally these time consuming and expensive procedures might operate in parallel, with statutory reviews being carried out on a child being looked after under the Children Act on one day and then under the 1993 Education Act on another day for a child with a statement of special educational needs.

Young people who stray across the frontiers of different agencies can enter uncharted territory and experience considerable delay in gaining access to relevant services (see Parsons, and Mitchell in this volume). The significant reorganisations of school management, status and curriculum, the incorporation of Further Education colleges, the introduction of purchaser/provider separation within Social Services and Health have created some additional short-term disruptions in communication and coordination. Services to young people with multiple problems may be much more sensitive to these organisational changes. The demise of link courses at Further Education colleges for year 11 pupils from both mainstream and special schools is an illustration of this.

Enormous friction is generated at the boundaries between and within agencies when dealing with a child with multiple problems. Not only do different professional cultures confront each other but, equally importantly, so do separate budget holders.

How does a children's home cope with an excluded young person when it is not staffed for day care? The answer is often with difficulty and high overtime costs that would be more appropriately spent on education.

The lack of a coherent framework for the division of responsibilities and functions between local authority departments, schools and health authorities is compounded by the different professional cultures such as between teachers and social workers. There is considerable ignorance of each other's professional background and statutory responsibilities. This is not rectified by most PGCE or DipSW courses. How many Heads of Year in schools are conversant with the needs of the children being looked after and their duties under the Children Act and the Education Act 1993 for participating in the care planning process?

A recent large-scale survey found that records of the educational careers of children in care were conspicuous by their absence (Fletcher-Campbell and Hall, 1990). It is common for social services departments not to possess a section on education in a case file which should be the key record of a child's life. The reasons for this are reflected by the fact that two separate studies have indicated that one in five social workers did not know whether the young person for whom they were case accountable had any educational qualifications (Biehal et al., 1992; Garnett, 1992).

This dislocation and fragmentation of key agencies divided by different professional priorities results, not surprisingly, in disrupted educational and care careers for excluded children. Access to resources in such circumstances tends to be unpredictable or by default. Whether an excluded child ends up in a residential special school many miles from home, in a Young Offender Institution or in a local Pupil Referral Unit will often owe as much to chance and geography as to careful planning. The arbitrary nature of the process is often disguised behind the terminology used by professionals. The label 'emotionally and behaviourally disturbed' has replaced 'maladjusted' and is of little more use or validity. Similarly, attempts to distinguish between 'disaffection' and 'learning difficulties' may be of value in turf wars between budget holders but do little to meet the needs of the large group of children who are excluded from achieving their potential (see also Booth in this volume).

Behaviour is often specific to a particular situation or environment. Given the range of health, social welfare and education needs of children with multiple problems then a flexible continuum of services is implied.

In organisational terms 'the overall picture is of services for children and families provided by and on behalf of different agencies, failing to mesh together and leaving a hole in the middle' (Jones and Bilton, 1993, p. 37). Excluded young people in the care system too often are falling down this hole:

> Up to a quarter of the 55,000 children and young people in the care system may be excluded or not attending school.
>
> (SSI and OFSTED, 1995, p. 3)

> Nearly 40 per cent of young people in children's homes in some authorities do not have access to a full-time education.
>
> (Audit Commission, 1994, p. 34)

> Three-quarters of all young people leaving the care system have no qualifications compared to less than one-twelfth in the general population.
>
> (Garnett, 1992, p. 63)

> A recent survey established that none of the children in the care system in their sample was judged by teachers as likely to achieve five GCSEs at Grade A–C compared to 38 per cent in the total school population.
>
> (SSI and OFSTED, 1995, p. 11)

> In the same survey it was established that in the 14–16 age group one-quarter were either permanently *excluded* or did not attend school.
>
> (SSI and OFSTED, 1995, p. 13)

> Only one or two young persons in a hundred in the care system will achieve a pass at A level.
>
> (Garnett, 1992, p. 63)

> One-half of all care leavers are unemployed after one year.
>
> (Jackson, 1995, p. 1)

> Over half of homeless young people may have been in the care system.
>
> (Jackson, 1995, p. 1)

It is indisputable that society is failing as a parent those who are the most vulnerable in the critically important duty to ensure educational achievement. This is not an indictment of individuals but rather the result of a systemic failure between education and social services. For social services departments to berate schools or for headteachers to demand greater powers to exclude is a damaging irrelevance that merely emphasises the impotence of our current professional structures to manage these young people effectively. Cost-shunting between agencies inevitably wastes scarce resources and intensifies the multiple problems of the young person (see also Parsons in this volume). Unfortunately the fault-lines between education and social services appear to be widening given the recent dramatic increase in permanent exclusions.

The associations between offending behaviour and educational status appear to be significant as both cause and effect (Graham, 1988); (see Searle, Stirling, and Cullingford and Morrison, in this volume). Exclusion or non-attendance at school obviously places young people more at risk in terms of involvement in substance abuse and offending (Graham, 1988). Equally, criminal activities including substance abuse can precipitate an exclusion from school.

Research and monitoring parallels departmental preoccupations both centrally and locally and consequently very little is known of the experiences of excluded young people who have multiple problems. These are often the children about whom knowledge should be shared between agencies. Yet we do not know how many of the total population of children looked after have statements of special educational needs or have been excluded. Virtually nothing is known of the destinations of many of these young people in the post-16 world except their disproportionate representation in prison populations and on the streets. Exclusion from school in years 10 or 11, when the chances of reintegration into a new school are often very limited, is extremely damaging to the transition to further education, Youth Training or employment. These young people are unlikely to meet the National Training and Education Targets and to be able to sustain themselves in Youth Training.

Paradoxically, although we are very concerned as a society about these disaffected and excluded groups, relatively little is known even in terms of scale. Given current estimates of exclusion and non-attendance for children of compulsory school age and the estimates for non-participation post-16, there may be between 125,000 and 150,000 young people not in education, training or employment between the ages of 14–17 (Dearing, 1995). The presence of such an ominously large pool of alienated and disadvantaged young people is a threat to the cohesion of communities and their quality of life and a significant constraint on economic success.

Given the failure of much of the traditional configuration of educational and social services in meeting the needs of young people who are excluded and who are beset with multiple problems, major changes are clearly necessary. In organisational terms the prerequisites for success are:

1   Integrated structures transcending departmental and agency boundaries;
2   Multi-disciplinary teams.
3   A flexible continuum of provision.
4   Local accountability.
5   Partnership between the public and private sectors.

CITIES IN SCHOOLS

Cities in Schools arose in the USA in the late 1970s as a response to the scale of disaffection with schools in inner cities. It was founded on a recognition of the need to broker all the resources of a local community in order to provide coordinated services. The movement was driven by a passionate commitment to the needs of individual young people. The school was seen as the last universal community institution and education the motive force for urban regeneration. It is now a highly successful and extensive organisation reaching over 100,000 young people in thirty-two states. The programmes span health, education and social welfare needs (Cities in Schools [Inc.], 1994).

CiS (UK) is an independent organisation based upon the American model but adapted to the political, social welfare and educational structures of the UK. Existing since 1990 it has expanded particularly rapidly since mid-1993 with over fifty projects being established in an eighteen-month period.

Its organisational structure is tailored to meet comprehensive needs of children with multiple problems. Rather than a single monolithic organisation with a command structure, it is a federation of autonomous charitable companies accountable to local boards of directors. Membership of these boards is drawn from local councils, social service departments, the business community, health services, the police, Training and Enterprise Councils, schools and relevant voluntary organisations. This enables the integration of service provision, local accountability and the best use of existing resources.

Operational management, business planning, staff recruitment, training, fund raising and evaluation are purchased from the Central Team of CiS (UK) through a detailed partnership agreement by the local CiS programmes, giving each local programme access to the national network for practice development and increased resources. It also minimises management costs for individual local programmes, enabling maximum resources to be deployed for direct services for young people.

Staff are recruited from a wide range of professional backgrounds including teaching, youth and community work, residential care, social work, education welfare and health.

The key groups of children and young people are those at risk of falling, or who have actually fallen, out of the education system through either non-attendance or exclusion, particularly those looked after by the local authority. The primary aim is to reintegrate them into mainstream education and training so that they can fulfil their potential. Since exclusion is often symptomatic of underlying problems, much of the work is concentrated on families and on reducing involvement in crime and drug and alcohol dependency and on preparation for independence.

Other CiS projects conform to the following principles which shape both the individual projects and the culture of the organisation. It is of paramount importance that the needs of a young person are dealt with in their entirety rather than from a single perspective, be it education, health or social services. Educational achievement for each individual is the goal but can be achieved only by recognising other issues, regarding relationships, self-esteem, appropriate behaviour, drug and alcohol use, that may be involved.

The right of all young people to mainstream educational environments is asserted constantly in CiS projects as are the advantages in terms of educational achievements, enhancement of life chances and benefits to the rest of the community.

The effectiveness of services has to be clearly demonstrated, particularly given the evidence regarding 'spontaneous remission' for perhaps two-thirds of young people displaying disruptive behaviour (Topping, 1983, p. 11).

In addition, value for money has to be established in the context of relatively costly services. All CiS projects receive an independent evaluation measured against agreed criteria and incorporating 'before and after' consumer surveys.

Family work with parents or carers is fundamental to successful reintegration into education. In many instances CiS project staff will undertake the basic social work tasks with a parent or carer, helping them to cope with a wide range of issues within the family. (Such work is always undertaken within the context of case accountability resting with the relevant local authority social worker.)

The promotion of equal opportunities is a key role for CiS staff. Evidence of disproportionate exclusion rates of, for example, African–Caribbean males is accumulating (Blyth and Milner in this volume; Knight, 1995; OFSTED, 1993a). In addition many young people with low self-esteem have restricted and stereotyped expectations of career paths for themselves. Exclusion from school can often diminish opportunities for participation in a whole range of activities, such as sport, and is a stigma in terms of perceptions by possible employers, training agencies or further education establishments.

The partnership approach is not confined to the organisational structure but permeates all work. Voluntary organisations such as CiS are adept at creating and sustaining networks across a disparate range of agencies. Significantly, CiS involves the resources of the business community ranging from small single person businesses to large national ones. Since the mid 1970s there has been an increasing involvement of businesses within mainstream education. They are also well placed to add value to projects for young people who have problems and who may be excluded from school. Without their input a whole-community approach cannot be achieved.

The contribution of the private sector ranges from significant cash donations and important contributions in kind, such as the provision of free office space, secretarial services and access to management training, and *pro bono* work on legal issues, auditing and marketing, to extended work experience and monitoring for excluded children, and representation on the board of management. In some cases, this involvement represents enlightened self-interest through a recognition that business cannot prosper without a trained workforce or more prosperous consumers or lower crime environments. In others it represents a strong commitment to giving young people another chance.

The concept of community involvement pervades the organisation and recognises that the needs of some individual young people outstrip the capability of a school or social work team acting in isolation.

If the problems of young people are often closely linked then a continuum of services is needed to prevent their precipitate transfer from one agency to another through processes such as permanent exclusion. Having established the organisational principles that are necessary, it is equally important to examine the structure and inter-relationship of the different kinds of provision for young people with multiple problems.

Both the strategic direction of the organisation and the inter-relationship of its projects and services are depicted in Figure 17.1. This pyramid is an adaptation of Topping's valuable work on the hierarchy of interventions (Topping, 1983).

Progression towards the apex of the pyramid represents increasing cost and more structured approaches. Clearly the more that resources can be progressively redeployed towards the base, the greater the long-term beneficial impact on greater numbers of children.

One of the major constraints on local authorities is that a disproportionate amount of their resources is committed to crisis interventions, often in very restrictive environments such as out of county/borough placements. The advantage of the CiS approach is that not only can significant resources be released at the alternative intervention stage for redeployment but this occurs within an integrated management structure with a clear strategic direction – the abolition of exclusion in all its forms.

While the bulk of CiS projects currently relate to the alternative intervention stage, several authorities have already been the beneficiaries of reintegration teams and a wide range of preventive initiatives partly funded by the cost effectiveness of alternative intervention projects.

The traditional services for young people with disruptive behaviour include residential and day special schools and off-site units.

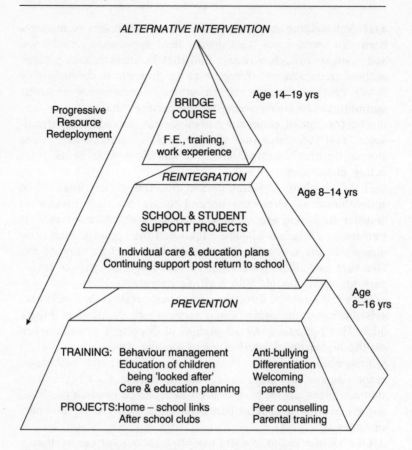

Figure 17.1   Continuum of CiS projects and services

The residential special-school sector may well follow the example of the residential child-care sector which has shrunk dramatically over the last decade. This will be for much the same reasons: high costs and a lack of demonstrable outcomes particularly where reintegration into local communities and progression into further education are concerned.

The off-site unit has traditionally created for the majority of permanently excluded 14–16 year olds as well as long-term non-attenders. These units experienced an extraordinary growth in the 1970s with ILEA alone possessing over 220 units with nearly

4,000 places (Topping, 1983, p. 35). This growth appears to have been unrelated to any marked increases in disruptive behaviour and exclusions and, as always, the existence of a resource creates its own demand whether it be bed spaces or motorways.

The 1993 Education Act required these units to operate with much greater clarity of purpose and curriculum and renamed them as Pupils Referral Units (Parsons, 1995, p. 22). In 1994 some 3,000 (39 per cent) of all permanently excluded secondary-age pupils attended these units (Parsons, 1995, p. 22).

Research and inspections (OFSTED, 1993, p. 9, 1995, pp. 5–6) have revealed a number of major weaknesses in this approach. The curriculum tends to be narrow and the quality of teaching can be reduced by the lack of specialist subject teachers (OFSTED, 1995, p. 6). Relatively few young people are reintegrated into mainstream primary and secondary schools (Parsons, 1995, p. 3; Graham, 1988, pp. 40–3). The primary aim of reintegration, particularly of younger pupils, is prevented by the presence of a group of 15- and 16-year olds who have experienced multiple exclusions and are not returning to secondary schools. This results in a wide range of ages in the one unit and creates a long-term out of school culture with inappropriate role models for younger pupils. Schools can absolve themselves of their responsibilities by the use of these units. Accommodation is often poor (OFSTED, 1993, p. 9; 1995, p. 5). Placements are not cost-effective. These is a risk of pupils and parents regarding the use of these units as a 'sin-bin' and staff may also become marginalised from mainstream professional development (OFSTED, 1993, p. 9). Academic achievement and progression into further education, training and employment are often unacceptably low (OFSTED, 1995, p. 13) In addition, over half of the units provide less than fifteen hours education a week (Parsons, 1995, p. 22). Many of these problems cannot be resolved by increasing the amount of resources avaliable as the model itself, no matter how good the staff are, is flawed fundamentally. The fact that another 2,000 pupils receive on average only five hours a week of Home Tuition (Parsons, 1995, p. 23) is a further indictment of traditional provision.

THE BRIDGE COURSE

The CiS Bridge Course was devised in the late 1980s initially for young people who were serious offenders and at risk of custody.

Without exception their mainstream schooling had broken down and they had been permanently excluded from several secondary schools. Several were also being 'looked after' by the local authority in either foster or residential care. Given that they had suffered some dislocation it was decided to establish a project without a base. Building on post-16 provision and the experience of link courses, a pilot scheme was devised that combined attendance for two days a week at a further education college on a discrete course with extended work experience. Recognition of the potential behavioural difficulties and the multiple needs of this group led to each young person being allocated a key worker in addition to the college lecturer team. These key workers would attend college on a rota basis and chase up any late arrivals in addition to undertaking any family and court work.

This pilot project ran for one term and had remarkable results that surprised the seasoned professionals who had known the young people over many years. In view of this it was decided to make the project full-time and to increase the number of groups of young people. It became established as an independent charity and over the next few years, extended to young people who were not offenders but whose schooling had broken down irretrievably.

In September 1993 this charity was subsumed within CiS and this model which had been adapted in the light of experience gained since 1989 was promoted as an alternative to off-site units and home tuition. The CiS course is now a full-time course for young people approaching their final year of compulsory education for whom the local education authority considers there is no appropriate mainstream school available owing to the irretrievable breakdown of schooling through non-attendance or permanent exclusion.

The constituent parts of the programme are: two days at college, two days related work experience and one day of a personal tutor session and a structured leisure or groupwork activity.

The objectives of the course are to:

1   Assist young people in improving their literacy/numeracy and life-skills.
2   Provide positive learning and educational experiences in their final year of compulsory education.
3   Achieve progression into further education, training or employment.
4   Prepare young people for independent living.

The curriculum is designed to be consistent with the requirements of section 298 of the Education Act 1993 and with Circular 11/94 (CiS [UK], 1995; DfE, 1994c).

A broad and balanced curriculum is offered that is relevant to individual learning needs. The core subjects of maths, English and information technology are augmented by vocational 'tasters', personal and social education and preparation for the world of work. The extended work experience is monitored through fortnightly progress meetings between the project manager, student and employer. In addition, a college lecturer will visit to assess the work undertaken in terms of competencies, to link educational issues between college and work experience, and to accredit learning through schemes such as the Vocational Access Certificate.

Other forms of accreditation used are of proven currency value such as: Word Power and Number Power, AEB Basic skills and the Youth Award Scheme. All students complete a high quality National Record of Achievement. Both the academic and vocational routes are emphasised in terms of post-16 education. Once the confidence of students has increased, opportunities for infill are negotiated to prepare for courses in the subsequent year.

Each student has a detailed education plan. This is written following an initial assessment of the student's learning achievements and agreed with the student and his or her parent(s) or carer(s). This individual action plan contains details and targets related to both educational and social welfare needs. The plan is formally reviewed each half term and renegotiated where necessary.

What makes the Bridge Course significantly different from other uses of further education provision is its highly structured approach encompassing family and educational needs, the emphasis on young people who have been labelled as the most disaffected and disruptive, and the role of the project manager.

The joint SSI and OFSTED report identified the reason for failing the educational needs of children in the care system as being 'the lack of one person responsible for fulfilling the role of parent in continuously pressing for improvement and inculcating in the child the importance of education' (SSI and OFSTED, 1995, p. 42).

The project manager, who may have a background in teaching, residential care, field social work, youth work, or the probation service, will be extremely experienced in working with young people who, in particular settings, display very challenging behaviour. The manager's role is to coordinate all aspects of the project, to be the personal tutor to each of the ten students, to work with parents and carers and to liaise with all relevant agencies.

In coordinating the project, the manager is responsible for a devolved budget covering the cost of college provision, transport costs, student activities and all administrative support costs. Flexible, devolved budgets are an organisational hallmark of CiS. Front-line staff who make key day-to-day decisions need swift access to funds. Equally, adolescents who may be living chaotic lives with crisis placement moves should not have their lives disrupted further through the slow grinding of bureaucratic processes to release money.

As personal tutor, the project manager ensures that each student has an individual tutorial each week covering any issues of concern to the young person. In this role the project manager will often undertake a considerable amount of family work to resolve difficulties which may be contributing to attendance and behavioural problems.

The project manager liaises with other agencies as some of these young people are caught up within both the criminal justice and care systems; this involves attending reviews, acting as the appropriate adult and generally ensuring that there is one person of sufficient professional stature to help to guide and support the young person.

Given the cost of such intervention and the need to demonstrate its effectiveness considerable emphasis is placed on evaluation and performance targets. This is achieved through concentrating on the recruitment and development of high quality staff and performance management and evaluation systems.

Hard data is collected on the young people's backgrounds, performance during the course, achievements and destinations. A consumer survey of their attitudes on issues such as education, employment and preparedness for independence is undertaken at the beginning and the end of the course.

In addition to individual performance targets (for both staff and students), targets are agreed with the main purchasers, LEAs or social services. These may include:

1   Attendance rates.
2   Punctuality.
3   Students dropping out of the project.
4   The numbers progressing into further education/employment/youth training.
5   Formal accreditation achieved.
6   The number of family visits.

A summary of the findings of an evaluation report in 1993–4 at three Bridge Courses operating in a large authority in the South of England, but spanning both urban and rural communities, is presented below (CiS [UK], 1994).

Just under a quarter of the students lived in a family with both natural parents compared to a national average of 70 per cent and is an indication of the level of family disruption experienced.

One-quarter were being 'looked after' by the local authority in contrast to a national average of 0.5 per cent. One Bridge Course had over one-third of students being 'looked after' and only one young person had parents who had not divorced. In addition, in this particular group of ten young people, four out of five of the girls had been sexually abused and three students had fathers who had committed suicide.

As might be expected, there was a great deal of movement in terms of accommodation during the year for this group. One student, for example, who was a resident at an adolescent psychiatric unit at the beginning of the course moved respectively into independent lodgings, semi-independent lodgings, an adult psychiatric hospital, bed-and-breakfast, and finally independent lodgings at the end of the course.

In total, nearly one-third (31 per cent) were living independently of parent(s)/carer(s) at the end of the course. This contrasts starkly with the national average of one in 200 of 16–17 year olds living independently.

The majority were excluded although significant numbers had been long-term non-attenders, in one case for almost three years. Several had previously been excluded from other schools and although they were now on the rolls of new schools they were refusing to attend. One student had attended more than ten schools as a result of changing care placements.

In terms of their perception of their secondary schooling over half of the students gave a positive view of the lessons (55 per cent) but two-thirds were negative regarding their teachers with only 21 per cent being positive.

The main loss from being out of school was contact with friends for more than one-third, with almost as many recording 'that they missed nothing'.

It is not surprising that other agencies were heavily involved in the lives of these young people with nearly half (48 per cent) being known to the police and Youth Justice teams and a similar proportion (45 per cent) being formally known to social services.

Attendance on the course was, considering their previous experience, very high. All three projects achieved overall attendance figures of more than 80 per cent. The vast majority of absences were authorised, often relating to agency involvement such as court appearances or health issues. If authorised absences were omitted then on one of the projects, for example, more than half of the students achieved 100 per cent attendance.

Comparative average attendance figures with school show a marked improvement from about 40 per cent to over 80 per cent. One student who had recorded a zero school attendance in the previous year achieved 88 per cent attendance on the course.

Broken down by course component, average attendance at work experience was 80 per cent, college 84 per cent and personal tutorial 89 per cent. There was an improvement in attendance in all curriculum components during the year.

There were positive first destinations for three-quarters of the students, in that 14 per cent went directly into employment, 24 per cent into further education and 38 per cent into Youth Training.

In terms of accredited achievements all students commencing the course in September achieved their National Record of Achievement. AEB Basic Skills, examinations in Numeracy, Literacy, Maths, English, World of Work and Life skills were entered at various levels. Other accreditations included Word Power and Number Power, Vocational Access Certificate, City and Guilds Communication Skills, Compact Certificate, Clait Modules and a range of certificates specific to particular colleges in, for example, First Aid, motor vehicles and computers.

The reaction of students to the teaching styles of further education lecturers was interesting, in that 91 per cent gave a positive rating in contrast to the 21 per cent to the teaching they had received in school. When lessons were assessed by subject content and length, 69 per cent of students rated them positively compared to 55 per cent in relation to school lessons.

Work experience is an important part of the curriculum and placements occurred in building, retail, offices, catering, mechanical, care, hairdressing, art and design, and working with animals. With some students there was a considerable turnover of placements but across the three projects the average number of placements was 1.85 per student. Over half had only one placement. Catering and mechanics represented 59 per cent of all placements. Choice of placement divided on a gender basis with all care placements being taken up by female students and all building placements by males. As might be expected given the high attendance rates, work experience was generally highly valued, particularly in the rural areas. Three-quarters of all responses relating to work experience were positive.

When it came to attitudinal change with regard to education, employment and training there appears to have been a significant shift. This was particularly the case in respect of education where two-thirds believed that they were more positive by the end of the course. In the project in the rural area this was over 80 per cent.

More positive attitudes towards employment and training were indicated by about half of the students although there was considerable variation between projects. Interestingly the higher the level of local unemployment, the greater the improvement in relation to training.

Open-ended questions were also asked in relation to personal development. The great majority of responses fell into the three areas of increased confidence, maturity and responsibility. A survey of the parents, carers and professionals working with these groups confirmed this belief that there had been a significant improvement in attitude, self-confidence, maturity and social skills.

The reason for the success of these projects lies in the harnessing of the more adult environment of further education colleges to a highly structured contractual approach by a single person who took responsibility for all aspects of these young people's lives. Clearly the project stands or falls according to the strengths and commitment of the project manager.

Bridge Courses are now operating in Cardiff, London, Norwich, Liverpool, Newport, Peterborough, Tredegar, Wisbech, Huyton,

Cambridge and Huntingdon and are proving equally effective in all of these very different locations.

Part of the attraction of this model for local authorities lies in its cost effectiveness. Where an off-site unit has unit costs of between £7,000 and £10,000 per pupil (OFSTED, 1993a, p. 4) – in some cases up to £17,000 per head where a true cost of the buildings and management costs is included – a Bridge Course costs between £4,000 and £4,500 depending on college fees and transport expenses. A group of ten students would therefore cost up to £45,000 for a full year with all costs, including the Project Manager's salary. Severing the nexus with a building completely both achieves integration into a mainstream educational environment and reduces costs significantly. These savings can then be redeployed into reintegration and preventive work with schools for younger children in order to reduce the number out of school in their final two years.

This basic Bridge model is being extended in a number of ways. A more intensive version for year 10 students is being piloted currently which involves three days a week in college, a career awareness programme, and a personal and social skills project operated in partnership with the youth service. It is expected that the shape of their year 11 course will be based much more on highly supported infill and a much greater range of individual choice following a successful year in college during year 10. Again this model is being used with groups of ten students who are deemed to be in most need by the local authority.

Other projects include operating a Bridge Course specifically for a children's home for young people currently placed out of county/borough in order to assist in the reintegration of those young people into their local community and to reduce local authority costs.

Similarly the Bridge model is being used by several pupil referral units to help them to focus on reintegration. In fact where a unit does create a 'revolving door' it is on the basis of excellent in-school support offered to schools and ultimately the need for capacity in units or out of authority special provision is dramatically reduced (see also Normington in this volume).

The major development for this model for excluded young people is to adapt it as part of a continuum from 14 to 19 ensuring that support continues post-16 for vulnerable groups of young people, such as those leaving care, but always within a mainstream environment. Young people excluded from education are far less likely to engage in Youth Training and further education post-16. Where they do, their retention rates are probably far below the average. CiS is working closely with a number of Training and Enterprise Councils to ensure that these groups are integrated into mainstream training and post-16 education.

The model itself requires continual refinement in the light of experience and formal inspection. It is important that the coherence of the educational experience is increased across the two main components of college and work experience. It is essential that the model adapts to become more challenging to the more able students and extends the range of subjects offered.

Bridging courses in various forms and for differing groups of young people have not been uncommon during the last fifteen years. The CiS Bridge Course is significantly different in both the level of problems experienced by the young people and the highly structured and intensive level of support offered to both college, student and family. CiS, through a strong commitment to the principles of integration and the entitlements of young people, has devised an extremely resilient model of support with excluded young people beset with difficulties who in turn can pose considerable challenges to existing working methods and organisational structures.

CONCLUSION

The conclusion is unequivocal: partnership and positive intervention can enable real success in education and life for these young people. The cost effectiveness of the Bridge Course will, if replicated on a large scale, enable a significant diversion of existing resources into prevention and early reintegration. The ideal is to eliminate exclusion in its present form. To achieve this will require major institutional and attitudinal professional reforms and the redeployment of resources. CiS will be striving with other agencies to achieve this through dynamic, locally accountable partnerships.

References

Advisory Centre for Education (1991) 'Exclusions', *ACE Bulletin*, no. 47, pp. 4–5.

Alanen, L. (1994) 'Gender and generation: feminism and the "child question"', in J. Qvortrup, M. Bardy, G. Sgritta, and H. Winterberger (eds) *Childhood Matters: Social Theory, Practice and Politics*, Aldershot: Avebury Press.

Alderson, K. (1994) 'Voices drove man to kill children with hammer', *The Times*, 24 September, p. 6.

Anderson, G. (1990) *Fundamentals of Educational Research*, London: Falmer Press.

Argyris, C. (1993) *Knowledge for Action: A Guide to Overcoming Barriers to Organisational Change*, San Francisco: Jossey–Bass.

Argyris, C. and Schön, D. A. (1974) *Theory in Practice*, San Francisco: Jossey–Bass.

Armstrong, D. and Galloway, D. (1992) 'On being a client: conflicting perspectives in assessment', in T. Booth, W. Swann, M. Masterton, and P. Potts (eds) *Policies for diversity in education*, London: Routledge.

Armstrong, D., Galloway, D. and Tomlinson, S. (1993) 'Assessing special educational needs: the child's contribution', *British Educational Research Journal*, 19, 2, pp. 121–31.

Association of Chief Education Social Workers and National Association of Social Workers in Education (1991) *Code of Principles and Practice*.

Association of Metropolitan Authorities (1995a) *Reviewing Special Educational Needs: Report of the AMA Working Party on Special Educational Needs*, London: AMA.

Association of Metropolitan Authorities (1995b) *Special Needs*, press release, 26 January, Ref. 6/95, London: AMA.

Audit Commission (1994) *Seen But Not Heard: Co-ordinating Community Child and Social Services for Children in Need*, London: HMSO.

Badger, B. (1992) 'Managing a disruptive school' in D. Reynolds, and P. Cuttance (eds) *School Effectiveness: Research, Policy and Practice* London: Cassell.

Ball, S. (1990) *Politics and Policymaking in Education*, London: Methuen.

Ball, S. (1993) 'Education markets, choice and social class: the market as a class strategy in the UK and the USA', *British Journal of Sociology of Education*, 14, 1, pp. 3–19.

Bardon, J. (1980) *The New Zealand Educational Psychologist: A Comparative Analysis*, New Zealand Council for Educational Research, University of Auckland, pp. 21–4.

Bardy, M. (1994) 'The manuscript of the 100-Years Project: towards a revision', in J. Qvortrup, M. Bardy, G. Sgritta, and H. Winterberger (eds) *Childhood Matters: Social Theory, Practice and Politics*, Aldershot: Avebury Press.

Barker Lunn, J. C. (1970) *Streaming in the Primary School*, Slough: National Foundation for Educational Research.

Barrett, G. (ed.) (1989) *Disaffection from School? The Early Years*, London: Falmer Press.

Barrett, M. (1980) 'The educational system: gender and class, in Barrett, M. (ed.) *Women's Oppression Today*, London: Verso.

Bass, E. and Davis, L. (1988) *The Courage to Heal*, London: Cedar Press.

Bebbington, A. and Miles, J. (1989) 'The background of children who enter local authority care', *British Journal of Social Work*, 19, 5, pp. 349–68.

Beecham, J. and Knapp, M. (1993) *Child Care Assessment in Social Services: A Study of the Costs*, Discussion Paper 982, Personal Social Research Unit, University of Kent, Canterbury.

Bell, G. (ed.) (1994) *Action Research, Special Needs and School Development*, London: David Fulton.

Bell, V. (1993) 'A continual contest: Foucault and feminism', in Bell, V., (ed.) *Interrogating Incest*, London: Routledge.

Bennathan, M. (1992) 'The care and education of troubled children', *Therapeutic Care and Education*, 1, 1, pp. 1–7.

Best, R. (1994) 'Teachers' supportive roles in a secondary school: a case study and discussion', *Support for learning*, 9, 4, pp. 171–8.

Biehal, N., Clayden, J., Stein, M. and Wade, J. (1992) *Prepared for Living? A Survey of Young People Leaving the Care of Three Local Authorities*, London: National Children's Bureau.

Binns, D. (1990) 'History and growth of traveller education', *British Journal of Educational Studies*, 38, 3, pp. 251–8.

Blyth, E. and Milner, J. (1990) 'The process of interagency work' in Violence against Children Study Group (editorial collective), *Taking Child Abuse Seriously*, London: Unwin Hyman.

Blyth, E. and Milner, J. (1993) 'Exclusion from school: a first step in exclusion from society?' *Children and Society*, 7, 3, pp. 20–34.

Blyth, E. and Milner, J. (1994) 'Exclusion from school and victim-blaming', *Oxford Review of Education*, 20, 3, pp. 293–306.

Blyth, E. and Milner, J. (1995) 'Young black people excluded from school', paper presented at Conference, *Current Developments in Child Care: Linking Practice with Research*, Leeds University, March.

Blyth, E. and Milner, J. (1996) 'Unsaleable goods and the education market', in C. Pole and R. Chawla-Duggan (eds) *Reshaping Education in the 1990s: Perspective on Secondary Schooling*, London: Falmer Press.

Booth, T. (1995) 'Mapping inclusion and exclusion: Concepts for all?', in C. Clark, D. Dyson and A. Millward (eds) *Towards Inclusive Schools?*, London: David Fulton.

Bourne, J. (1989) *Moving into the Mainstream: LEA Provision for Bilingual Pupils*, London: NFER Nelson.

Bourne, J., Bridges, L. and Searle, C. (1994) *Outcast England: How Schools Exclude Black Children*, London: Institute of Race Relations.

Bowers, T. (1994) 'Strangely familiar', *Managing Schools Today*, 3, 7, pp. 3–5.

Boykim, W. and Toms, F. D. (1985) 'Black child socialisation: a conceptual framework', in H. P. McAdoo, and J. L. McAdoo (eds) *Black Children: Social, Educational and Parental Environments*, London: Sage.

Brandt, G. L. (1986) *The Realisation of Anti-racist Teaching*, Lewes: Falmer Press.

British Broadcasting Corporation (1993) 'A class apart', a *Panorama* programme, 15 March.

Bronfenbrenner, U. (1979) *The Ecology of Human Development*, Cambridge, Mass: Harvard University Press.

Broom, D. (1988) 'Asians beat whites in O levels', *The Times*, 6 October, p. 3.

Bullock, R., Little, M. and Milham, S. (1994) 'Children's return from state care to school', *Oxford Review of Education*, 20, 3, pp. 307–16.

Burgess, R. (1989) 'Grey areas: ethical dilemmas in educational ethnography', in R. Burgess (ed.) *The Ethics of Educational Research*, London: Falmer Press.

Burgess, R. G. (1984) *In the Field*, London: Allen & Unwin.

Burns, R. B. (1977) 'The self-concept and its relevance to academic achievement', in D. Child (ed.) *Readings in Psychology for the Teacher*, London: Rinehart & Winston.

Burns, R. B. (1982) *Self-Concept Development and Education*, London: Holt, Rinehart & Winston.

Carlen, P. (1985) 'Out of care into custody', in P. Carlen, and A. Worrall (eds) *Gender, Crime and Justice*, Milton Keynes: Open University Press.

Carlen, P., Gleeson, D. and Wardhaugh, J. (1992) *Truancy: the Politics of Compulsory Schooling*, Buckingham: Open University Press.

Carpenter, B. (1994) *Early Intervention: Where are we now?*, Oxford: Westminster College.

Carroll, H. C. M. (ed.) (1977) *Absenteeism in South Wales: Studies of Pupils, their Homes and their Secondary Schools*, Swansea: University College of Swansea Faculty of Education.

Centrepoint (1992) *No Way Back*, London: Centrepoint.

Channel 4 (1993) *Free for All*, 2 March.

Chartered Institute of Public Finance and Accountancy (1993) *Education Statistics 1992–3: Actuals incorporating the Handbook of Unit Costs*, London: CIPFA.

Christenson, S., Yesseldyke, J. E., Wang, J. J. and Algozzine, B. (1983) 'Teacher attributions for problems that result in referral for psycho-educational evaluation', *Journal of Educational Research*, 76, pp. 174–80.

Cicourel, H. V., and Kitsuse, J. I. (1968) 'The social organisation of the highschool and deviant adolescent careers', in E. Rubington and M. S. Weinberg (eds) *Deviance: the Interactionist Perspective*, New York: Macmillan.

Cities in Schools (Inc.) (1994) *Annual Report*, Alexandria, VA: CiS.

Cities in Schools (UK) (1994) *Evaluation Report*, Cambridge: CiS.

Cities in Schools (UK) (1995) *The Bridge Course: A Curriculum Framework*, Cambridge: CiS.

Clarke, M. (1986) 'Education and welfare issues in co-ordination and co-operation', *Pastoral Care in Education*, 4, 1, pp. 51–9.

Clegg, S. R. (1989) *Frameworks of Power*, London: Sage.

Cline, T. (1989) 'Making case conferences more effective: a checklist for monitoring and training', *Children and Society*, 3, 2, pp. 99–106.

Coard, B. (1971) *How the West Indian Child is made Educationally Subnormal in the British School System*, London: New Beacon Books.

Cohen, J. (1995) 'Expelled boy takes private school to court', *Sunday Times*, 30 April, p. 10.

Cohen, R. and Hughes, M. (with Ashworth, L. and Blair, M.) (1994) *School's Out: the Family Perspective on School Eexclusion*, London: Family Service Units, Barnardos.

Colton, M. and Heath, A. (1994) 'Attainment and behaviour of children in care and at home', *Oxford Review of Education*, 20, 3, pp. 317–27.

Commission for Racial Equality (1985) *Birmingham LEA and Schools: Referral and Suspension of Pupils*, London: CRE.

Commission for Racial Equality (1986) *Teaching English as a Second Language: Report of a Formal Investigation in Calderdale LEA*, London: CRE.

Commission for Racial Equality (1992) *Set to Fail? Setting and Banding in Secondary Schools*, London: CRE.

Condon, P. (1995) cited in *The Times*, 8 July, p. 4.

Connolly, P. (1995) 'Racism, masculine peer-group relations and the schooling of African–Caribbean infant boys', *British Journal of Sociology of Education*, 16, 1, pp. 75–92.

Cooper, P. (1993) *Effective Schools for Disaffected Students*, London: Routledge.

Cooper, P., Upton, G. and Smith, C. (1991) 'Ethnic minority and gender distribution among staff and pupils in facilities for pupils with emotional and behavioural difficulties in England and Wales', *British Journal of the Sociology of Education*, 12, 1, pp. 77–94.

Cottle, T. J. (1978) *Black Testimony: Voices of Britain's West Indians*, London: Wildwood House.

Coxon, P. (1988) 'A primary approach to misbehaviour', *Special Children*, no. 24, October, pp. 22–3.

Cullingford, C. (1993) 'Children's attitudes to bullying', *Education 3–11*, 21, 2, pp. 54–60.

Cullingford, C. and Brown, G. (1995) Children's Perceptions of Victims and Bullies, *Education 3–13*, 23, 2, pp. 11–17.

Cullingford, C. and Morrison, J. (1995) 'Bullying as a formative experience: the relationship between the experience of school and criminality', *British Educational Research Journal*, 21, 5, pp. 547–60.

Curtis, M. J. and Meyers, J. (1985) 'Best practices in school-based consultation', in A. Thomas and J. Grimes (eds) *Best Practices in School Psychology*, Washington, DC: National Association for School Psychologists.

Davie, L. (1979) 'Deadlier than the male? Girls' conformity and deviance in school', in L. Barton and R. Meighan (eds) *Schools, Pupils and Deviance*, Driffield: Nafferton Books.

Davie, R. (1977) 'The interface between education and social services', in DHSS and Welsh Office, *Working Together for Children and Families*, London: HMSO.

Davie, R. (1989) 'Behaviour problems and the teacher', in T. Charlton and K. David (eds) *Managing Misbehaviour*, Basingstoke: Macmillan.

Davies, B. (1986) *Threatening Youth: Towards a National Youth Policy*, Milton Keynes: Open University Press.

Davies, B. (1990) 'Agency as a form of discursive practice: a classroom scene observed', *British Journal of Sociology of Education*, 11, 3, pp. 341–61.

Davis, L. (1985) *Caring for Secondary School Pupils*, London: Heinemann Educational.

Dawson, N. (1994) *The 1994 Survey of Educational Provision for Pregnant Schoolgirls and Schoolgirl Mothers in the Leas of England and Wales*, Bristol: Department of Education, University of Bristol.

Dearing, R. (1995) *Review of 16–18 Qualifications*, London: Sir Ron Dearing, July.

Denzin, N. K. (1978) *The Research Act* (2nd edition), New York: McGraw Hill.

Department for Education (1992a) *Exclusion: a Discussion Paper*, London: DfE.

Department for Education (1992b) *Choice and Diversity: A New Framework for Schools*, Cm 2021, London: HMSO.

Department for Education (1993) *A New Deal for 'Out of School' Pupils*, press release 126/93, London: DfE.

Department for Education (1994a) *Pupil Behaviour and Discipline*, Circular No. 8/94, London: DfE.

Department for Education (1994b) *Exclusions from School*, Circular No. 10/94, London: DfE.

Department for Education (1994c) *The Education by LEAs of Children Otherwise than at School*, Circular No. 11/94, London: DfE.

Department for Education (1994d) *Code of Practice on the Identification and Assessment of Special Educational Needs*, London: DfE.

Department for Education (1994e) *Our Children's Education: The Updated Parent's Charter 1994*, London: HMSO.

Department for Education (1994f) *The Education (Special Educational Needs) (Information) Regulations*, London: DfE.

Department for Education (1995) 'Grants for Education Support and Training (GEST) Scheme, Truancy and Disaffected Pupils Category', *Directory of Approved Projects 1994–5*, London: DfE.

Department for Education and Department of Health (1994a) *Children with Emotional and Behavioural Difficulties*, Circular No. 9/94, DH LAC (94) 9, London: DfE and DoH.

Department for Education and Department of Health (1994b) *The Education of Sick Children*, Circular No. 12/94, DH LAC(94) 10, London: DfE and DOH.

Department for Education and Department of Health (1994c) *The Education of Children Looked After by Local Authorities*, Circular No. 13/94, DH LAC (94) 11, London: DfE and DoH.

Department of Education and Science (1989) *Discipline in Schools, Report of the Committee of Inquiry chaired by Lord Elton*, London: HMSO.

Department of Education and Science (1991) *The Education (Pupils' Attendance Records) Regulations, 1991*, Circular No. 11/91, London: DES.

Department of Education and Science (1992) *Education in Social Services Establishments: A Report by HMI*, 4/92/NS, London: DES.

Department of Health (1980) *Single and Homeless*, London: HMSO.

Department of Health (1991) *Children in the Public Care, A Review of Residential Child Care*, Utting Report, London: HMSO.

Department of Health (1992a) *Children Act Report*, London: HMSO.

Department of Health (1992b) *Choosing with Care: The Report of the Committee of Enquiry into the Selection, Development and Management of Staff in Children's Homes* (Warner Report), London: HMSO.

Department of Health (1993) *One Year of the Children Act*, London: HMSO.

Department of Health and Social Security and Welsh Office (1977) *Working Together for Children and Their Families*, London: HMSO.

Department of Health and Social Security and Welsh Office (1988) *Working Together*, London: HMSO.

Dimenstein, G. (1992) *Brazil: War on Children*, London: Latin America Bureau.

Dineen, B. (1993) 'Teachers pay high price for classroom control', *Yorkshire Post*, 8 March, p. 9.

Draper, L. (1995) 'Huge leap in school exclusions', *Sheffield Telegraph*, 10 March, p. 5.

Duncan, C. (1988) *Pastoral Care: An Anti-Racist/Multi-Cultural Perspective*, Oxford: Blackwell.

Earl Marshal School (1993a) *Policy on Exclusions*, Sheffield: Earl Marshal School.

Earl Marshal School (1993b) *Lives and Love and Hope: A Sheffield Herstory*, Sheffield: Earl Marshal School.

Eaton, M. J. and Houghton, D. M. (1974) 'The attitudes of persistent teenage absentees and regular attenders towards school and home', *Irish Journal of Psychology*, 2, 3, pp. 159–75.

Ehrenreich, B. and English, D. (1979) *For Her Own Good: 150 Years of the Experts', Advice to Women*, London: Pluto Press.

Elshtain, J. B. (1981) *Public Man, Private Woman*, Oxford: Martin Robertson.

Erikson, E. (1977) *Childhood and Society*, London: Paladin.

Eron, L. D., Huesmann, L. R., Dubow, E., Romanoff, R. and Yarmel, P. W. (1987) 'Aggression and its correlates over 22 years', in D. Crowell, I. Evans and C. O'Donnell (eds) *Childhood Aggression and Violence*, New York: Plenum Press.

Evans, N. (1977) 'The professional stance of teachers', in DHSS and Welsh Office, *Working Together for Children and Their Families*, London: HMSO.

Everhart, R. (1983) *Reading, Writing and Resistance: Adolescence and Labor in a Junior High School*, New York: Routledge & Kegan Paul.

Farmer, E. and Parker, R. A. (1991) *Trials and Tribulations*, London: HMSO.

Farrington, D. and West, D. J. (1990) 'The Cambridge study in delinquent development: a long-term follow up of 411 London males', in H. J. Kerner and G. Kaiser (eds) *Criminality: Personality, Behaviour and Life History*, Berlin: Springer Verlag.

Firth, H. (1992) 'Has recent education/social services legislation enhanced the educational opportunities of a child in "Care"?', unpublished M.Sc. dissertation, University of Reading.

Firth, H. (1993) *Listening to Children Project*, Educational Support Services, Winchester, Hampshire County Council.

Firth, H. (1995a) *Annual Review of the Education Support Service, 1995*, Social Service Library, Winchester, Hampshire County Council.

Firth, H. (1995b) *Children First: A Framework for Action*, Winchester, Hampshire County Council.

Fletcher, B. (1993) *Not just a Name*, London: National Consumer Council and Who Cares? Trust.

Fletcher-Campbell, F. (1990) 'In care? In school?' *Children and Society*, 4, 4, pp. 365–73.

Fletcher-Campbell, F. and Hall, C. (1990) *Changing Schools? Changing People? The Education of Children in Care*, Slough: National Foundation for Educational Research.

Fogelman, K., Tibenham, A. and Lambert, L. (1980) 'Absence from school', in L. Hersov and I. Berg (eds) *Out of School: Modern Perspectives in Truancy and School Refusal*, Chichester: John Wiley.

Foucault, M. (1977) *Discipline and Punish: The Birth of the Prison*, London: Allen Lane.

Frederickson, N. (1990) 'Systems work in EP practice: a re-evaluation', in N. Jones, and N. Frederickson (eds) *Refocusing Educational Psychology*, London: Falmer Press.

Frederickson, N. (1993) 'Using soft systems methodology to re-think special needs', in A. Dyson, and C. Gains (eds) *Rethinking Special*

Needs in Mainstream Schools: Towards the Year 2000, London: David Fulton.

Gale, I. and Topping, K. (1986) 'Suspension from high school: the practice and its effects', *Pastoral Care*, November, pp. 215–24.

Galloway, D. (1976) 'Size of school, socio-economic hardship, suspension rate and persistent and unjustified absence from school', *British Journal of Educational Psychology*, 46, 1, pp. 40–7.

Galloway, D. (1982) 'A study of pupils suspended from school', *British Journal of Educational Psychology*, 52, pp. 205–12.

Galloway, D. (1985) *Schools and Persistent Absentees*, Oxford: Pergamon.

Galloway, D., Armstrong, D. and Tomlinson, S. (1994) *The Assessment of Special Educational Needs; Whose Problem?* London: Longman.

Galloway, D., Martin, R. and Wilcox, B. (1985) 'Persistent absence and exclusion from school: the predictive power of school and community variables', *British Educational Research Journal*, 11, 1, pp. 51–61.

Galloway, D., Mortimore, P. and Tutt, N. (1989) 'Enquiry into discipline in schools, University of Lancaster', in N. Jones (ed.) *School Management and Pupil Behaviour*, London: Falmer Press.

Galloway, D., Ball, T., Blomfield, D. and Seyd, R. (1982) *Schools and Disruptive Pupils*, London: Longman.

Garner, M., Petrie, I. and Pointon, D. (1990) *LEA Support Services for Meeting Special Educational Needs*, London: Special Educational Needs National Advisory Council.

Garner, P. (1994) 'Exclusions from school: towards a new agenda', *Pastoral Care in Education*, 12, 4, pp. 3–9.

Garnett, L. (1992) *Leaving Care and After*, London: National Children's Bureau.

Garnett, L. (1994) *The Educational Attainments and Destinations of Young People 'looked after' by Humberside County Council,* unpublished report by Humberside Social Services and Humberside Education Services.

Gibson, A. and Barrow, J. (1986) *The Unequal Struggle*, London: CSS Publications.

Gill, D. (1986) *Staff Sharing Scheme*, Department of Education, Wellington, New Zealand.

Gillborn, D. (1992) *'Race', Ethnicity and Education*, London: Unwin Hyman.

Gillham, B. (1981) *Problem Behaviour in the Secondary School*, London: Croom Helm.

Glaser, B. G. and Strauss, A. L. (1967) *The Discovery of Grounded Theory*, New York: Aldine.

Gleeson, D. (1992) 'School attendance and truancy', *Sociological Review*, 40, 3, pp. 437–90.

Gordon, J. L., Casey, A. and Christenson, S. L. (1985) 'Implementing a re-referral intervention system: part I, the model', *Exceptional Children*, 51, 5, pp. 377–84.

Graham, J. (1988) *Schools, Disruptive Behaviour and Delinquency: A Review of Research*, Home Office Research Study No. 96, London: HMSO.

Grice, A. and Hymas, C. (1994) 'Teachers told to crack down on unruly children', *Sunday Times*, 2 January, p. 1.

Grunsell, R. (1980) *Beyond Control? Schools and Suspension*, London: Writers and Readers, in association with Chameleon Books.

Guardian (1994) 'In his own words', 21 June, p. 7.

Guba, E. B. and Lincoln, Y. S. (1987) 'Naturalistic enquiry', in M. J. Dunkin (ed.) *The International Encyclopedia of Teaching and Teacher Education*, Oxford: Pergamon Press.

Hackett, G. (1992) 'Brent seeks ruling on exclusions', *Times Educational Supplement*, 17 July, p. 2.

Hammersley, M. (1984) 'The researcher exposed: a natural history', in R. Burgess (ed.) *The Research Process in Educational Settings: Ten Case Studies*, London: Falmer Press.

Hammersley, M. (1990) *Reading Ethnographic Research: A Critical Guide*, London: Longman.

Hargreaves, A. (1994) *Changing Teachers, Changing Times*, London: Cassell.

Hargreaves, D. (1967) *Social Relations in a Secondary School*, London: Routledge & Kegan Paul.

Hayden, C. (1993) 'The work of an under-eights team within social services', Report No. 25, Social Services Research and Information Unit, University of Portsmouth.

Hayden, C. (1994a) 'Research into school exclusions', *Young Minds Newsletter*, 18, pp. 13–14.

Hayden, C. (1994b) 'Primary age children excluded from school: a multi-agency focus for concern', *Children and Society*, 8, 3, pp. 132–47.

Hayden, C. (forthcoming) *Children Excluded from Primary School: 'Unmarketable' or 'exceptional'?*, Milton Keynes: Open University Press.

Heath, A. F., Colton, M. J. and Aldgate, J. (1989) 'The educational progress of children in and out of care', *British Journal of Social Work*, 19, 6, pp. 447–60.

Heath, A. F., Colton, M. J. and Aldgate, J. (1994) 'Failure to escape: a longitudinal study of foster children's educational attainment', *British Journal of Social Work*, 24, 3, pp. 241–60.

Hedges, A. (1985) 'Group interviewing', in R. Walker (ed.) *Applied Educational Research*, Aldershot: Gower.

Hendrick, H. (1990) 'Constructions and reconstructions of British childhood: an interpretative survey, 1800 to the present', in A. James, and A. Prout (eds) *Constructing and Reconstructing Childhood*, London: Falmer Press.

Her Majesty's Inspectorate (1989) *A Survey of Provision for Pupils with Emotional/Behavioural Difficulties in Maintained Special Schools and Units*, London: DES.

Hibbett, A. and Fogelman, K. (1988) *Early Adult Outcomes of Truancy II: the Effects of Truancy after Allowing for Other Factors*, National Child Development Study, User Support Group Working Paper 3, Social Statistics Research Unit, City University, London.

Hibbett, A. and Fogelman, K. (1990) 'Future lives of truants: family formation and health related behaviour', *British Journal of Educational Psychology*, 60, pp. 171–9.

Hibbett, A., Fogelman, K. and Manor, O. (1990) 'Occupation and outcomes of truancy', *British Journal of Educational Psychology*, 60, pp. 23–36.

Hills, J. (1993) *The Future of the Welfare State: A Guide to the Debate*, York: Joseph Rowntree Foundation.

Hirst, A. (1993) 'Teachers may hush up attacks', *Huddersfield Daily Examiner*, 25 March, p. 7.

Holloway, W. (1989) *Subjectivity and Method in Psychology*, London: Sage.

Hood-Williams, J. (1990) 'Patriarchy for children: on the stability of power relations in children's lives', in L. Chisholm, P. Buchner, H. Kruger and P. Brown (eds) *Childhood, Youth and Social Change: A Comparative Perspective*, London: Falmer Press.

Huesmann, L. R., Eron, L. D. and Lefkowitz, M. M. (1984) 'Stability of aggression over time and generations', *Developmental Psychology*, 20, pp. 1120–34.

Hugill, B. (1993) 'Inner city school funds slashed', *Observer*, 31 October, p. 3.

Humphries, S. (1981) *Hooligans or Rebels? An Oral History of Working Class Childhood and Youth 1889–1939*, Oxford: Blackwell.

Imich, I. (1994) 'Exclusions from school: current trends and issues', *Educational Research*, 36, 1, pp. 3–11.

Inner London Education Authority (1985) *Equal Opportunities for All?*, London: ILEA.

Jackson, S. (1987) *The Education of Children in Care*, Bristol: University of Bristol, School of Applied Social Studies.

Jackson, S. (1989) 'Residential care and education', *Children and Society*, 2, 4, pp. 335–50.

Jackson, S. (1994) 'Educating children in residential and foster care', *Oxford Review of Education*, 20, 3, pp. 267–79.

Jackson, S. (1995) *Transforming Lives: The Crucial Role of Education for Young People in the Care System*, Tory Laughland Memorial Lecture, Royal Society of Arts, 29 June.

James, C. L. R. (1994) *Beyond a Boundary*, London: Serpent's Tail.

John, P. J. (1991) 'Problem behaviour: an investigation into students' perceptions of schooling', unpublished paper, Bristol: University of the West of England Library.

John, P. J. (1993) 'Damaged goods? An interpretation of excluded pupils' perceptions of schooling', unpublished thesis, Bristol: University of the West of England Library.

Jones, A. (1993) 'Becoming a "girl": post-structuralist suggestions for educational research', *Gender and Education*, 5, 2, pp. 157–66.

Jones, A. and Bilton, K. (1993) *Shape Up or Shake Up? The Future of Services for Children in Need*, London: National Children's Bureau.

Jones, A. and Bilton, K. (1994) *The Future Shape of Children's Services*, London: National Children's Bureau.

Jordan, E. (1995) 'Fighting boys and fantasy play: the construction of masculinity in the early years of school', *Gender and Education*, 7, 1, pp. 69–86.

Kahan, B. (1977) 'Summary of the first six months', in DHSS and Welsh Office, *Working Together for Children and Their Families*, London: HMSO.

Kahan, B. (1979) *Growing up in Care*, Oxford: Blackwell.

Kavanagh, S. (1988) 'The true cost of caring', *Foster Care*, 56, pp. 8–10.

Kelly, A. (1988) 'Ethnic differences: science choice, attitudes and achievement in Britain', *British Educational Research Journal*, 14, 2, pp. 113–26.

Kingston, P. (1995) 'Nowhere to turn', *Guardian Education*, 13 June, pp. 2–3.

Knapp, M. (1986) 'The relative cost-effectiveness of public, voluntary and private providers of residential child care', in A. J. Culyer, and B. Jonsson (eds) *Public and Private Health Services*, Oxford: Blackwell.

Knapp, M., Drury, C., Fenyo, A., Gould, E., McCrone, P. and Salter, C. (1993) *The Cost-Effectiveness of Intermediate Treatment*, Report to the Department of Health, Personal Social Services Research Unit, University of Kent, Canterbury.

Knight, R. (1995) *Educational Provision for Excluded Pupils*, Slough: National Foundation for Educational Research.

Kyriacou, C. (1990) 'Establishing the trustworthiness of naturalistic studies', *Research Intelligence*, 37, p. 36.

Kyriacou, C. and Normington, J. (1994) 'Exclusion from high schools and the work of the outside agencies involved', *Pastoral Care in Education*, 12, 4, pp. 12–15.

Lane, D. (1989) 'Violent histories: bullying and criminality', in D. Tattum and D. Lane (eds) *Bullying in Schools*, Stoke-on-Trent: Trentham.

Lane, D. A. (1990) *The Impossible Child*, London: Trentham Books.

Lawrence, J., Steed, D. and Young, P. (1978) 'Non-observational monitoring of disruptive behaviour in a school', *Research Int. Journal*, 4, p. 38.

Lawrence, J. and Steed, D. (1986) 'Primary school perception of misbehaviour', *Educational Studies*, 12, 2, American Educational Studies Association,University of Cincinnati, Ohio.

Lawrence, J., Steed, D. and Young, P. (1984) *Disruptive Children: Disruptive Schools?* London: Routledge.

Lees, S. (1986) *Losing Out: Sexuality and Adolescent Girls*, London: Hutchinson.

Levy, A., and Kahan, B. (1991). *The Pindown Experience and the Protection of Children, The Report on the Staffordshire Child Care Enquiry*, Staffordshire County Council.

Lloyd Bennet, P. (1993) 'Stockpiling the unsaleable goods', *Education*, 13 September, pp. 126–7.

Lloyd-Smith, M. (ed.) (1984) *Disrupted Schooling*, London: John Murray.

Lloyd-Smith, M. (1993) 'Problem behaviour, exclusions and the policy vacuum', *Pastoral Care in Education*, 11, 4, pp. 19–24.

Lloyd-Smith, M. and Davies, J. (eds) (1995) *On the Margins: the Educational Experiences of 'Problem' Pupils*, Stoke-on-Trent: Trentham.

Longworth-Dames, S. M. (1977) 'The relationship of personality and behaviour to school exclusion', *Educational Review*, 29, 3, pp. 163–77.

Lortie, D. (1975) *School Teacher*, Chicago: Chicago University Press.

Lovey, J., Docking, J. and Evans, R. (1993) *Exclusion from School: Provision for Disaffection at Key Stage 4*, London: David Fulton.

Lowe, C. (1989) 'Coping strategies and pupil discipline', in N. Jones (ed.) *School Management and Pupil Behaviour*, London: Falmer Press.

Lowenstein, L. F. (1990) 'Dealing with the problem of expelled pupils', *Education Today*, 40, 4, pp. 35–7.

Mac an Ghaill, M. (1988) *Young, Gifted and Black*, Milton Keynes: Open University Press.

Mac an Ghaill, M. (1994) *The Making of Men*, Milton Keynes: Open University Press.

McLean, A. (1987) 'After the belt: school processes in low-exclusion schools', *School Organisation*, 7, 3, pp. 303–10.

McManus, M. (1987) 'Suspension and exclusion from high school: the association with catchment and school variables', *Research in Education*, vol. 38, pp. 51–63.

McManus, M. (1990) *Troublesome Behaviour in the Classroom,* London: Routledge.

McManus, M. (1995) *Troublesome Behaviour in the Classroom: Meeting Individual Needs*, 2nd edition London: Routledge.

Maginnis, E. (1993) 'An inter-agency response to children with special needs – the lothian experience – a Scottish perspective', paper presented at National Children's Bureau conference, *Exclusions from School: Bridging the Gap Between Policy and Practice*, 13 July, London.

Maines, B. and Robinson, G. (1988) *B/G Steem a Self esteem Scale with Locus of Control Items*, Bristol: Lame Duck Publishing.

Major, J. (1993) Party Political Broadcast (all four television channels), 20 February.

Mason, M. and Rieser, R. (1990) *Disability Equality in the Classroom: a Human Rights Issue*, London: Inner London Education Authority.

Maxime, J. E. (1984) 'Some psychological models of black self-concept', in S. Ahmad, J. Cheetham and J. Small (eds) *Social Work with Black Children and their Families*, London: Batsford.

Mayall, B. (1994a) 'Children in action at home and at school', in B. Mayall (ed.) *Children's Childhoods: Observed and Experienced*, London: Falmer Press.

Mayall, B. (1994b) 'Introduction' in B. Mayall (ed.) *Children's Childhoods: Observed and Experienced*, London: Falmer Press.

Mayet, G.-H. (1992) 'What hope is there for children with learning and behavioural difficulties?', *Concern*, 81, Summer, p. 3.

Mearns, D. and Thorne, B. (1988) *Person-Centred Counselling in Action*, London: Sage.

Measor, L. and Woods, P. (1984) *Changing Schools: Pupils' Perspectives on Transfer to a Comprehensive*, Milton Keynes: Open University Press.

Millham, S., Bullock, R., Josie, K. and Haak, M. (1986) *Lost in Care*, London: Gower.

Mirza, H. S. (1992) *Young, Female and Black*, London: Routledge.

Mongon, D. (1988) 'Behaviour units, maladjustment and student control', in R. Slee (ed.) *Discipline and Control: A Curriculum Perspective*, Melbourne: Macmillan.

Mortimore, P., Davies, J., Varlaam, A. and West, A. (1983) *Behaviour Problems in Schools: An Evaluation of Support Centres*, London: Croom Helm.

Mortimore, P., Sammons, P., Stoll, L., Lewis, D. and Ecob, R. (1988) *School Matters? The Junior Years*, London: Open Books.

Munro, N. (1993) 'Truancy table chaos looms', *Times Educational Supplement (Scotland)*, 26 November, 1412, p. 1.

Murgatroyd, S. (1980) *Helping the Troubled Child: Interprofessional Case Studies*, London: Harper & Row.

Muschamp, Y., Pollard, A. and Sharpe, P. (1992) 'Curriculum management in primary schools', *Curriculum Journal*, 3, 1, pp. 21–39.

National Association for the Care and Resettlement of Offenders (1993) *Exclusions: A Response to the DfE Discussion Paper*, London: NACRO.

National Association of Head Teachers (1994) *Permanent Exclusions*, press release, December.

National Children's Bureau (1992) *Childfacts*, London: NCB.

National Union of Teachers (1992) *Survey on Pupils' Exclusions: Information from LEAs*, May, London: NUT.

National Union of Teachers (1993) *Special Needs Support Services under Threat*, July, London: NUT.

Netten, A. and Beecham, J. (1993) *Costing Community Care: Theory and Practice*, Personal Social Services Research Unit, University of Kent, Canterbury.

Netten, A. and Smart, S. (1993) *Unit Costs of Community Care*, Personal Social Services Research Unit, University of Kent, Canterbury.

Newson, J. and Newson, E. (1976) *Seven Years Old in the Home Environment*, London: Allen & Unwin.

Norman, M. (1993) 'When gun law comes to school', *The Times*, 25 March, p. 16.

Normington, J. (1992a) 'Return to school from an assessment centre', in G. Vulliamy and R. Webb (eds) *Teacher Research and Special Educational Needs*, London: David Fulton.

Normington, J. (1992b) 'Exclusion from high school and the multi-disciplinary work of the support agencies involved', unpublished M.Phil. thesis, University of York.

Norwich, B. (1994) *Segregation and Inclusion, English LEA Statistics 1988–92*, Bristol: Centre for Studies on Inclusive Education.

Nottinghamshire County Council (1991) *Pupil Exclusion from Nottinghamshire Secondary Schools*, Nottingham: NCC.

O'Leary, J. (1995) 'Parents failing in duty to discipline, say headteachers', *The Times*, 31 May, p. 6.

Oakley, A. (1994) 'Women and children first and last: parallels and differences between children's and women's studies', in B. Mayall (ed.) *Children's Childhoods: Observed and Experienced*, London: Falmer Press.

Office for Standards in Education (1993a) *Education for Disaffected Pupils: a Report from the Office of Her Majesty's Chief Inspector of Schools*, London: OFSTED.

Office for Standards in Education (1993b) *Exclusions: a Response to the DfE Discussion Paper*, London: OFSTED.

Office for Standards in Education (1993c) *School Inspection Manual*, London: OFSTED.

Office for Standards in Education (1995) *Pupil Referral Units: The First Twelve Inspections*, London: OFSTED.

Oldersma, J. and Davis, K. (1991) 'Introduction' to K. Davis, M. Leijenaar and J. Oldersma (eds) *The Gender of Power*, London: Sage.

Oldman, D. (1994) 'Childhood as a mode of production', in B. Mayall (ed.) *Children's Childhoods: Observed and Experienced*, London: Falmer Press.

Oliver, M. (1990) *The Politics of Disablement*, London: Macmillan.

Olweus, D. (1980) 'The consistency issue in personality psychology revisited with special reference to aggression', *British Journal of Social and Clinical Psychology*, 19, pp. 377–90.

Olweus D. (1991) 'Bully/victim problems among school children', in D. J. Pepler and K. H. Rubin (eds) *The Development of Childhood Aggression*, London: Lawrence Erlbaum Associates.

Orbach, S. (1995) 'When therapy goes willingly to school', *Guardian*, Weekend section, 7 January, p. 8.

Osuwu-Bempah, J. (1994) 'Race, identity and social work', *British Journal of Social Work*, 24, 2, pp. 123–36.

Parsons, C. (1994) 'Debris management in primary school exclusion', paper presented at the BERA annual conference, Oxford, September.

Parsons, C., Benns, L., Hailes, J. and Howlett, K. (1994) *Excluding primary School Children*, London: Family Policy Studies Centre.

Parsons, C., Hailes, J., Howlett, K., Davies, A. and Driscoll, P. (1995) *National survey of Local Education Authorities' Policies and Procedures for the Identification of, and Provision for, Children who are Out of School by Reason of Exclusion or Otherwise*, Final report to the Department for Education, Canterbury: Christ Church College.

Paterson, F. (1989) *Out of Place*, London: Falmer Press.

Peagram, E. (1991) 'Swings and roundabouts: aspects of statementing and provision for children with emotional and behavioural difficulties', *Maladjustment and Therapeutic Education*, 9, 3, Winter, pp. 160–8.

de Pear, S. (1994) 'The link between special needs and exclusions. Why?', unpublished MEd dissertation, London: West London Institute, College of Brunel University.

Pedersen, E. (1966) 'Student characteristics and the impact of perceived teacher-evaluation on the level of educational aspiration of adolescents', unpublished Ed.D. thesis, Harvard University, Cambridge, Mass.

Phares, V. (1992) 'Where's Poppa?' *American Psychologist*, May, pp. 656–64.

Phoenix, A. (1991) *Young Mothers*, London: Polity Press.

Pitman, J. (1995) 'Asia's academic stars', *The Times*, 12 May, p. 17.

Plummer, K. (1983) *Documents of Life*, London: Allen & Unwin.

Preston, B. (1993a) 'Teachers must learn to play safe', *The Times*, 27 Febuary, p. 15.

Preston, B. (1993b) 'Reforms failing to raise standards in urban schools', *The Times*, 28 October, p. 5.

Preston, B. (1994a) 'Expulsions spiral as schools fight "yob culture"', *The Times*, 25 October, p. 1.

Preston, B. (1994b) 'Judge tells school to take back pupil expelled after strip', *The Times*, 29 October, p. 4.

Prout, A. and James, A. (1990) 'A new paradigm for the sociology of childhood? Provenance, promise and problems', in A. James, and A. Prout (eds) *Constructing and Reconstructing Childhood*, London: Falmer Press.

Pye, J. (1991) *Invisible Children*, Oxford: Oxford University Press.

Qvortrup, J. (1990) 'A voice for children in statistical and social accounting: a plea for children's right to be heard', in A. James, and A. Prout (eds) *Constructing and Reconstructing Childhood*, London: Falmer Press.

Qvortrup, J. (1994) 'Childhood matters: an introduction', in J. Qvortrup, M. Bardy, G. Sgritta, and H. Winterberger (eds) *Childhood Matters: Social Theory, Practice and Politics*, Aldershot: Avebury Press.

Rabinowicz, J. (1993) 'Examining the new Education Bill: implications for exclusions', paper presented at National Children's Bureau conference, *Exclusions from School: Bridging the Gap Between Policy and Practice*, London, 13 July.

Randal, G. (1989) *Homeless and Hungry*, London: Centrepoint.

Reid, K. (1985) *Truancy and School Absenteeism*, London: Hodder & Stoughton.

Reid, K. (1986) *Disaffection from School*, London: Methuen.

Reid, K. (1989) *Helping Troubled Pupils in Secondary Schools*, Oxford: Blackwell.

Reid, K., Hopkins, D. and Holly, P. (1988) *Towards the Effective School*, Oxford: Blackwell.

Reynolds, D. (ed.) (1985a) *Studying School Effectiveness*, Lewes: Falmer.

Reynolds, D. (1985b) 'The Effective School' *Times Educational Supplement*, 20 September, Features, p. 25.

Reynolds, D. and Sullivan, M. (1981) 'The comprehensive experience', in L. Barton, and S. Walker (eds) *Schools, Teachers and Teaching*, Lewes: Falmer Press.

Reynolds, D., Jones, D., St Leger, S. and Murgatroyd, S. (1980) 'School factors and truancy', in L. Hersov and I. Verg (eds) *Out of School*, Chichester: John Wiley.

Robinson, G. and Maines, B. (1988) *You Can, You Know You Can!*, Bristol: Lame Duck Publishing.

Robinson, K. (1992) 'Classroom discipline: power, resistance and gender. A look at teacher perspectives', *Gender and Education*, 4, 3, pp. 273–87.

Robinson, V. (1987) 'A problem analysis approach to decision-making and reporting for complex cases', *Journal of the New Zealand Psychological Service Association*, 8.

Robinson, V. (1993) *Problem Based Methodology: Research for the Improvement of Practice*, Oxford: Pergamon Press.

Robson, C. (1993) *Real World Research*, Oxford: Blackwell.

Rodgers, B. (1990) 'Behaviour and personality in childhood as predictors of adult psychiatric disorder', *Journal of Child Psychology and Psychiatry*, 31, pp. 393–414.

Rousseau, J. J. (1956) *Emile*, translated by B. Boxley, London: Dent (first published 1762).

Rutter, M. (1991) 'Services for children with emotional disorders', *Young Minds Newsletter*, 9, p. 1–5.

Rutter, M. and Smith, D. (1995) *Psychosocial Disorders in Young People*, London: John Wiley.

Rutter, M., Maugham, B., Mortimore, B. and Ouston, J. (1979) *Fifteen Thousand Hours: Secondary Schools and their Effects on Children*, London: Open Books.

Sampson, J. and Lamb, J. H. (1992) 'Crime and deviance in the life course', *Annual Review of Sociology*, 18, pp. 63–84.

Sawicki, J. (1991) *Disciplining Foucault: Feminism, Power and the Body*, London: Routledge.

Schön, D. A. (1983) *The Reflective Practitioner: How Professionals Think in Action*, New York and London: Basic Books, HarperCollins.

Schön, D. A. (1987) *Educating the Reflective Practitioner*, San Francisco: Jossey–Bass.

Schön, D. A. (1991) *The Reflective Turn: Case Studies in and on Educational Practice*, New York and London: Columbia University, Teachers College Press.

Schostak, J. (1983) *Maladjusted Schooling*, Lewes: Falmer Press.

Schutz, A. and Luckmann, T. (1974) *Structures of the Life World*, London: Heinemann Educational.

Schutz, W. (1978) *FIRO Awareness Scales Manual*, New York: Consulting Psychologists' Press.

Scottish Office (1989) *Effective Intervention: Child Abuse, Guidance on Co-operation in Scotland*, London: HMSO.

Searle, C. (1994) 'The culture of exclusion', in J. Bourne, L. Bridges, and C. Searle (eds) *Outcast England: How Schools Exclude Black Children*, London: Institute of Race Relations.

Secondary Heads Association (1992) *Excluded from School: A Survey of Secondary School Suspensions*, Bristol: SHA.

Seddon, J. (1992) *I Want You to Cheat*, Buckingham: Vanguard Press.

Sinclair, R. (1994) 'The Education of Children in Need', paper presented at the Third International Child Care Conference, Birmingham, 22 March.

Sinclair, R., Grimshaw, R. and Garnett, L. (1994) 'The education of children in need: the impact of the Education Reform Act 1988, the Education Act 1993, and the Children Act 1989', *Oxford Review of Education*, 20, 3, pp. 281–92.

Sivanandan, A. (1994) 'Introduction' in J. Bourne, L. Bridges, and C. Searle (eds), *Outcast England: How Schools Exclude Black Children*, London: Institute of Race Relations.

Smith, D. and Tomlinson, S. (1989) *The School Effect: A Study of Multi-Racial Comprehensives*, London: Policy Studies Institute.

Smith, P. and Thompson, D. (eds) (1991) *Practical Approaches to Bullying*, London: David Fulton.

Social Services Inspectorate and OFSTED (1995) *The Education of Children Who are Looked After by Local Authorities: a Joint Report Issued by the Social Services Inspectorate and the Office for Standards in Education*, London: Department of Health/OFSTED.

Social Services Select Committee (1984) *Children in Care*, London: HMSO.

Stedman Jones, G. (1971) *Outcast London*, Oxford: Oxford University Press, p. 222.

Stein, M. and Carey, K. (1986) *Leaving Care*, Oxford: Blackwell.

Stirling, M. (1992a) 'The Education Reform Act and EBD children', *Young Minds Newsletter*, 10, March, pp. 8–9.

Stirling, M. (1992b) 'How many pupils are being excluded?', *British Journal of Special Education*, 19, 4, pp. 128–30.

Stirling, M. (1993) 'A "Black Mark" against him? Why are African–Caribbean boys over represented in the excluded population?', *Multi-Cultural Education Review*, 15, pp. 3–6.

Stoll, P. and O'Keefe, D. (1989) *Officially Present*, Oxford: Institute of Economic Affairs.

Strain, M. (1995) 'Autonomy, schools and the constitutive role of community: towards a new moral and political order for education', *British Journal of Education Studies*, 43, 1, pp. 4–19.

Strauss, A. L. (1986) *Qualitative Data Analysis for Social Scientists*, Cambridge: Cambridge University Press.

Swann, W. (1987) '"Firm links should be established ..." a case study of conflict and policy-making for integration', in T. Booth, and W. Swann (eds) *Including Pupils with Disabilities: Curricula for All*, Milton Keynes: Open University Press.

Thomas, J. B. (1973) *Self-Concept in Psychology and Education: A Review of the Research*, Slough: National Foundation for Educational Research.

Times Educational Supplement (1991) 'Excluding a stitch in time', 3905, p. 13.

Times Educational Supplement (1994), Editorial, 17 June, p. 8.

Times Educational Supplement (1995) 'Time to care about these in care', McParlin and Graham, 13 October, p. 13.

Tizard, B., Blatchford, P., Burke, J., Farquhar, C. and Plewis, I. (1988) *Young Children at School in the Inner City*, London: Lawrence Erlbaum Associates.

Todman, J., Justice, S. and Swanson, I. (1991) 'Disruptiveness and referral to the Educational Psychology Service', *Educational Psychology in Practice*, 6, 4, January, pp. 199–202.

Tomlinson, S. (1981) *Educational Subnormality, a Study in Decision-Making*, London: Routledge & Kegan Paul.

Tomlinson, S. (1982) *A Sociology of Special Education*, London: Routledge & Kegan Paul.

Topping K. (1983) *Educational Systems for Disruptive Adolescents*, New York: St Martins Press.

Troyna, B., and Siraj-Blatchford, I. (1993) 'Providing support or denying access? The experience of students designated as ESL and SN in a multi-cultural secondary school', *Educational Review*, 45, 1, pp. 3–11.

Troyna, B., and Williams, I. 91987) *Racism, Education and the State*, Beckenham: Croom Helm.

Tutt, N. (1992) Presentation at seminar, 'The Education of Children in Care', organised by Leeds City Council Social Services Department and Leeds University, Leeds University 2 March.

Urwin, C. (1984) 'Power relations and the emergency of language', in J. Henriques, W. Holloway, C. Urwin, C. Venn, and V. Walkerdine (eds) *Changing the Subject: Psychology, Social Relations and Subjectivity*, London: Methuen.

Utting, D., Bright, J. and Henricson, C. (1993) *Crime and the Family: Improving Child-Rearing and Preventing Delinquency*, London: Family Policy Studies Centre.

Varnava, G. (1995), Interviewed as president of the National Association of Head Teachers, on BBC Radio 4 *Today* programme, 28 July.

Wagner, P. (1995) *School Consultation: Frameworks for the Practising Educational Psychologist*, London: Kensington and Chelsea Education Psychology Service.

Walker, T. G. (1994) 'Educating children in the public care: a strategic approach', *Oxford Review of Education*, 20, 3, pp. 339–47.

Walkerdine, V. (1984) 'Developmental psychology and the child-centred pedagogy', in J. Henriques, W. Holloway, C. Urwin, C. Venn, and V. Walkerdine *Changing the Subject: Psychology, Social Regulation and Subjectivity*, London: Methuen.

Walkerdine, V. (1989) 'Developmental psychology and the child-centred pedagogy: the insertion of Piaget into early education', in P. Murphy, and B. Moon (eds) *Developments in Learning and Assessment*, London: Hodder & Stoughton.

Walkerdine, V. (1990) 'Sex, power and pedagogy', in V. Walkerdine *Schoolgirl Fictions*, London: Verso.

Walkerdine, V. and Lucey, H. (1989) *Democracy in the Kitchen*, London: Virago.

Webb, R. (1994) *After the Deluge: Changing Roles and Responsibilities in Primary School*, report of research commissioned by the ATL, London: Association of Teachers and Lecturers.

Westera, J. (1985) 'Evaluation of the Staff Sharing Scheme', unpublished Diploma in Educational Psychology report, University of Auckland, New Zealand.

Westwood, S. (1990) 'Racism, black masculinity and the politics of space', in J. Hearn, and D. H. J. Morgan (eds) *Men, Masculinities and Social Theory*, London and Winchester: Unwin Hyman.

White, J. L., Moffitt, T. E., Earls, F. E., Robin, L. and Silva, P. A. (1990) 'How early can you tell? Predictors of childhood conduct disorder and adolescent delinquency', *Criminology*, 28, 4, pp. 507–33.

Who Cares? Trust (1995) Conference, *Seen and Heard: Educated and Employed*, 3–4 May, Royal Hotel, Hull.

Williamson, J. (1991) 'An extra radiator? Teacher's views of support teaching and withdrawal in developing the English of bilingual pupils', *British Journal of Educational Studies*, 15, 3, pp. 315–26.

Willis, P. (1977) *Learning to Labour: How Working Class Kids Get Working Class Jobs*, Aldershot: Saxon House.

Woodhead, M. (1990) 'Psychology and the cultural construction of children's needs', in A. James, and A. Prout (eds) *Constructing and Reconstructing Childhood*, London: Falmer Press.

Woods, P. (1979) *The Divided School*, London: Routledge & Kegan Paul.

Woods, P. (1986) *Inside Schools: Ethnography in Educational Research*, Routledge.

Wright, C. (1987) 'The relations between teachers and Afro–Caribbean pupils: observing multiracial classrooms', in G. Weiner, and M. Arnot (eds) *Gender Under Scrutiny: New Enquiries in Education*, London: Open University/Unwin Hyman.

Yorkshire Post (1993) 'Damages claim ahead over "banished" pupil', 6 July, p. 4.

Young, S. (1994) 'Exclusion "bias" to be investigated', *Times educational Supplement*, 1 July, p. 11.

Zahran, H. A. S. (1967) 'The self-concept in the psychological guidance of adolescents', *British Journal of Educational Psychology*, 37, pp. 225–9.

Index

DATE DUE